SLAVERY
AND ITS
CONSEQUENCES

Slavery and its Consequences: Racism, Inequity and Exclusion in the USA edited by Lawrence Edward Carter, Sr., Jodi L. Henderson, and Tina Davis

Published by SlaveFree Today, Inc.
312 Crosstown Rd, Suite 166
Peachtree City, GA 30269

journalofmodernslavery.org

Book cover and layout design by The Book Designers

Limited Edition Hardcover ISBN: 979-8-9867696-0-8
Hardcover: 979-8-9867696-1-5
Paperback ISBN: 979-8-9867696-2-2
eBook ISBN: 979-8-9867696-3-9

Journal of Modern Slavery special issue
ISSN: 2833-7689 (print)
2833-7670 (online)

SLAVERY
AND ITS
CONSEQUENCES

Racism, Inequity
& Exclusion in the USA

EDITED BY
LAWRENCE EDWARD CARTER SR.
JODI L. HENDERSON · TINA DAVIS

a special issue of the Journal of Modern Slavery

CONTENTS

PREFACE

In 2020, as the world was collectively facing the pandemic, the single incident of police brutality that took place in Minneapolis reached most people's screens. Watching the seconds and minutes of George Floyd's murder was horrific beyond words. It felt as if our hearts stopped. The subsequent protests it triggered against racism and police brutality in the US and internationally showed that millions of people regardless of race were beginning to understand on a deeper level that this is everyone's problem. It concerns us all. We at the *Journal of Modern Slavery* felt compelled to take action. It was important to respond to the racially motivated hate crime and racial injustice that also took the lives of Ahmaud Arbery, Breonna Taylor and too many others before and since, and that daily harms so many people in different ways. A very concrete way we could do that was to share our platform. We decided to initiate a special issue that looks deeper into the racial injustices and systemic racism that has been a part of the United States throughout the country's history from the beginning of slavery in 1619 and up until today.[1] And in the process, as we wished to explore a wider range of subjects, the special journal issue grew into a book.

When we were thinking of who to invite to be the guest editor, we were looking for a person who has played a central part in creating change over many years, a person with a broad and progressive mind, who can speak about the country's slavery

---

1 We also want to acknowledge the exploitation Native Americans have experienced, which we wish to address in a future publication.

history and its impact with authority and first-hand experience. We were so delighted when Dr. Lawrence Edward Carter Sr., Professor of Religion and founding Dean of the Martin Luther King Jr. International Chapel at Morehouse College in Atlanta, Georgia accepted our invite. We couldn't have found a more knowledgeable, experienced and generous guest editor to lead this special issue book. Dr. Carter, a moral cosmopolitan who have institutionalized a pedagogy of peace, has lived through segregation, been a part of the civil rights movement, and has tirelessly exerted himself to educate hundreds of thousands of people about the philosophy and legacy of his mentor, Martin Luther King Jr., about non-violence and much more.[2]

Slavery and Its Consequences cover a wide variety of subjects tied in different ways to the overall theme of the book, and they are presented in different formats, such as the poem *We Knew* by Stephanie Dunn; the photo essay from the 2008 Democratic National Convention by Naje Lataillade; and Charles Finch's essay where he takes a new look at the peculiar institution of slavery, as well as academic articles on black lives matter in music; the birth and re-birth of black activist athletes; Afro-American Folk Sources and Slave Visions of Heaven and Hell; on Radicalizing Cain, Demonizing Blackness and Legalizing Discrimination; a Black church response to gender-based violence and sexual exploitation of Black women, girls and queer folks and more. The book also presents a literary review of the woke; an interview with Dr. Carter on the peacebuilder project he created about the three giants, Gandhi, King and Ikeda, as well as two dialogues; one about Black publishing with Paul Coates and Barry Beckham; and a

---

2 Dr. Carter 's track record as an educator, faith leader and community-builder extends far beyond what is noted in the text.

dialogue with Herbie Hancock, Wayne Shorter and Esperanza Spalding on jazz, freedom and Buddhism.

We are incredibly grateful towards each contributor of this anthology who in their own unique way have helped make the book a powerful mix of perspectives based on their intellectual knowledge, lived experiences and wisdom. It weaves together multiple threads as they link to the historical slavery and the racism and discrimination that has followed. Aside from the historical perspectives, you meet defiance, self-reflection, faith, pride, resilience, dignity, courage, humour, humanity and hope between the pages of this book. This, however, does not take away from the graveness of the topic it sets out to address, which is there as a consistent undercurrent.

The legacy of slavery and its troubling history that has shaped the nation, which Orville Vernon Burton writes about in the article, *American Slavery Historiography*, is ever-present in the book's many contributions. The book sets out to grapple with the influence slavery has had on America and on the world, and the ways that this manifests today.

We are aware that there are many more subjects that could and very possibly should have been addressed in a book with this theme, and we hope we will be able to somehow address that in the future.

Slavery and Its Consequence is very much born out of our mutual belief that a book can bring about change, and we sincerely hope this anthology will serve as a catalyst for much needed discussions about systemic racism and the transformation we deem so necessary.

Tina Davis   Jodi L. Henderson
London, UK   Atlanta, USA

JOURNAL OF MODERN SLAVERY SPECIAL ISSUE

SLAVERY AND ITS CONSEQUENCES: RACISM, INEQUITY AND EXCLUSION IN THE USA

Introduction by Guest Editor
The Rev. Dr. Lawrence Edward Carter Sr.
September 2022

Having devoted my life's work to serving as a pastor and an educator, I understand that slavery includes not only the physical shackles used to subjugate human beings, but also the mental, emotional, social, political and economic limitations imposed to catch and keep people in various states of bondage. My ministry—from and beyond the pulpit—and my teaching— inside and outside the classroom—include a search for an answer to the nagging question: How can humankind eradicate slavery in all forms and experience the freedom that grants us the right to be and become our best selves? I continue to ask and listen for a response.

That is why I am so honored and grateful to serve as guest editor of this issue of the *Journal of Modern Slavery*. Through a collection of well-researched and thought-provoking articles, compendia, interviews, a photo essay and a poem, the contributors examine aspects of the history of slavery, as well as some of the ways it and its consequences are still having a negative impact around the globe. Their work, which represents perspectives from academic and professional disciplines, includes discourse about slavery, racism, inequity and exclusion through the lens of religion, culture, scholarship and human trafficking. Taken together, the submissions help illumine modern-day slavery as a humanitarian crisis that deserves ongoing inquiry and conversation—but most of all, courageous action to bring it to an end.

Religion

The thesis of Lewis V. Baldwin's article, ***A Home in Dat Rock: Afro-American Folk Sources and Slave Visions of Heaven and Hell***, is that "African slaves in America shaped a more humane and realistic set of values than their white oppressors where heaven and hell were concerned." He cites songs, sermons and interviews that show how slaves' experiences as abused and exploited people shaped their understanding of heaven as freedom – a literal paradise where they would one day find security, intimacy with God, retribution for the wrongs done to them, reunion with friends and family, and/or eternal rest. Baldwin also cites sources that show how slaves' understanding of the Bible's moral codes shaped their views about hell. Many believed that because they were the oppressed, they would not go to hell, but that "every slaveholder will infallibly go to hell, unless he repents."

Drawing on his experience as an attorney, biblical scholar, and minister, Joel B. Kemp argues in ***Racializing Cain, Demonizing Blackness & Legalizing Discrimination: Proposal for Reception of Cain and America's Racial***

Caste System that the ongoing oppression of Black people can be traced to a faulty interpretation of the story of Cain recorded in Genesis 4. Through a construct he calls the "3Ds of Blackness" – the author's "terminology to capture a constellation of pejorative attributes assigned to Black Americans as part of the construction of racial castes in this nation" – Kemp shows how views of Black people as dangerous, deviant, and depraved have been established by religion and perpetuated by law.

Culture

We Knew, a poem by Stephane Dunn, reminds readers of the ways in which Black men and women down through the ages have testified to the truth that still rings urgently in the collective consciousness today: "In the beginning/ We knew/All Black Lives Matter."

The Sounds of Freedom: A Dialogue on the Poison of Racism, the Medicine of Jazz, and a Buddhist View of Life is the transcript of an interview conducted by Taro Gold with three eminent jazz artists: Wayne Shorter, Herbie Hancock, and Esperanza Spalding. The artists not only have in common musical careers in the same genre, but also the practice of Nichiren Buddhism. Gold engages them in a wide-ranging conversation that includes insights on how jazz embodies the Buddhist principle of "changing poison into medicine" – a strategy that can be adopted by social justice movements to create positive change.

In *Black Publishing: An Interview with Paul Coates and Barry Beckham*, Jodi Henderson engages the highly regarded publishers in a conversation about the history and future of their industry. They talk about their place in the long legacy of black publishing and how they were inspired by the civil rights and social justice movements of the 1960s to start their own efforts to bring books by and about Black people to market. While Coates and Beckham applaud the efforts of white publishing houses that acquire and promote works by Black writers, they believe that because of their "fierce independence" there will always be a role for Black publishers as champions of Black voices.

Dealing with the Devil and Paradigms of Life in African American Music unpacks Anthony Pinn's assertion that "a haunting and eerie narrative of the battle for human's soul [is] firmly lodged in the lyrics of African American music." To make his case, Pinn explores the work of several blues and rap music artists and demonstrates how their lyrics recognize and address the tension between angelic and demonic personalities – but do so in ways that differ vastly from the approach of African American spirituals in understanding and resolving this epic struggle.

Stephanie Shonekan contends that Black music "has always and consistently amplified and spotlighted the mattering of Black lives." In *Black Lives Have Always Mattered in Black Music*, she selects and analyzes 10 songs by Black artists that span more than a century, from slavery to the early 2020s. For each, Shonekan outlines the historical context in which the song was created and explores how the artists, by using their music to respond to racial discrimination and oppression, sparked awareness, roused emotions, inspired hope, and spurred activism for social justice.

Ron Thomas' *The Birth—and Rebirth—of Black Activist Athletes: They Refused to Lay Their Burdens Down* highlights the many ways in which Black athletes have and continue to face and respond to racism – all while exhibiting grace and prowess in their respective sports. With a combination of stories and photographs of noteworthy Black activist-athletes over the past 200 years, Thomas reveals how these men and women not only played to win their games, but also worked to overcome discrimination.

In his photo essay, **To Hope, Fourteen Years Later**, Naje Lataillade shares some of the images he captured at the s 2008 Democratic National Convention in Denver, Colorado, where the party nominated Barack Obama as its candidate for President of the United States. In the piece, the photographer and documentarian also turns the lens on himself—sharing insights into his feelings as, 14 years later, he reflects on that historic time and considers what it means in today's political climate to have hope.

Scholarship

Charles S. Finch III posits in **A New Look at Slavery: "The Peculiar Institution,"** that "slavery is slavery, wherever and whenever you find it." In a brief overview of the history of slavery from 4,000 BC to the mid-20th century, Finch explores how the practice of human bondage manifested differently in northeast Africa, western Asia, and North, Central, and South America. He explains that in the southern United States, where whites referred to slavery as their "peculiar institution," owning human beings was rooted in economic gain—a factor that made slavery hard to eradicate and ensured its negative impacts would last long after it was legally abolished.

In *American Slavery Historiography*, Orville Vernon Burton explores the evolution of the field of slave history. With the caveat that "because history entails all the past of all of humankind, historians will never be able to attain the whole Truth," Burton catalogs the works of slavery historians from various backgrounds and differing, often controversial, points of view—including many whose research and conclusions have been much-debated and debunked. In addition to a broad array of authors, the historiography covers a broad array of topics about slavery, including its economic, moral, political, social, psychological, cultural, legal and gender-specific causes and impacts.

Leah Creque's *Literary Review of the Woke 2019-2021* highlights the contributions of a pantheon of Black writers whose works of fiction and nonfiction provide "historical context of the foundation that was laid for public awareness at home and abroad of the continual plight of African Americans." Her comprehensive list documents a robust Black literary movement that began with slave narratives and continues with 21st century books by authors whose exploration of Black life is helping to catalyze the "waking up" of America in the aftermath of the murder of George Floyd.

Gender-Based Violence

Brandon Thomas Crowley begins his article, *Modern Slavery by Another Name: A Black Church Response to Gender-Based Violence and the Human Trafficking of Black Women, Girls, and Queer Folx for the Purpose of Sexual Exploitation*, by agreeing with Princeton University Professor Eddie S. Glaude Jr.'s assessment that the Black church is dead. As evidence of this death, Crowley names the Black church's failure to acknowledge and support Black women and Black LGBTQIA+ survivors of gender-based violence. He then offers "queering"—a "tool used to reconsider or reinterpret a thing or concept from a perspective that intentionally rejects the traditionally opp-ressive categories of sexuality and gender"—as a way the Black church can awaken from her death with a calling to do spiritual justice.

My contribution to this book on slavery and its consequences is captured in **Blueprints for Improved Communities** – an interview Dr. Tina Davis conducted with me to explore my perspectives about how humankind can create a better world, and how we can draw from the timeless teachings of the three peacebuilders Gandhi, King and Ikeda to tackle the challenges we face as a world community today. I share some of my experiences of racism and how I have witnessed change over the years on matters related to racial injustices from the time I grew up in Dawson, Georgia, and Columbus, Ohio in the 40s and 50s; how Martin Luther King Jr. influenced my life; and my work as Dean of the Martin Luther King Jr. International Chapel at Morehouse College.

I also discuss my calling to establish the Gandhi King Ikeda Institute for Ethics and Reconciliation, which celebrates and promotes the philosophies of these three men from three different faith traditions: Mohandas Karamchand (Mahatma) Gandhi, a Hindu; Martin Luther King Jr., a Christian; and Daisaku Ikeda, a Buddhist. From their respective spiritual worldviews, they came to the same conclusion: Peace is the only way to heal the world—a commitment I share and a goal I work toward every day.

I trust that readers will find, as I did, much in this book issue of the *Journal of Modern Slavery* that inspires them to ask and seek answers to old and new questions about what it means to be human—indeed, what it means, what it will take for everyone to finally be free.

Peace and blessings.

Rev. Dr. Lawrence Edward Carter Sr.
Dean, Martin Luther King Jr. International Chapel
Professor of Religion
College Archivist and Curator

Morehouse College
Atlanta, Georgia

"WE KNEW"

"WE KNEW"

Stephane Dunn

David Walker said it in an eighty-seven page appeal
   We must rise up & free ourselves

Harriet Tubman lived it
   stole herself back to herself then gave black lives
   to themselves

Sojourner preached it
   ain't the black women too and the men

God whispered it to Nat Turner
   Righteous indignation is correct

Frederick Douglass told Lincoln to recognize it

Du Bois wrote we need education the vote and
   the bullet to protect it

Ida B Wells put it in the press
   don't live or buy where they kill us

Zora Neale Hurston and Langston Hughes celebrated it

Ali rhymed it and fought it

Kwame Ture
Tommie Smith
And the Black Panthers Black Power saluted it
   On the world stage
   In American cities and Mississippi

Fannie Lou Hamer stood up and testified on it
Thurgood Marshall argued it in the Supreme Court

Lorraine Hansberry
Amiri Baraka
Sonia Sanchez
Nikki Giovanni
Jimmy Baldwin
and Toni Morrison immortalized it in word

Mary Turner
Medgar Evers
Malcolm X
Martin King
Cynthia Carole Denise Addie Mae Carole
    on a Sunday morning
    and Emmett Till in Money
    were murdered to hide it

But we knew
Before hashtags
Before televised revolution and murder
Before the Movements
Before slave ships & the auction block
Before 1619
Before Jamestown
Before our kidnapping
In the beginning
We knew
All Black Lives Matter

BLACK LIVES HAVE ALWAYS MATTERED IN BLACK MUSIC

Stephanie Shonekan

In the summer of 2020, after the public killing of African American George Floyd, mainstream society in the United States, along with millions of people around the world, suddenly woke up to the injustice of racism in the United States. Pundits have speculated about the reasons why this particularly terrible episode finally hit the bullseye of awareness and empathy.

It appeared that a societal shift had occurred. After 400 years, the population of Americans who seemed moved by racial injustice multiplied. It could not have been just the fact that this Black man had been killed by the police, and that it was captured, recorded, and shared on social media. That had happened many times before, and even earlier that same year with Ahmaud Arbery.

George Floyd was different. Most have posited that the reason why George Floyd hit a nerve was that it happened in the midst of the unprecedented global COVID-19 pandemic, when folks were at home, undistracted, and could therefore absorb the footage undisturbed. Suddenly, people who had turned away from Trayvon Martin, Eric Garner, Sandra Bland,

Rekia Boyd, Philando Castile, Tamir Rice, Michael Brown, and so many others sat up and "woke" up.

The "Black Lives Matter" hashtag quickly became popular beyond the consciousness of Black folks. The hashtag and the ensuing movement had been created by Alicia Garza, Opal Tometi, and Patrisse Cullors in 2013 to remind Black people that despite George Zimmerman's acquittal of the killing of 17 year old Trayvon, that we still mattered.

Though the movement had grown consistently since 2013, it had been vilified by the FBI as a group of extremists, and by a certain demographic of Americans who had either distanced themselves or ignored the movement altogether. Again and again, I saw the founders defend their movement as not the diminishing of the mattering of other groups, but a necessary focus on the mattering of Black lives, which seemed in jeopardy, as demonstrated by these killings.

Walking through the neighborhood of my college town in 2020, I was struck by the number of BLM signs that popped up in front yards. For the first time in my memory, I saw evidence of solidarity, or at least the appearance of a shared concern for the lives of Black folks.

Certainly since the beginning of the twenty-first century, scholars of legal studies, Black Studies, political science, history, sociology, and journalists and writers[1] have written about the state of the American nation that these publicly visible atrocities and other aspects of the systemic racism have exposed. In the twenty-first century, as much of this discourse has been published, the #BlackLivesMatter movement has served as the accompanying activist platform where athletes, politicians,

---

1 Michelle Alexander, Keona Ervin, Saidiya Hartman, Frank Wilderson, Fred Moten, William Darrity, Robin D.G. Kelley, Ta-Nehisi Coates, Jelani Cobb, Nikole Hannah-Jones, among others

filmmakers, visual artists, and grassroots organizers have found their voices. This expansion has crossed over the Black World to find alignment in places like Palestine and Nigeria, where the most recent youth movement, #EndSars, was inspired by the #BlackLivesMatter movement, and resulted in the terrorist killing of several young activists by the Nigerian police force.

And yet, what Cullors, Garza and Tometi are saying with their hashtag is not new. Throughout reconstruction, Jim Crow segregation, the Civil rights movement, Black Power, and the building of a critical race theoretical framework to deal with rising disparities in the criminal justice system, Black revolutionary icons like Harriet Tubman, Marcus Garvey, Sojourner Truth, W.E.B. Du Bois, Booker T. Washington, Langston Hughes, Diane Nash, Rosa Parks, Martin Luther King, Malcolm X, John Lewis, Al Sharpton, Jesse Jackson, Maxine Waters, and across the Diaspora like Nelson Mandela, Wole Soyinka, Walter Rodney, Eric Williams, and Paul Gilroy, have been raising their voices to the injustices that have sprouted inexorably from the construction of race and the extension of this construct into sturdy and enduring racist systems and policies.

Apart from a few prominent allies like John Brown, Andrew Goodman, Michael Henry "Mickey" Schwerner, and Grace Lee Boggs, mainstream America has remained on the sidelines, observing when the intensity of the volume has been raised. However, 2020 and George Floyd marked a shift, an expanding of the boundaries where US mainstream society, and indeed other societies around the world, finally started recognizing or considering that it is time to do what it will take to underscore or amplify the fact that, like all other lives, Black lives should matter too.

One arena that has always and consistently amplified and spotlighted the mattering of Black lives is Black music. This is why I often point to my trusty pile of music albums when I am asked what people can do or when I am asked where people can go to start with the self-education that is critical to the raising of awareness.

People tend to be moved to empathy when they come into close proximity to a situation. Black music has the power to shorten that distance because Black musicians have adapted to each iteration of injustice and infused their music with edifying and enlightening information about the global historical relevance of the Black struggle.

Arguably, no American artistic form has captured the history of the struggle for racial equality as consistently and substantially as Black American music. Before and since reconstruction, while many white Americans remained resistant to the notion of full citizenship for African Americans and attacked the value of their musical expression by creating minstrelsy and promoting extensive campaigns against what they saw as the decadence of "race music" or "negro music," Black people continued to create and disseminate their music.

In the second decade of the twenty-first century, as the nation, and indeed the world, seemed to wake up and pay attention to the injustices against Black lives highlighted by the #BlackLivesMatter movement, Black artists have continued to carefully document their experiences, from slavery to the current period.

This essay focuses on ten songs, spanning over a century, from "Lift Ev'ry Voice and Sing" written by James Weldon Johnson and his brother Rosamond to "Freedom" by Beyoncé and Kendrick Lamar. How has the message about Black lives mattering remained consistent in American music history, and what devices and nuances have artists utilized in expressing this message as the painful racial history has evolved?

It is difficult to arrive at ten songs, because for every ten, there are hundreds more. Every genre of African American music has captured the mattering of Black life. The blues, jazz, art music, rock n roll—all have offered intimate glimpses into the complexities of African American experiences.

For purposes of this essay, I will focus on mostly secular music—soul, R&B, and hip hop—with one offering from sacred and another from jazz. It is important to note that Black music begins to chart Black life with the Negro spirituals. Songs like "Wade in the Water" and "Sometimes I Feel Like a Motherless Child" were critical cultural foundations for African Americans and their survival in the United States.

Into these songs they poured their pain and their hopes, and out of these songs the humanity and dignity of the enslaved can be imagined. Bernice Johnson Reagon explains that these early Negro folk songs stand "today not simply as the sole American music, but as the most beautiful expression of human experience born this side of the seas. ... [I]t still remains as the singular spiritual heritage of the nation and the greatest gift of the Negro people."[2]

Indeed, these songs remain at the root of all the music that has captured the lives and humanity of Black people. "Wade in the Water" reminds us of the deep spirituality of Black Americans and their aspirations for escape and freedom. "Sometimes I Feel Like a Motherless Child" reflects the

---

2 Bernice Johnson Reagon, ed. *We'll Understand it Better By and By: Pioneering African American Gospel Composers* (Washington and London: Smithsonian Institution Press, 1992) 4.

deep nostalgia for family and a homeland, both tangible concepts of which they had been robbed.

The ten songs that follow are descendants of these early, iconic Negro folk songs. I must admit upfront that one artist—Nina Simone—will take up three spots on this precious list of ten songs. The austerity of the exercise notwithstanding, she, along with seven others, offer different and distinct angles of why and how Black lives matter.

I will also pull from a handful of contemporary books published during the #BlackLivesMatter era as scholars have been able to reflect on how the current historical moment of the twenty-first century has resulted from centuries of white supremacy while Black lives have been disdained and discounted.

"LIFT EV'RY VOICE"
by James Weldon and Rosamond Johnson (1900):
The Notion of Citizenship

In February 2017, the Oakwood Aeolians, a renowned choir from Oakwood University, a historically Black college (HBCU) in Alabama, performed at the University of Missouri. They began with a rendition of "the Negro National Anthem," also known as "Lift Ev'ry Voice and Sing."

As they began to sing, all the Black folks in the hall promptly stood up. Most of the white folks remained seated, looking confused. This moment was a reminder that not everybody relates to that song as a "National Anthem."

It is almost a mirror image of why many African Americans continue to question the validity of the "Star Spangled Banner." Both songs began as heartfelt poems deeply connected to a pride in American identity. Inspired by the 1814 US defense of Fort Henry from British naval ships, Francis Scott Key wrote the poem "Defense of Fort M'Henry," which, when set to music by his brother-in-law, became the "Star-Spangled Banner." This rousing song about US sovereignty failed to represent the perspective of all citizens, and particularly those who were viewed as property.

Arguably, the most enduring counter-anthem to the "Star Spangled Banner" is "Lift Every Voice and Sing," which fits a unique Black identity that is rooted in America.

Written as a poem by James Weldon Johnson and set to music by his brother J. Rosamond Johnson in 1900, what the brothers called the "Negro National Hymn" was adopted by the NAACP as an anthem in 1919. In 2000, former NAACP president and longtime Civil Rights activist Julian Bond published an anthology of reflections on this anthem.

One of these was a reflection by African American historian John Hope Franklin who cited the last lines of the song, "true to our God/true to our native land," a reminder to Black folks that America is indeed their home: "Whenever I hear the words, I can hear James Weldon Johnson admonishing me to keep the faith," Franklin wrote.[3] This resolve to claim the United States as home by Black Americans belies the conditions of exclusion that African Americans have consistently faced since slavery.

In his book *The Color of Law*, Richard Rothstein writes about the endurance of racism and discrimination embedded in the "history of racial exclusion. When we consider problems that arise when African Americans are absent in significant numbers from schools that whites attend, we say we seek

---

3 Julian Bond and Dr. Sondra Kathryn Wilson. *Lift Every Voice and Sing: A Celebration of the Negro National Anthem; 100 years, 100 voices* (New York: Random House, 2001).

diversity, not racial integration. When we wish to pretend that the nation did not single out African Americans in a system of segregation specifically aimed at them, we diffuse them as just *people of color.*"[4]

William Darrity's book on reparations, *From Here to Equality,* similarly expands on this condition: "Not only do Black Americans have reduced opportunities to obtain quality education; they also receive less of a payoff for any credential they earn.

The persistence of wage and employment discrimination and racial wealth inequality ensures that America's dice are loaded against Blacks in two ways... at each level of educational attainment Blacks have an unemployment rate two times that of whites. Blacks with some college education or an associate's degree frequently rate lower than whites who never finished high school. Job prospects for recent Black college graduates... remain comparatively grim."[5]

Given the sustained reality of racial inequality and inequity cited by Rothstein and Darrity above, how can one national anthem—the "Star Spangled Banner"—written by a slave master reflect the realities of the descendants of those who were enslaved and who have not yet attained equal access to full citizenship? "Lift Ev'ry Voice" as a Negro National Anthem insists that there is a different, legitimate, national identity that represents a people who continue to look back at their painful history while looking up to a spiritual power for the fortitude they will need to keep moving forward.

---

4 Richard Rothstein. *The Color of Law: A Forgotten History of How Our Government Segregated America* (New York: WW Norton, 2017), xvii.

5 William A. Darrity and A. Kristen Mullen. *From Here to Equality: Reparations for Black Americans in the Twenty-First Century* (Chapel Hill, NC: University of North Carolina Press, 2020), 231.

"STRANGE FRUIT"
by Billie Holiday (1939):
Active Violence against the Black Body

Perhaps no song plunders the visceral horrors of injustice against Black people through the violence against the Black body better than Billie Holiday's "Strange Fruit," written by Jewish teacher Abel Meeropol in 1937 and recorded by Holiday in 1939. Her voice plunges to haunting depths as it communicates the terror of African American life and death.

The song paints a horrific picture of lynched bodies of African Americans, a reality captured by writers like Ida B. Wells in the late 1800s to early 1900s when she documented cases of lynching in Memphis, Tennessee. In her book *Caste*, Isabel Wilkerson explains the terror that Black people faced after reconstruction with the rise of the Ku Klux Klan, during what Du Bois called the "seven mystic years": "It was largely Black efforts to rise beyond their station that set off the backlash of lynchings and massacres … and the imposition of Jim Crow laws to keep the lowest caste in its place. A white mob massacred some sixty Black people in Ocoee, Florida, on Election Day in 1920, burning Black homes and businesses to the ground, lynching and castrating Black men, and driving the remaining Black population out of town after a Black man tried to vote."[6]

The violence on Black bodies in the United States took various unimaginably horrific forms, as Wilkerson elaborates that "from slavery well into the twentieth century, doctors used African-Americans as a supply chain, for experimentation, as subjects deprived of either consent or anesthesia. Scientists

---

6 Isabel Wilkerson. *Caste: The Origins of Our Discontents (New York: Random House, 2020), 228-229.*

injected plutonium into them, purposely let diseases like syphilis go untreated to observe the effects, perfected the typhoid vaccine on their bodies, and subjected them to whatever agonizing experiments came to the doctor's minds."[7]

So "Strange Fruit" imagines the realities of a country where these Black bodies were violated for medical research and profit, or simply for being Black. The lyrics set to a beautiful melody recount sensory signifiers that encode the smell of burning flesh, and macabre imagery of bulging eyes and twisted mouths of unimaginable pain and fear of innocent American fathers, brothers, mothers, and sisters, sons and daughters as they faced certain death.

David Margolick's book on the biography of the song explains the impact the rendering of this song had to move people to action: "whether they protested in Selma or took part in the March on Washington or spent their lives as social activists, many say that it was hearing 'Strange Fruit' that triggered the process" of activism.[8]

The span of time between reconstruction and the Black Lives Matter movement keeps "Strange Fruit" relevant to Black life. The brutal beating of Rodney King, the 41 shots that were directed at Amadou Diallo, the choking of Eric Garner and George Floyd, and the scores of murders of unarmed Black people by members of the police force indicates that Black bodies still lack value.

As the Trump campaign called for previous eras when America was once great, Black Americans wondered when the country was truly great for all. Eddie Glaude writes that

---

7 Wilkerson, 147.

8 David Margolick. *Strange Fruit: The Biography of a Song* (New York: Ecco, 2001), 6.

"the nation had turned its back on whatever vision of the country Black Lives Matter put forward. Police were still an ominous presence in many Black communities. ... All the while, 40% of America delighted in Trump's presidency. They had told themselves the lie that Black and brown people threatened their way of life, and now they were poised to make America white again."[9]

"TRIPTYCH: PRAYER, PROTEST, PEACE"
by Max Roach and Abbey Lincoln (1960): Response to State Violence (internal, emotional, psychological)

In 1959, jazz drummer Max Roach and lyricist Oscar Brown, Jr. began to work on a collaborative project. It was to be a musical and artistic response to the ugliness of segregation and racism. The album was released as "We Insist: Max Roach's Freedom Now Suite" by Candid Records in 1960, in the midst of the Civil rights movement.

Other collaborators on the album include percussionist Babatunde Olatunji, saxophonists Coleman Hawkins and Walter Benton, trumpeter Booker Little, trombonist Julian Priester, and most importantly vocalist Abbey Lincoln. According to jazz scholar Ingrid Monson, this album "is perhaps the best-known jazz work with explicitly political content."[10]

Most critics agree that Abbey Lincoln brought an urgency to the album that set it apart from the rest of the jazz albums of that time. In the third track, "Triptych: Prayer, Protest, Peace," she

---

9 Eddie S. Glaude, Jr. *Begin Again: James Baldwin's America and its Urgent Lessons for Our Own* (New York: Crown/Penguin Random, 2020), 21.

10 Ingrid Monson. *Freedom Sounds: Civil Rights Call Out to Jazz and Africa* (New York: Oxford University Press, 2007), 172.

vocalizes the deep painful experience of being Black in America. The song is divided into three parts: Prayer, Protest, Peace.

When I listen to this, I am transported to the belly of the slave ship, the earnest reach for a spiritual power that will lead us out, the deep moans and screams of anger and distress, and the yearning for peace. But I understand this because I am moved to prayer, protest and peace every time I, or my children, or my husband encounters racism or sexism, which are the results of slavery, colonialism, imperialism.

If "Strange Fruit" shows us what the violence against Black people looks like, Triptych reveals the emotional impact of this long history. Eddie Glaude explains that "many Black people did not forget, and carried that sense of history experienced in the moment when something triggers the recollection that collapses past and present. History and time blur as the traumas of the present call forward a litany of past betrayals.

Slavery, Jim Crow, lynching, police killings, prisons, Black ghettos, failed schools, and the people who sanctioned it all packed into one pile of American shit."[11] When Lincoln gets to the "Protest" part of the track, we experience the despair, the anger that has been "piled" like layers on top of Black folks over generations, smothering the life out of them. Douglas Blackmon describes these layers as "Black reenslavement"[12] because each layer is like a return to the beginning.

William Darrity and Kristen Mullen define these layers of micro- and macroaggressions: "Microaggressions range from insults and jokes depicting people of color as scofflaws or as stupid or incompetent to the experience of being physically

---

11 Glaude, 153.

12 Douglas A. Blackmon. *Slavery by Another Name: The Re-Enslavement of Black Americans from the Civil War to World War II* (New York: Anchor Books, 2008).

present but excluded from a conversation and hearing racial slurs and innuendos. Macroagressions range from racial profiling and public humiliation to physical violence that threatens life and limb."[13]

Triptych captures the effect of this reality for Black folks. "Prayer" represents the hope and faith with which Black people have to begin every new day, before the agonized screams and frenzied drumming of the inevitable reality of the "Protest" section. The exhaustion of this perpetual, traumatic cycle comes in the "Peace" section as Lincoln and Roach settle back into heavy sighs and calmer beats.

"MISSISSIPPI GODDAM"

by Nina Simone (1964): Response to State Violence
(external, vocal, urgent)

While "Triptych" captures the internal psychological reaction to state violence without words, Nina Simone's "Mississippi Goddam" is an urgent, wordy, militant external reaction.

After the Civil War, and the Emancipation Proclamation of 1865, there was a brief period of hope for African Americans. Freedom had been gained, but was short-lived as African Americans contended with restrictive and racist Jim Crow laws, horrific lynchings, and insurmountable barriers to access the so-called American Dream. By the 1950s and '60s, this reality was in full swing, with some shocking watershed moments, such as the murder of 14 year old Emmett Till in 1955, the Alabama church bombing that killed four little girls

---

13 Darrity and Mullen, 252.

in 1963 and the assassination of Civil rights activist Medgar Evers also in 1963.

This bloody southern landscape is the backdrop against which Nina Simone wrote and released her incredible statement song "Mississippi Goddam" in 1964. Like other African American artists, she was responding to racial injustice with music that was urgent and moving.

But this song went further than other musical offerings because it drew close attention to the irony of a country that stood for certain altruistic values that were not applicable to all citizens. In this stinging song, Simone embeds her urgent message in what she calls "a showtune."

That juxtaposition sheds a harsh, bright light on the tragic reality and the need to step up the Civil Rights Movement. Darrity relays the resistance to the civil rights movement: "For many southerners, the right to enslave Black people was both a pocketbook issue and a matter of stubborn principle. For them, the assumption that all men, Black or white, stood on equal footing was fundamentally wrong."[14]

Unwilling to wait for the tide of history to turn against these racist realities, Simone pushes forward, against the tendency to "go slow," with the move to advocate for full citizenship. Like so many songs Simone wrote, "Mississippi Goddamn" is bold, irreverent and honest.

---

14 Darrity and Mullen, 168.

"CHANGE IS GONNA COME"

by Sam Cooke (1964): History and Hope

Released in 1964, "A Change is Gonna Come" was written by Sam Cooke after a harrowing encounter with the ugliness of racism. Turned away from a hotel and arrested for protesting this unjust treatment, he turned to his craft, reaching back to the hope and aspiration of his spiritual gospel roots, to envision a time when a man like him might live in the United States without a fear of being targeted because of the color of his skin.

Inspired by Bob Dylan's classic 1963 song "Blowin' in the Wind," which asks big questions about how long these questions about human life, dignity, and peace would be left unanswered, Cooke anchors his song in a similar time/historical framework, opening with the start of his own life's trajectory: "I was born by the river, in a little tent/Oh, and just like the river/I've been running ever since."

But while Dylan leaves the answers "blowin' in the wind," Cooke resolves that a change will indeed come: "But I know a change is gonna come. Yes it will." One can almost hear the resolve in the exclamation mark after that last line.

This song, which has been covered by so many other artists—including Al Green, Otis Redding, Patti LaBelle, and Bettye LaVette—combines history and hope, and remains as a reminder of the incremental progress that has been made since the arrival of Africans in the Americas, and certainly since the Civil Rights Movement of the 1960s, when this song was birthed.

In 2020, a white colleague grew impatient with me when I expressed sadness and surprise at the lack of an institutional response to yet another racist killing. "Why are you so surprised?" she asked, exasperated at me. Her question caught me off-guard because I thought I had done something wrong by not being like her—able to shrug it off and sigh and say to myself, "oh well, it is just another example of white supremacy."

As I processed our interaction in that conversation, I shook off the guilt because my inclination, like Sam Cooke's song, is to acknowledge the injustice, remain deeply moved by each fresh iteration of violence, and continue to hope for change, even in the midst of the historical facts and present reality of the endurance of White supremacy.

"FOUR WOMEN"

by Nina Simone (1966): Black Women/Say Her Name/
Intersectionality

Pushing back firmly against the trend of second-wave feminism, scholars like Kimberlé Crenshaw and Britney Cooper have highlighted the importance of nuance and detail in the study of racial and gender identity. In her classic essay "Mapping the Margins: Intersectionality, Identity Politics, and Violence," legal scholar Crenshaw writes "Although racism and sexism readily intersect in the lives of real people, they seldom do in feminist and antiracist practices.

And so, when the practices expound identity as woman or person of color as an either/or proposition, they relegate the identity of women of color to a location that resists telling."[15] Nina Simone's 1966 song "Four Women" embodies this telling.

---

15 Kimberlé Crenshaw. "Mapping the Margins: Intersectionality, Identity Politics, and Violence against Women of Color." *Stanford Law Review*, vol. 43, no. 6, (1991). 1241.

As Crenshaw suggests, it is problematic—and even unjust – to see Black women as either just Black or just women. This impulse to see Black women through only the lens of race or sex erases essential parts of their identities. Simone addresses this historical tendency in "Four Women" by lovingly embracing the unique identities of four Black women: Aunt Sarah, Siffronia, Sweet Thing, and Peaches.

Each character has her own recognizable, personal history that is embedded in the history of this nation. Aunt Sarah is the nurturer, the tradition bearer, on whose strong back this country was built. Her resilience to keep standing, in spite of the strikes that inflict her "again and again," is noted by Simone.

Saffronia is the Black woman who struggles with the complex parts of her biracial identity, because her rich, white planter father "forced [himself on her] mother one night." This stanza recalls the actual sexual violence inflicted on enslaved women. What, Simone urges us to ask, is the psychological product of this violence?

Sweet Thing represents another kind of resilience, a study of survival where this character is forced to use the very body that has been violated by white supremacy to survive.

And lastly, Peaches is a culmination of the entire cast, serving as a reminder of each terror that has been meted out against Black women through history. She's angry, not in a surface stereotypical way, but because the micro-and macro-aggressions she and her ancestors have faced over time are just layers of trauma on every fiber of her Black existence.

This song is Simone's reminder that Black women must matter, as Black and as women, as mothers, daughters, workers, providers, and saviors. Every time I have played this song in class, my students sit up and say they recognize each of the characters, who appear in their generation and in the generations of their mothers and grandmothers.

If the four women were a composite character, she might be heard in Abbey Lincoln's screams and sighs on "Triptych," or she might be Billy Holiday or Ida B. Wells who sang about or witnessed lynchings of Black bodies. In the chapter titled "An Unloved Woman," in her book *Wayward Lives, Beautiful Experiments*, Saidiya Hartman frames a scene where Ida Wells was removed from a train:

> She fought like a tiger. They clutched her hands and feet, dragging her through the aisle, tearing her traveling coat... the white passengers stood on their seats and clapped when she was ejected. She was not a lady. She was not a woman. She was a Negro. ... A darky damsel and a Black cow were strangely equivalent and indicative of the category crisis she embodied. What kind of woman was she, if a woman at all? ... As Ida Wells experienced directly, a colored woman could be labeled a prostitute, cursed as a 'slanderous and dirty-minded mulatress' and threatened with castration ... she exchanged stories with other Black women about the insults, the obscene propositions, the hateful glances, the lustful eyes, the threats of grievous harm. ... The very words 'colored girl' or 'Negro woman' were almost a term of reproach.[16]

Each of Nina Simone's four women is seen and humanized in this scene. Other artists have attempted to bring nuance to

16 Saidiya Hartman. 2020. *Wayward Lives, Beautiful Experiements: Intimate Stories of Social Upheaval* (New York: WW Norton, 2020), 38-40.

the Black woman's identity, but few have been as successful as Simone in "Four Women."

"THE MESSAGE"
by Grand Master Flash (1982): Inner-City Realities and Reaganomics

Hip hop pioneer Grandmaster Flash and the Furious Five released "The Message" in 1982. This marked the beginning of conscious rap as it sharpened the lens on what was happening in certain parts of the United States.

Rap and hip hop had been birthed in the late 1970s out of a need to create innovative dance music and express raw emotions and frustrations about what was happening to young African Americans and Latinos in the Bronx. The musical culture spread quickly to other cities across the country.

According to critics, the Ronald Reagan administration and its neo-liberal economic policies wreaked havoc on these Black and brown communities that were already being ravaged by the crack epidemic. Tracing the rise of Reagan and his impact on Black and brown communities, Eddie Glaude focuses on how Reagan, as a presidential candidate "declared, 'Let's make America great again' and the majority of white America got in line. ... The passage of time between 1975, when Reagan left the governorship, and the 1980 election allowed the majority of the country to forget his negative reaction to the Black freedom movement."[17]

As federal dollars were spent on building highways to cut

---

17 Glaude, 150-152.

through the most depressed sections of cities, these communities were disrupted and dispersed. Some political theorists have concluded that the wealth that "Reaganomics" was designed to build up, did not trickle down to these communities.

DJ Grandmaster Flash and his posse of MCs led by Melle Melle responded with "The Message," a socially conscious song about what it was like to live in these devastated communities. It is a narrative about the effects of "Reagonomics" on the sanctity and security of the community, which, "like a jungle" has people struggling to survive on streets with "broken glass" where landlords and the repo man are an ever-present threat.

In *The Color of Law*, Richard Rothstein tracks how these neighborhoods became deteriorated from the 1940s onward: "Decisions to permit toxic waste facilities in African American areas did not intend to intensify slum conditions, although this was the result. The racial aspect of these choices was a desire to avoid deterioration of white neighborhoods when African American sites were available as alternatives.

The welfare of African Americans did not count for much in this policy making."[18] In fact, Rothstein's research took him to the archives where he found evidence that: "the government had purposely used public housing to ensure that African Americans were concentrated away from white neighborhoods."[19]

"The Message" also highlights the psychological damage to an entire generation of Americans: "Don't push me cos I'm close to the edge, I'm trying not to lose my head." This is a refrain that continues echoing into the twenty-first century.

---

18 Rothstein, 55.

19 Rothstein, 242.

"N.I.*.*E.R (THE SLAVE AND THE MASTER)"

by Nas (2008): A Proud Retrospective Reminder

While Grandmaster Flash and the Furious Five approached their song as a narrative snapshot of the urban Black landscape of the 1980s, Nas' 2008 song "N.I.*.*E.R (The Slave and the Master)" traces the history of Black people to their African roots and reminds us that the society has established a false construct of Black people.

Nas states in this song that "this history don't acknowledge us/We was scholars long before colleges." It is a reminder of Gramsci's writings on hegemony and power, and of the organic intellectual, who brings folk knowledge from outside the borders of formal education.

An organic intellectual himself, Nas subversively turns to the notorious N word to invert the usual connotation and to lift up the collective chin of Black folks in the United States. "They say we N-I Double G-E-R/ We are much more," This follows the example of Tupac's "Words of Wisdom" where the word is redefined as "Never Ignorant, Getting Goals Accomplished."

In 2015, although there was general discontent with a campus that allowed racist behaviors from some segments of the community, the student movement at Mizzou was triggered by the hurling of this word at the student body president who happened to be Black. The editorials and comment sections of the local paper exposed the underbelly of a white college-town with residents who did not understand the etymology of the word. Why, they lamented simplistically, did African-Americans have a problem with the word when they used it in their rap songs all the time.

One of the most loaded and problematic words in US cultural history is "Nigger." The articulation of the word has often been the trigger for extreme racial tension at different times and in different parts of the country. This term, with its deep roots in slavery, is still used with the purpose of demeaning African Americans.

Interestingly, at a certain point in the 1990s, the word was "reclaimed," repurposed, and redefined by the young African Americans who formed the critical hip hop generation. Thus, a variant of the word was employed in vernacular and in hip hop lyrics. That seemed to indicate to some members of the mainstream audience, one of the largest groups to purchase hip hop music, that the word could be utilized by all.

However, the six-letter word and its variants, have become cultural signifiers that connote everything from hatred to camaraderie, with inherent rules and parameters for who can use them and what they ultimately mean. Nas' treatment of the word in this song is smart and provocative, leaving no ambiguity about the pride and dignity of Black people.

"FREEDOM"
by Beyoncé ft Kendrick Lamar (2017):
Freedom Dreams Deferred

In the second decade of the twenty-first century, the Black Lives Matter hashtag, created by three Black women, evolved into a movement as the roll call of murders and acquittals continued. Artists like J. Cole, Lauryn Hill, Kendrick Lamar, and Childish Gambino, following in the footsteps of other American artists before them, have responded with clarity and urgency.

Beyoncé's *Lemonade* album reflects the evolution of an artist arriving at this epiphany of what the music can do for the movement. It is both a personal awakening and a public political statement about Black liberation and social justice. Joining her on the song "Freedom," Kendrick Lamar skewers the media portrayals of Black folks and communities and provides a sharp critique of police brutality.

Beyonce's verses signal the reverberations of the history of the enslaved, ancestors who waded in water to escape the chains of bondage, and she asks with the same urgency of Nina Simone: "Freedom, where are you?" It is a question that good citizens must continue to ask on behalf of marginalized and oppressed groups as the twenty-first century marches on. And, as Beyonce sings, that inquiry must be accompanied by hope because "winners don't quit on themselves."

It is pertinent to mention that this song includes samples from the collections of ethnomusicologists John Lomax and Alan Lomax. One is a brief sample from a song called "Stewball" by "prisoner #22" and the other is a small section from "Collection Speech/Unidentified Lining Hymn" (1959), recorded by Alan Lomax, performed by Reverend R.C. Crenshaw. These inclusions point to the historical tragedies of unjust incarceration rates and the important position of the Black church in the push for liberation.

The song ends with a recording of Jay-Z's grandmother at her 90th birthday celebration, saying, "I was served lemons but I made lemonade." This is a reminder of the terrible, sour history that sets the prelude for this call for freedom.

"I WISH I KNEW HOW IT WOULD FEEL TO BE FREE"

by Billy Taylor and Nina Simone: Freedom Aspirations

I conclude this list with my third Nina Simone song. The events of January 6, 2021 at the Capitol revisit the national focus on race, identity, and the concept of freedom. Who gets called a patriot, a hero, a traitor? What is a riot, a protest, or an insurrection? Semiotics and semantics, words and meaning, signifiers and signified, positionality, cultural context and knowledge – all of these concepts are critical to helping us get to the roots of the cultural knowledge that binds us and separates us.

At the heart of the matter, when we think about what happened on January 6, 2021, we should consider what "freedom" means? The 1964 song by Billy Taylor and Nina Simone "I Wish I Knew How It Would Feel To Be Free" allows us to interrogate this concept. The shifting amoebic unfixed meaning of freedom is at the core of the problems that this country continues to face, which are captured in all the preceding nine songs.

In 1964, jazz pianist Billy Taylor composed "I Wish I Knew How It Would Feel To Be Free." According to Brian Zimmerman in *Jazziz Magazine*, "this would become Taylor's most famous composition, which he originally wrote for his daughter, Kim.

The song, with its stately melody and strong gospel roots, was embraced by leaders of the Civil Rights Movement as a message of peace and dignity."[20]

---

20 Brian Zimmerman. "Billy Taylor - 'I Wish I Knew How It Would Feel to Be Free.'" 2019. *JAZZIZ Magazine*. July 24, 2019. https://www.jazziz.com/billy-taylor-i-wish-i-knew-how-it-would-feel-to-be-free/.

Nina Simone recorded it in 1967, bringing her signature commitment and resolve to the lyrics, a convincing and compelling case for the rights of citizens to be free. The rich tones of her voice reflect the aspirations for freedom that so many African Americans have felt before and after that song was released.

There is a line that Simone always sings with emphasis: "I wish I could say all the things I should say." This line is reflective of the social and psychological impact of living in a country where you have to be careful what you say, how you live, in order to progress, to get a job, a bank loan, or simply to stay safe.

Many artists have covered this song over the years and their treatment of this line has uncovered various aspects of white positionality. For instance, Mary Travers of Peter, Paul, and Mary tweaks the line slightly to "I wish I could say all the things *I know* I should say" (my emphasis). This change brings attention to the position of white women in American history and the struggle for freedom. It begs the question of what are the things left unsaid when acts of racism happen? And what have been the voting patterns of white women in the last few elections, which have attempted to disenfranchise Black folks?

Another important line in this song is "Remove all the bars that keep us apart." Again, Simone signals the different barriers to advancement that have been mounted by segregationist policies driven by white supremacy. For instance, John Denver changes this line to "remove every doubt that keeps us apart," as if he, as a white man, is trying to convince African Americans that the "bars" are simply figments of the imagination.

And so, when Nina sings this song, we should all imagine what her yearnings are for freedom as a Black woman. We can and should do the work to imagine what freedom looked like for Erica Garner, Sandra Bland, and the mothers like Mamie Till, mother of Emmet Till, who lost their children to this horrific violence. We should consider the work of Alicia Garza, Patrisse Cullors, Opal Tometi, Stacey Abrams, Shonda Rhimes, Cori Bush, Kamala Harris, and others.

As we find nuance and meaning in the notion of freedom, we can begin to advocate for an America that may at some point live up to its ideals. As Angela Davis writes in her book, *Freedom is a Constant Struggle*, "it is in collectivities that we find reservoirs of hope and optimism."[21]

These ten songs, each a giant in the soundtrack of the Black experience in the United States, are a miniscule cross section of a vast spectrum of Black American music. These ten songs have been presented here as a reminder that the music has always framed the stories and the journeys of Black life. The songs offer a unique, illuminating portal into Black life for those who are not Black. But it is important to emphasize that this music is first and foremost for Black folks themselves.

From its African roots, African American music has always functioned as a form of entertainment, education, edification, and worship. Within these ten songs is pain enough, but there is also love, joy, determination, and faith.

This essay began with a reflection on race during the COVID crisis. As America gaped and gasped at the George Floyd killing and the racial inequities that became clear in the response to the pandemic, Black folks were turning to

---

21 Angela Davis. *Freedom is a Constant Struggle* (New York: Haymarket Books, 2016), 49.

the music to cope. DJs D-Nice and ?uestlove spun sets on Instagram live, attracting thousands—and in some cases, hundreds of thousands—of mostly Black folks to tune in, join the raucous commentary and share nostalgic memories of the music that has brought us thus far.

Also, Timbaland and Swizz Beatz kicked off their Verzuz webcast series, hosted on Instagram and airing on YouTube and Facebook. Each episode featured a pair of Black music icons who sang along to their big hits in a sort of friendly battle style. Millions of people, again largely the Black community, tuned into these shows, rooting for their favorites of the battle, sharing commentary on Twitter and other social media platforms, and finding ways to survive the lockdown and pandemic through these moments of joy.

While mainstream America contended with their own new awakening to racial trauma, Black people turned within, congregated on social media to interact with the music and with each other, thereby reminding themselves of how much their complex humanity matters.

A NEW LOOK AT SLAVERY— THE "PECULIAR INSTITUTION"

Charles S. Finch III, M.D.

One can trace the history of slavery at least to the beginning of historical times, about 4,000 BC. For most of the period afterward, slaves were war captives in northeast Africa and western Asia. There was no economic dependence on slavery such as would be seen in North, Central, and South America after the Columbian voyages that began in 1492 and during the ensuing conquests.

That said, the Aztecs were known to raid other peoples for captives for the purposes of human sacrifice. Still, the people of Mesoamerica were mostly farmers and artisans working their own lands and their own trades.

As for the attitudes of Europeans toward Africans, prior to the seventeenth century, there existed no widespread, generic attitudes concerning black inferiority among Europeans. Those Europeans who had any contact with West Africa encountered powerful, well-organized states with all the attributes of civilization as it was understood at that time.

The African slave trade launched by Portuguese mariners around 1440 was confined to the transport of slaves into Europe until the sixteenth century, and at that time, there was still a steady flow of European slaves into the eastern realms controlled by the Turkish Ottoman Empire. The exclusive trade in black Africans, especially across the Atlantic, would not begin until the early sixteenth century.

SLAVERY AND ITS CONSEQUENCES

When Portugal and Spain invaded Central and South America, their first acts were to enslave the indigenous populations. These people, who had never experienced such mass enslavement, died by the thousands, so much so that they were in real danger of being wiped out. The problem was so dire that in the early 1500s, the Spanish Bishop Bartolomé de las Casas intervened on behalf of the local people and got the Spanish Crown to agree to obtain its slaves from Africa. His famous plea was based on the assumption that Africans could better withstand the rigors of plantation slavery. Yet even the stature and influence of Las Casas could not halt the onerous oppression of the indigenous peoples of the Americas.

Slavery came to North America in 1619, twelve years after the founding of Jamestown, Virginia in 1607. It readily took root in what would become America's southern states, from what is now Virginia to Texas. Although slavery was practiced throughout the English colonies and subsequently in the American states, it took its greatest hold in the eleven states that would eventually form the Confederate States of America.

The plantation system became entrenched in the South because it enriched the plantation landholders to an immense degree. This system did not take root to the same extent in the states north of Maryland, where trade and a budding industrial economy rapidly established themselves. The Virginian aristocracy, which produced several American presidents, was particularly enriched by this plantation economy. Virginia's aristocracy arose to the political forefront of America's British colonies and later took the lead in the American Revolution and the Constitutional Convention.

Washington, Jefferson, Madison, and Monroe are all revered names in American history. They were four of the first five presidents of the new United States of America, and each was a slaveholder, which is perhaps the reason that the abolitionist movement did not gain traction until all of them had died.

In the period after the War of 1812, when the British threat to America had receded, an increasingly contentious conflict between North and South gathered steam. Abolitionists in the North became increasingly vocal, and the slaveholding South became increasingly adamant about preserving its "peculiar institution," its quaint name for slavery. Southern justifications for enslaving "the Negro" became ever more strident, with countless assertions about slavery saving the captured Africans from the indignities of being Africans, savages unequipped for the demands of freedom or self-government.

In addition, white women were said to need protection from the potential sexual aggressions of black male slaves, and indeed from black males anywhere and everywhere, slave or free. At the same time, southern white males felt completely empowered to sexually abuse black women whenever and wherever they pleased.

No southern white man, including the above-mentioned founding fathers, was considered to be a man until he had had a sexual encounter with a black woman. In fact, George Washington was called the "stallion of the Potomac" for his unrestrained sexual license with both black and white women. It was said that southern white plantation owners would marry a suitable white woman, father two or three children with her, and then spend the rest of their "intimate time" with black slave women.

Jefferson in particular was notorious in this regard, as his well-known relationship with Sally Hemings demonstrates. She was a slave girl on Jefferson's plantation with whom Jefferson became enamored, so much so that he took her with him to France where he was ambassador for the newly formed United States of America. She attracted a lot of attention in France, which was just emerging from its own revolution. It is said that she could have remained in France as a free woman had she so chosen, but she had children by a slave father back in Virginia whom she could not bring herself to abandon. There are Hemings descendants in Virginia to this day.

Though Jefferson was, as has been said, enamored with Sally Hemings, to his dying day he never emancipated her. Men like Aaron Burr—Thomas Jefferson's vice-president who nevertheless who could not abide him—said Jefferson was a man who espoused lofty principles, as seen in the Declaration of Independence, but never lived by them.

For nearly 60 years after Thomas Jefferson and Aaron Burr's intense, heated debates regarding slavery, the slavery question divided the North and the South into two mutually hostile regions. Men like Henry Clay attempted to dampen this intersectional hostility by passing the Missouri Compromise in 1820.

Missouri was a slave territory on the verge of being admitted to the Union. The admission was being forestalled by non-slaveholding states in the North that were determined to prevent an upset in the balance of power. The admission of Missouri would have created twelve slave states against eleven non-slaveholding states. The contentious issue was resolved by the simultaneous admission of Maine into the Union, creating an equal number of slave and non-slave states. For the next 40 years, a new state admitted in a non-slaveholding region of the expanding country had to be counter-balanced by the admission of a new slave state.

Events such as the Dred Scott Decision of 1857 were intended to resolve the impasse but only intensified it and hastened the onset of the American Civil War. Dred Scott and his wife were slaves who traveled with their owner to the free states of Illinois and Wisconsin. In these venues, Scott sued for his freedom multiple times between 1843 and 1857, without success. Scott's case gained such notoriety that it eventually ended up in the Supreme Court under Chief Justice Roger B. Taney. Taney and six of his fellow justices ruled against Scott, keeping Scott and his wife enslaved and infuriating Northern abolitionists while making Dred Scott a *cause célèbre* for the abolitionists. The Dred Scott decision is considered one of the driving events that led to the Civil War four years later.

It was abundantly clear that North and South were locked in an irreconcilable conflict over slavery. After the Dred Scott case, war seemed inevitable, and so it was in 1861 when Southerners fired on the federal Fort Sumter in South Carolina.

Four years of bloody conflict ensued, resulting in the deaths of more than one million people. That was the highest number of causalities that the United States had ever sustained in a war and remains so to this day.

With Lee's surrender at Appomattox, the Confederacy—made up of eleven Southern states—was defeated. In the Emancipation Proclamation of 1863, all black slaves were formally freed by the Union, but slavery continued in the Confederate states until the war ended in 1865.

The Thirteenth, Fourteenth, and Fifteenth Amendments to the Constitution awarded the freed slaves the ostensible benefits of full citizenship, but this lasted only while Federal troops occupied the South. In 1877, President Rutherford B. Hayes pulled out all Federal troops from the eleven states. By this time, the former Confederate States had rejoined the Union, and in a contentious presidential election, Hayes negotiated the troop withdrawal in exchange for Southern electoral-college votes. It won him the election, but it meant that the South, freed from Federal restraints, could inaugurate a systematic repression of the new black "citizens" that was hardly less vicious than the slave-holding regime before it.

This vicious repression continued until the advent of the Civil Rights Movement in 1955, with the Montgomery bus boycott led by Dr. Martin Luther King, Jr., the emerging leader of the Southern Christian Leadership Conference. Even with the landmark civil rights legislation of the 1960s, the legacy and lingering effects of American slavery and post-slavery political repression have been felt up to the present day.

Slavery in the Western world continued in Brazil until 1888, when it was legally outlawed in that country. From the beginning of the Atlantic slave trade in the mid-fifteenth century to its termination in the mid-nineteenth century, an estimated fifty to eighty million Africans were wrested from their homelands and transshipped to the New World. It is also estimated that one-third of all the black people captured and taken from their African homelands died before ever reaching the New World.

Conditions on the slave ships were horrific beyond belief, with Africans packed in the cargo holds like sardines and forced to live amidst their own filth. Those who died were simply thrown overboard. Sharks seemed to know which ships were slave ships because they followed them and devoured all the dead humans thrown into the sea.

More than a few Africans preferred death to slavery and simply jumped overboard at the first opportunity, but the trade was still very lucrative for the companies that owned the slave ships. While Northerners prided themselves as having outlawed slavery, it was Northern shipping companies that were leased to carry slaves from Africa.

Slavery was also a prominent feature of the Islamic world until well into the twentieth century. Islam came into being in 622 A.D. with the Hegira of Prophet Mohammad, and slavery, already present in the Arabian lands of early Islam, extended with the spread of Islam to the far corners of the Old World. During the early period of Islam, however, Muslims did not racialize slavery. They took slaves from everywhere that Islam expanded—Europe, Africa, Western Asia, and India.

Slavery continued in Saudi Arabia until it was outlawed in 1948, making Saudi Arabia one of the last countries in the world to maintain legalized slavery. However, from roughly 1650 on, almost all the slaves entering the Islamic world were brought from Africa. Africa came to be seen, it might be said, as "the land of slaves," and it is a difficult truth to accept that even after Europe outlawed and suppressed slavery wherever possible, African nations wanted to keep the trade going.

Guns were one of the most prized commodities that African slave traders obtained from their European counterparts. They used these against local enemies and against peoples who could be raided for slaves.

When the coastal areas of West Africa had been largely depleted by slave raiding, raiding continued deep in the interior. Europeans, susceptible to malaria and possessing limited cultural knowledge, could not carry slave raiding and trading so far inland, so their coastal African partners carried out the wars and raids in the interior to obtain slaves.

Slavery is slavery, wherever and whenever you find it. Nonetheless, in manifested differently in different locales. In the Americas, a plantation economy took hold in ways that produced a particularly brutal way of life for the slaves. The Arab world lacked a plantation economy as extensive as the one that existed in the Americas, but slavery was omnipresent there too, although slaves' status differed.

Many of the Islamic armies enlisted slave soldiers led by slave generals. Occasionally, a particularly able slave could ascend to a rank equivalent to prime minister. Moreover, it was not unknown for high-ranking slaves to marry free-born women. Children born of such unions assumed the status of their mothers. Slaves who ascended to high ranks in the state were often more trusted than non-slaves of high rank. Their loyalty to their patrons, therefore, was absolute.

Not all slaves accepted their fate passively. There were several slave uprisings in the United States, the most notorious one being the rebellion led by Nat Turner in Virginia. Turner brought to life all the latent fears of white people because he and his band killed every white person they could find. In all, fifty-nine whites were killed by Nat Turner and his followers.

The most extensive and successful slave revolts transpired in Brazil and the Caribbean. Slaves in the forested regions of Brazil rose up in a body and defeated every Portuguese army sent against them. Furthermore, they accomplished what no group of blacks ever had in the Western Hemisphere—they founded their own state, Palmares. Palmares remained an independent state for ninety-four years, an unprecedented phenomenon in the New World.

Outside of Brazil, there were numerous other slave uprisings in the Western Hemisphere. The most successful group was the Maroons of Jamaica, who managed to escape slavery and set up their own independent state in the hills. To this day, the Maroons have never been conquered and maintain a quasi-independent way of life in the lands they fought for and won.

That said, there was never a slave-created state within a state like Palmares, which was unique in terms of its size, organization, and ability to defend itself for nearly a century. In 1791, slaves rebelled in the northern regions of Saint Domingue, which would later become Haiti. The revolution they launched created the independent nation of Haiti in 1804—the only nation state to emerge from a slave rebellion. Haiti was the first black independent nation state in the Americas, and the second independent state in the hemisphere.

In one form or another, slavery could be found on every inhabited continent in the world. It was not until the nineteenth century that it became recognized as a blight and stain on civilization everywhere. Even so, it could not be completely eradicated from the globe until the mid-twentieth century. As indicated earlier, it left an imprint on American society that has not been fully transcended or erased. Is it true to say that all actions have consequences, individual or collective, immediately or eventually? Because in the end, everything balances out in the universe.

AMERICAN SLAVERY HISTORIOGRAPHY[1]

Orville Vernon Burton

In 1965 historian Bennett H. Wall observed that in the field of U.S. history only "three important monographs have been concerned solely with the subject of slavery." They were Ulrich B. Phillips's *American Negro Slavery* (1918), Kenneth M. Stampp's *The Peculiar Institution* (1956), and Stanley M. Elkins's *Slavery* (1959). When Wall was writing, the multivolume *History of the South* series had five volumes (now it has ten). In spite of all those volumes, Wall's conclusion was that "The literature of slavery reveals much heat on the question of morality but little illumination of other aspects of the institution."[2]

Wall did not include the historian John Hope Franklin and his books, *The Free Negro in North Carolina, 1790-1869* (1943) or

---

1 After my dear friend Charles Joyner and I had presented papers together on slavery in upcountry and low country South Carolina at an American Studies conference in Canada, Richard Wentworth, then director of the University of Illinois Press, asked us to edit a new volume on State and Local Histories of Slavery, similar to Elinor Miller and Eugene D. Genovese, eds., *Plantation, Town, and Country: Essays on the Local History of American Slave Society* (Urbana, 1974), updated after the explosion in slavery studies in the 1980s and 1990s. Joyner and I began soliciting essays and had begun an introduction for the volume, but Joyner passed away in 2016. I have drawn on our historiographical discussion in that joint introduction and have included much of the work and ideas of Chaz Joyner, a great historian and folklorist of slavery. I dedicate this essay to my friend Chaz Joyner. I am also grateful for suggestions and comments by Jeff Forett and Larry McDonnell (both of whom have challenged my own work), colleagues Stephanie Hassell and Lee Wilson, Peter Eisenstadt, David Moltke-Hansen, Gavin Wright, my research assistant Alexander Bowen, my daughter Beatrice Burton who is also a historian studying how slavery is presented to the general public, and my editor and wife Georganne Burton who has helped me to clarify any unwieldy ideas.

2 Bennett H. Wall, "African Slavery," in *Writing Southern History: Essays in Honor of Fletcher M. Green*, eds. Arthur S. Link and Rembert W. Patrick (Baton Rouge: LSU Press, 1965), 182 (first quote), 177 (second quote), and 181 (third quote).

From Slavery to Freedom (1947).[3] Franklin did pioneering work on slavery's origins in Africa, then into the Western Hemisphere, various migrations within the U.S., enslaved workers' struggles for freedom, and the on-going quest for racial equality. It was little noticed at the time, but it has been a best-seller ever since the academy woke up to African American scholarship.

A similar reception met the work of W. E. B. Du Bois. Du Bois was the first African American to earn a Ph.D. in history at Harvard University (1895) and is now recognized as an intellectual genius.

Since 1965, so much has been written about American slavery that the sheer volume of the bibliography is daunting. Any attempt, such as this one, to characterize major themes, controversies, and disagreements of this historiography is likely to result in oversimplification. The latest historiographical essay that I am aware of is the 2020 review essay by Vanessa M. Holden and Edward E. Baptist, "Nineteenth-Century Enslavement of Africans and African Americans in the United States," in *Reinterpreting Southern Histories: Essays in Historiography.*[4] That first-rate essay covers more topics, such as gender and intersectionality; this essay takes a longer view.

Other relevant articles in the same volume are Catherine Clinton and Emily West, "Gender and Sexuality in the Old South," and Harry L. Watson and John D. Majewski, "On the Banks of the James or the Congaree: Antebellum Political

---

3 John Hope Franklin, *The Free Negro in North Carolina, 1790-1860* (Chapel Hill: The University of North Carolina Press, 1943) and *From Slavery to Freedom: A History of African Americans* (New York: Knopf, 1947).

4 Vanessa M. Holden and Edward E. Baptist "Nineteenth-Century Enslavement of Africans and African Americans in the United States," in *Reinterpreting Southern Histories: Essays in Historiography*, eds. Craig Thompson Friend and Lorri Glover (Baton Rouge: LSU Press, 2020), 99-138.

Economy," and Sarah E. Gardner and David Moltke-Hansen, "The Transformation of Southern Intellectual History."[5]

Another compilation of the historiography of slavery is the publication of bibliographies once a year in the journal *Slavery & Abolition*. University of Virginia historian Joseph Miller, until his death in 2019, marshalled and published a list of all books and essays appearing during each year, and that important contribution has been continued by Thomas Thurston of the Gilder Lehrman Center for the study of Slavery, Resistance, and Abolition at Yale University.[6] The last bibliography was compiled in volume 47 for 2020 and includes works published in 2019. The bibliography is always a summary of the previous calendar year, and thus I assume there will be future ones. The *Journal of Southern History* also publishes an annual list, including a section on scholarship on African American history (among many more categories) published in journals the previous year.

Any compilation of slavery studies must concede the diversity and difficulties, but that is only a beginning. When Peter Parish suggested that we should check our "intellectual grandfathers," he did not know how visceral those words could be.[7]

Parish neglected grandmothers. He also neglected Black grandfathers, who could not even get into segregated archives until the late 1960s and early 1970s in some of the former Confederate states. Moreover, documents from enslaved

5 Catherine Clinton and Emily West, "Gender and Sexuality in the Old South," and Harry L. Watson and John D. Majewski, "On the Banks of the James or the Congaree: Antebellum Political Economy," and Sarah E. Gardner and David Moltke-Hansen, "The Transformation of Southern Intellectual History" in *Reinterpreting Southern Histories*, eds. Craig Thompson Friend and Lorri Glover, 139-265 and 168-187 and 534-562.

6 Thomas Thurston, "Slavery: Annual Bibliographical Supplement 2019," *Slavery & Abolitionism* 41, no. 4 (2020): 877-997, https://www.tandfonline.com/doi/abs/10.1080/0144039X.2020.1834317.

7 Peter J. Parish, *Slavery: History and Historians* (New York: Harper & Row, 1989), x-xi.

people are mostly missing in the archives; what archives have are sources from the enslavers. Nonetheless, scholars have continued to find new ways to read these sources against the grain, providing us with an increasingly nuanced understanding of the lives of Black Americans, both enslaved and free. Historians need to be aware of how tricky this can be. We conduct research of the documents, and our profession honors "archival research."

With this in mind, I start this endeavor humbly, admitting that there is too much for this essay to cover, and that topics on slavery go in too many directions. With this review I am implicating myself in a process that has been going on ever since the professionalization of history in the late 19th century (and perhaps ever since Herodotus). I believe there is a value in the attempt.

With the explosion of slavery studies in the late twentieth century and early 21st century, groups of historians, as if marking their territory, fell into different camps, challenging others' interpretations. There is merit in each of the scholarly traditions under consideration, and critiques of new ideas often mean amplification and elucidation. Yet, some of the work may have a tendency to overstate a particular interpretation in order to command attention. "Either/or" can replace "both/and" in the debates, leading to misunderstanding rather than clarification.

Today no clear demarcations mark categories of interpretations. Slavery studies are now wide open, some with an emphasis on gender and the body, others on cultural wars, others revisiting the older schools of inquiry on the profitability of enslaving workers or the amount of agency that enslaved people possessed.

Current interest in the New York Times "1619 Project" and the reactions to that project opened the subject of historiography to the general public. According to its website, the project "aims to reframe the country's history by placing the consequences of slavery and the contributions of black Americans at the very center of our national narrative."[8]

Secondary teaching of US History usually covers slavery as it existed in the antebellum period of cotton production, so the 1619 Project was an important corrective; we all should know that slavery was endemic in colonial life and early America. What the project does not recognize is that slavery in the future United States long antedated the importation of the first Africans to Virginia.

Indigenous people held enslaved people before Europeans arrived, and early in the colonial era Indigenous people also made up the majority of the people enslaved by European newcomers. Nevertheless, it was after 1619 that people of African descent became an ever-greater share of the enslaved population, beginning to dominate by the late 17th century. And yet, while Native American enslavement died out in the east, it continued in the west.[9]

As the 1619 Project emphasizes, slavery affected, and still influences, all of American history. As is often the case, those

---

8 "The 1619 Project," *The New York Times*, August 14, 2019, https://www.nytimes.com/interactive/2019/08/14/magazine/1619-america-slavery.html. Since completion of this essay, there is now a book with extended chapters, Nikole Hannah-Jones, *The 1619 Project: A New Origin Story* (New York: One World, 2021).

9 Columbus brought back Indians from the New World to be sold in the slave markets of Seville. Spain began importing enslaved Africans to the New World in 1502 and at least by 1513, the Spanish government was selling licenses for the slave trade. Alan Gallay, *The Indian Slave Trade: The Rise of the English Empire in the American South, 1670–1717* (New Haven: Yale University Press, 2002); Andres Resendez, *The Other Slavery: The Uncovered Story of Indian Enslavement in America* (New York: Houghton Mifflin Harcourt, 2016) documents the enslavement of Native Americans from European invasion to early twentieth century; Brett Rushfoth, *Bonds of Alliance: Indigenous and Atlantic Slaveries in New France* (Chapel Hill: University of North Carolina Press, 2012).

wanting a paradigm shift may overstate their position. It is factual that slavery was a central part of US history, but scholars debate whether it was the absolute center. When facts and opinions bump against each other, pushback is inevitable.

The pushback against the 1619 Project includes mentions of particular historical inaccuracies, but, more important, it has resisted the idea of the centrality of slavery to US History. The reaction has gone too far—resisting any teaching of African American history, as if it were not part and parcel of American History as a whole.

One response to the 1619 Project is the "1776 Project." This abbreviated history of the U.S. rightly honors the Declaration of Independence, the Constitution, and the rule of law. Its agenda, however, is evident in an adjoining website, which states its goal as "Overturning Critical Race Theory and the 1619 Project." The creators want schools to teach a "patriotic vision of America and its history," which, of course, many currently do, even while teaching about slavery in U.S. history.[10]

Another recent development, which is, fortunately, creating a new line of historiography, is a reexamination of the history of colleges and universities, many of which developed with or because of slavery, and that is both northern and southern schools. Craig Steven Wilder, *Ebony and Ivy: Race, Slavery, and the Troubled History of America's Universities* (2013), and Leslie Harris, Alfred Brophy, and James T. Campbell, *Slavery*

---

10 *1776 Project*, https://1776project.org/. See also, *1776 Project PAC*, https://1776projectpac.com/about/; The President's Advisory 1776 Commission, *The 1776 Report*, January 2021, https://trumpwhitehouse.archives.gov/wp-content/uploads/2021/01/The-Presidents-Advisory-1776-Commission-Final-Report.pdf. Part of the pushback points out that most immigrants to the US arrived after slavery. On protection of slavery as one of the causes of the American Revolution, see Woody Holton, *Liberty Is Sweet: The Hidden History of the American Revolution* (New York: Simon and Schuster, 2021).

and the University (2019), and others have been examining the legacy of slavery in our institutions of higher education.[11]

The Universities Studying Slavery (USS) consortium includes Clemson University. *Call My Name, Clemson: Documenting the Black Experience in an American University Community* (2020), by Rhondda Robinson Thomas, combines history and memoir to consider this institution's founders, who were integral in slavery and racist ideology, and also the enslaved people and convict-lease workers who erected its buildings.[12]

Slavery and racism, intricately related, are the ugliest of stains on the character of a nation "birthed in liberty." Any attempt to understand our national character, or to understand racism, or even to understand the development of liberty and democracy, requires an understanding of American slavery back to the first Spanish slaving raids in Florida. Yet, because slavery is difficult to look at, many contend that the easiest, most bearable course of action is to ignore the hideous wound. For centuries, that is pretty much what we as a nation did.

In many ways we still do. There was a Civil War, there were plantations. There were "servants." There were even some vaguely defined "race problems," but we (those of us who are white Americans) are "past all that now." That lie is confronted in the 1619 Project.

---

11 Craig Steven Wilder, *Ebony and Ivy: Race, Slavery, and the Troubled History of America's Universities* (London: Bloomsbury, 2013); Harris, Brophy, and Campbell, eds., *Slavery and the University: Histories and Legacies*, (Athens: UGA Press, 2019).

12 Rhondda Robinson Thomas, *Call My Name, Clemson: Documenting the Black Experience in an American University Community* (Iowa City: University of Iowa Press, 2020). See also, Furman University Task Force on Slavery & Justice, *Seeking Abraham: A Report of Furman University's Task Force on Slavery and Justice, Second Edition* (2019), https://www.furman.edu/about/wp-content/uploads/sites/2/2019/11/Seeking-Abraham-Second-Edition.pdf; "Universities Studying Slavery," *The University of Virginia*, 2013, https://slavery.virginia.edu/universities-studying-slavery/.

If one reaction to trauma is to deny its importance, to forget the past and move on, another is to demand acknowledgement (as in our remembrance of the attack on 9/11). No national reckoning, no reconciliation, can come without the total openness to admit and deal with this sin on America's soul. Moreover, most historians today agree that slavery also provided the concepts of race that created Jim Crow and still hold power today. The racial ideas developed during slavery have defined critical aspects of American culture ever since, knowingly or not.

Without understanding slavery, we will never understand ourselves and the world we live in now. If we forget the past, we will *never* move on. Someone, somewhere, has to probe the festering sores if we are ever to be healed.

Historians seeking to understand why the morally shameful monster of human enslavement developed in and with America have offered varying interpretations. Each raised different problems and sharpened the debate as new insights fueled new debates. Then too, the vehemence with which scholars made their arguments indicated how intensely they saw the social, moral, and spiritual stakes of understanding slavery.

As the debates on slavery unfolded, historians examined different sorts of sources and evidence, with different approaches and methods, and offered varying theories and definitions, and different goals—all worthwhile. Historians thus create historiography. As Gavin Wright observed in a 2019 article: any given text is "a product of its times and a suggestive motivator for ours." And so, it is for readers today to understand the historical record the best we can.[13]

---

13 Gavin Wright, "Slavery and Anglo-American capitalism revisited," *The Economic History Review* 73, no. 2 (2020), 355.

In the first half of the twentieth century, the leading white historian of slavery was Yale's Georgiaborn scholar Ulrich Bonnell Phillips. His *American Negro Slavery* (1918) and *Life and Labor in the Old South* (1928) were prime examples of the nadir of American race relations after the era of Reconstruction. Phillips saw slavery as a benign system, a "school for civilizing savages."[14]

In 1915 Carter G. Woodson, an African American scholar, and the second Black person to receive a Ph.D. at Harvard, founded the Association for the Study of Negro Life and History (now Association for the Study of African American Life and History). In 1922 Woodson published *The Negro in Our History*, which should have opened a new branch of historiography, but did not take hold in the general white reading public at that time.[15] Woodson recommended that people interested in Black history read Du Bois, William Pickens, and Kelly Miller. Woodson also published the work of Alrutheus Ambush Taylor in his *Journal of Negro History.*[16] Although writing specifically on Reconstruction, Taylor looked back to slavery as part of his major studies.[17]

Sadly, it was Phillips's work (and the works of his many Ph.D. students) that set the standard on the subject until the

14 Ulrich B. Phillips, *American Negro Slavery: A Survey of the Supply, Employment and Control of Negro Labor as Determined by the Plantation* (Baton Rouge: LSU Press, 1966; orig. publ. 1918), 291; Phillips, *Life and Labor in the Old South* (Boston: Little, Brown and Co., 1963; orig. publ. 1929).

15 Carter G. Woodson, *The Negro in Our History* (Washington, DC: Associated Publishers, 1922), 329.

16 See W. E. B. Du Bois, *The Souls of Black Folk* (Chicago: A.C. McClurg & Co, 1904); William Pickens, *The New Negro* (New York: The Neale Publishing Co., 1916); Kelly Miller, *Race Adjustment* (New York: The Neale Publishing Co., 1908), and *Out of the House of Bondage* (New York: The Neale Publishing Co., 1914).

17 *The Negro in South Carolina During the Reconstruction* (1924) and *The Negro in the Reconstruction of Virginia* (1926) were first serialized in Carter G. Woodson's Journal *of Negro History* because university presses would not publish Taylor. Taylor's journal articles were bound as a book with the Association for the Study of Negro Life and History's imprint. His third book, published after receiving his Ph.D. from Harvard, was *The Negro in Tennessee, 1865-1880* in 1941 (Washington, D.C.: Associated Publishers).

1950s. It was the dominant depiction of slavery in American history textbooks (as well as among many historians). Between the two world wars, historians held, and the general public accepted, that slavery was good for the enslaved people! No reputable historian now believes that slavery was a positive good for the enslaved workers, but Phillips's point of view dominated US history and culture.[18] During this nadir of American race relations, the history profession, as almost every archive, was for white historians only.

Phillips, who died in 1934, was still venerated in the mid-1950s as a towering figure in the profession, and his mastery of plantation records was considered almost heroic. He produced a number of Ph.D. students, and many did important state studies of slavery, generally in line with Phillips's interpretation.

Not all white historians agreed with Phillips. Herbert Aptheker, *American Negro Slave Revolts* (1943), proved that many enslaved people revolted against this supposedly benign system.[19] Economists Alfred H. Conrad and John R. Meyer and a few historians as diverse as Lewis C. Gray, Charles Sydnor, and Richard Hofstadter challenged Phillips on various points, but few historians attempted a full-scale study of American slavery in the nearly four decades after World War I.[20]

---

18 Phillips, *American Negro Slavery*, 291, 35, 4244, 342. For explications of Phillips's life and works see Eugene D. Genovese, "Ulrich Bonnell Phillips and His Critics," Foreword to Phillips' *American Negro Slavery* (Baton Rouge: LSU Press, 1966); Genovese, "Race and Class in Southern History: An Appraisal of the Work of Ulrich Bonnell Phillips," *Agricultural History* 41, no. 4 (Oct. 1967): 34558; John Herbert Roper, *U.B. Phillips: A Southern Mind* (Macon: Mercer University Press, 1984); Merton L. Dillon, *Ulrich Bonnell Phillips, Historian of the Old South* (Baton Rouge: LSU Press, 1985); and John David Smith, *An Old Creed for the New South: Proslavery Ideology and Historiography, 18651918* (Westport: Greenwood Press, 1985).

19 Herbert Aptheker, *American Negro Slave Revolts* (New York: International Publishers, 1943).

20 Lewis C. Gray, in *History of Agriculture in the Southern United States to 1860*, 2 vols. (Washington, D.C.: Carnegie Institution, 1933), studied the origins of the plantation system and found them to be capitalistic. Charles S. Sydnor, *Slavery in Mississippi* (New York: D. Appleton & Co., 1933), and Richard M. Hofstadter, "U.B. Phillips and the Plantation Legend," *Journal of Negro History* 29, no. 2 (Apr. 1944): 109-24.

The historiography of slavery in the academic community changed in 1956 when Kenneth M. Stampp published *The Peculiar Institution*. For a young historian to take on U. B. Phillips, the professional icon, and Phillips's widely accepted interpretation of slavery, was bold. Stampp had to command the argument and the evidence, and he did. He mastered even more plantation records than Phillips, and, more importantly, he did so with great sensitivity to what all the evidence actually portrayed. Stampp addressed issues of economics, finding that slavery was profitable for enslavers. He also looked beyond economics, at the institution as a blight on the ideals of America.

Stampp wholeheartedly rebuked Phillips's theories. In doing so, he challenged the provincialism and racism of his and prior generations. He provided a striking intellectual force in his departure from the old racial and social myths that simply assumed Black inferiority. Stampp denied Phillips's contention that slavery exhibited a progression from savagery to civilization. Rather, he described the institution as an oppressive means of economic exploitation.

He depicted the enslaved workers as captives violently uprooted from an organic position in a viable African society and placed in a New World. His study was evidence-driven, for instance using slave newspaper advertisements with descriptions of the enslaved with scars and brands. He also had interpretive skills and an understanding of such modern social sciences as sociology and psychology.

Many contemporary white readers were moved by a passage in which Stampp declared, "I have assumed that the slaves were merely ordinary human beings, that innately Negroes *are*, after all, only white men with black skins, nothing more, nothing less." As the author intended, it gave a new and different meaning to the white construction of the "otherness" of Black people. It gave the story of the enslaved a relevance to whites it had never seemed to have before.

Few whites in the 1950s had thought of enslaved people innately like themselves. All too often what people, both white and Black people, knew of Africa was what they had read in H. Rider Haggard novels and seen in the Tarzan movies and in travelogues about "the Dark Continent." To most white readers, however, Africans and their descendants were innately different and even innately inferior.

By causing white readers to identify with the enslaved and by helping them to see how "the master class, for its own purposes, wrote chattel slavery, the caste system, and color prejudice into American custom and law," *The Peculiar Institution* affected its readers as few works of scholarship had ever done before.

Stampp's phrase, "white men with black skins," was, of course, offensive to those who asserted and fostered Black pride, and who understood both that the history of African Americans was different than that of white Americans, and that past and culture made a difference. At the same time, Stampp meant to awaken white people to their own prejudice, and the phrase was inspiring to white readers who grew up in a segregated southern community and opposed the horrors of segregation and racism that they witnessed firsthand.[21]

---

21 Kenneth M. Stampp, *The Peculiar Institution: Slavery in the Ante-Bellum South* (New York: Vintage Books, 1956), vii-viii, and p. 23.

SLAVERY AND ECONOMICS

A study of economics and slavery in England, *Capitalism and Slavery* (1944), by Eric Williams of Trinidad, influenced slavery studies thereafter. In this examination of the British Caribbean and Atlantic slave trade, Williams argued that the huge profits from enslaved labor and the slave trade enabled the development of capitalism and the industrial revolution in England. He found that it was only when the profits derived from industrialized England grew greater than the profits from slavery, that abolitionism rose as a force in England. It took a while, but Williams's model finally found resonance with historians in the U.S.[22]

By the mid-1960s the historiography accepted the moral repugnance of slavery. The debate became focused on economics. Many historians agreed that human bondage made possible the industrial revolution and created great wealth in the emerging capitalist democracy of the United States. While some economic historians argued that capitalism did or would have developed in America without slavery, most agreed that slavery in America did provide the labor for that foundation.

Within the "slavery as a business" topic, the issue began as a simple question of whether or not slavery was profitable. Economists entered this fray in 1958 with an article by Alfred Conrad and John Meyer, "The Economics of Slavery in the Ante Bellum South." They announced that the answer was yes and that any other view could not stand against the facts.[23]

---

22 Eric Williams, *Capitalism and Slavery* (1944; repr., Chapel Hill: University of North Carolina Press, 1994). Williams (1911-1981) served as the first prime minister of independent Trinidad and Tobago beginning in 1962 until his death. Prior to entering politics, he was a professor of social and political science at Howard University.

23 Alfred H. Conrad and John R. Meyer, "The Economics of Slavery in the Ante Bellum South," *The Journal of Political Economy* April 1958. Vol LXVI, No. 3.

Historians, however, would not concede the field to the economists or the cliometricians. The leading historical figure of the 1960s was the young Marxist historian Eugene D. Genovese, who not only drew upon Phillips (without the racist baggage) but also upon the Italian philosopher Antonio Gramsci's work on cultural hegemony. As a Marxist, Genovese was drawn to the white planter class of the Old South who formulated the only (except for the more spiritual and moral New England Transcendentalists) critique of emerging U.S. capitalism in their pro-slavery arguments.

In *The Political Economy of Slavery: Studies in the Economy and Society of the Slave South* (1961), and also *The World the Slaveholders Made: Two Essays in Interpretation* (1969), Genovese shaped the work on slavery studies thereafter. In a later edition of *The Political Economy* (1989), Genovese stated emphatically that his work was not "the economics of slavery" but the "political economy of slavery."

With his argument that southern slavery was precapitalistic and seigniorial, Genovese claimed that slavery retarded economic growth and industrial development in the South.[24] With the influence of his wife, Elizabeth Fox-Genovese, Eugene Genovese modified somewhat his arguments about the precapitalistic South. It emerged as a development of "merchant capital"—a form of capital that is a political economic *relation*, not a thing.

His examination of merchant capital compared slavery with serfdom, wage labor, or other labor-forms in which an economic surplus can be extracted. In wage labor, that surplus

---

24 Genovese, *The World the Slaveholders Made: Two Essays in Interpretation* (Middleton: Wesleyan University Press, 1988) and *The Political Economy of the Slavery: Studies in the Economy and the Society of the Slave South* (Middleton: Wesleyan University Press, 1989), 3. In a 1995 H-Net review, Genovese denied calling the South seigniorial, although he certainly used the word in other contexts, but that is the term that has stuck.

took the form of *profit,* derived from *labor power.* Under slavery, though, it was not just the result of labor that merchant capital commanded—it was labor itself, incarnated in human form, with all its merits and demerits, potentialities, and problems. In mature form, that labor came to reflect brutal paternalistic management, something Fox-Genovese's work on family culture helped Genovese understand.[25]

Many accepted Eugene Genovese's and Elizabeth Fox-Genovese's revised arguments that slavery in the American South was part of the capitalist system but really not of it (some critics saw this revision as merely semantic). Nor were the Genoveses alone in such arguments that slavery was not generally profitable and that it ultimately retarded economic growth.

Urban historian Richard Wade, in *Slavery in the Cities* (1964), insisted that slavery as an institution was fundamentally incompatible with urbanization and industrial development, and the historical sociologist Barrington Moore, Jr., in *Social Origins of Dictatorship and Democracy* (1966), made much of the capitalist/precapitalist split.[26] Fred Bateman and Thomas Weiss, in *A Deplorable Scarcity* (1981), traced the failure of large-scale southern industrialization to the precapitalist reluctance of Southern planters to invest in industry.[27]

---

25 Elizabeth Fox-Genovese and Eugene D. Genovese, *Fruits of Merchant Capital: Slavery and Bourgeois Property in the Rise and Expansion of Capitalism* (New York: Oxford University Press, 1983); Elizabeth Fox-Genovese's *Within the Plantation Household: Black and White Women of the Old South* (Chapel Hill: University of North Carolina Press, 1988) focused on enslaved and non-slaveholding women of the South, compared to women of the North.

26 Richard C. Wade, *Slavery in the Cities* (New York: Oxford University Press, 1967); Barrington Moore, Jr., *Social Origins of Dictatorship and Democracy: Lord and Peasant in the Making of the Modern World* (Boston: Beacon Press, 1966). As early as 1976, economic historian Claudia Goldin disputed Wade's findings. See Claudia Dale Goldin, *Slavery in the American South, 1820-1860: A Quantitative History* (Chicago: University of Chicago Press, 1976).

27 Fred Bateman and Thomas Weiss, *A Deplorable Scarcity: The Failure of Industrialization in the Slave Economy* (Chapel Hill: University of North Carolina Press, 2017).

This interpretation did not go unchallenged of course. In 1970, Robert Starobin entered the debate with his book, *Industrial Slavery in the Old South*, a study of the business of slavery, of working conditions, and of resistance.[28] Kenneth Stampp's student James Oakes, in *The Ruling Race* (1982), provided the sternest critique of Genovese's early works and then continued the onslaught in his second, more sophisticated book, *Slavery and Freedom* (1992). Oakes's primary concern, however, was less with capitalism than with aristocracy.[29]

Genovese and those who argued slavery was not profit-driven had the goal posts moved in 1974 with the publication of Robert Fogel and Stanley Engerman's two volume *Time on the Cross*.[30] This magnum opus of quantitative economic history made bold claims for the economic vitality of slavery, its profitability, and the efficiency of its work force. The authors wrote that enslaved people typically produced 35 percent more with the same inputs than did northern family farms. Moreover, Fogel and Engerman claimed that an enslaved person could typically expect to receive 90 percent of the profits of their labor over his or her lifetime. They never did explain how this could happen, nor how a system could profit by returning so much income to a labor force unable either to buy its products or purchase stock.

Nevertheless, their analysis left the impression that slavery, while morally abhorrent, was not so bad. The work provoked a firestorm of criticism from economists as well as

---

28 Robert S. Starobin, *Industrial Slavery in the Old South* (New York: Oxford University Press, 1970).

29 James Oakes, *The Ruling Race: A History of American Slaveholders* (New York: Knopf, 1982) and *Slavery and Freedom: An Interpretation of the Old South* (New York: W. W. Norton & Co., 1998).

30 Robert Fogel and Stanley Engerman, *Time on the Cross: The Economics of American Negro Slavery* (New York: W. W. Norton & Co., 1974).

historians such as Kenneth Stampp, Herbert Gutman, and Gavin Wright.[31] Not all these scholars disagreed with the fundamental conclusion that slavery was a relatively healthy capitalist economic system, but they all disparaged Fogel and Engerman's work for vagueness, improper techniques, unwarranted inferences, and false conclusions.

Many scholars identified gross errors of omission and commission in *Time on the Cross*. Fogel, however, refused to retreat; in his *Without Consent or Contract* (1989) he blamed much of the acerbic reaction to *Time on the Cross* on its moral implications. One of the "findings" in *Time on the Cross* was that enslaved workers were internalizing white values. He was convinced that for some academics that "finding" was taken to be an insult and was judged with an air of moral repugnance.[32]

A more temperate analysis of the issue was offered by Gavin Wright in *The Political Economy of the Cotton South: Households and Wealth in the Nineteenth Century* (1978). While Wright agreed that slavery was profitable for enslavers, he did so in a more nuanced and reasoned way. Moreover, he never denied the institution's brutality.[33]

In 1989, Michael Tadman included demography as well as manuscript sources to examine white speculation in the internal slave trade, *Speculators and Slaves: Masters, Traders, and Slaves in the Old South*.[34] In 1999 Walter Johnson's *Soul*

---

31 See Paul A. David, Herbert G. Gutman, Richard Sutch, Peter Temin, Gavin Wright, *Reckoning with Slavery* (New York: Oxford University Press, 1976).

32 Robert Fogel, *Without Consent or Contract: The Rise and Fall of American Slavery* (New York: W. W. Norton & Co., 1989).

33 Wright, *The Political Economy of the Cotton South and Wealth in the Nineteenth Century* (New York: W. W. Norton & Co., 1978).

34 Michael Tadman, *Speculators and Slaves: Masters, Traders, and Slaves in the Old South* (Madison: University of Wisconsin Press, 1989).

by Soul: Life Inside the Antebellum Slave Market analyzed the commodification in the New Orleans slave market and por-trayed the heart-wrenching drama of people up for sale.[35]

Other work on the slave trade followed, such as Daina Berry's *The Price for Their Pound of Flesh: The Value of the Enslaved, from Womb to Grave, in the Building of a Nation* (2015) and Alexandra Finley's *An Intimate Economy: Enslaved Women, Work, and America's Domestic Slave Trade* (2020).[36] Stephanie Jones-Rogers, *They Were Her Property: White Women as Slave Owners in the American South* (2019), showed the important role of women in the capitalistic profits from holding enslaved workers, and Jennifer L. Morgan, *Reckoning With Slavery: Gender, Kinship, and Capitalism in the Early Black Atlantic* (2021) examined the role given to enslaved women in developing capitalism.[37]

Other work in the line of arguments for slavery as a cap-italist enterprise included Edward E. Baptist, *Creating an Old South* (2002) and Adam Rothman, *Slave Country* (2005).[38] In 2011, Seth Rockman (*Scraping By*, 2009), co-hosted with Sven Beckert a conference at Brown University on "Slavery's Capitalism."[39] Soon after the conference, three major studies

---

35 Walter Johnson, *Soul by Soul: Life Inside the Antebellum Slave Market* (Cambridge: Harvard University Press, 1999).

36 Daina Ramey Berry, *The Price for Their Pound of Flesh: The Value of the Enslaved, from Womb to Grave, in the Building of a Nation* (Boston: Beacon Press, 2017); Alexandra J. Finley, *An Intimate Economy: Enslaved Women, Work, and America's Domestic Slave Trade* (Chapel Hill: University of North Carolina Press, 2020).

37 Stephanie Jones-Rogers, *They Were Her Property: White Woman as Slave Owners in the American South* (New Haven: Yale University Press, 2019); Jennifer L. Morgan, *Reckoning with Slavery: Gender, Kinship, and Capitalism in the Early Black Atlantic* (Durham: Duke University Press, 2021).

38 Edward E. Baptist, *Creating an Old South: Middle Florida's Plantation Frontier before the Civil War* (Chapel Hill: University of North Carolina Press, 2002); Adam Rothman, *Slave Country: American Expansion and the Origins of the Deep South* (Cambridge: Harvard University Press, 2005).

39 Seth Rockman, *Scraping By: Wage Labor, Slavery, and Survival in Early Baltimore* (Baltimore: Johns Hopkins University Press, 2009).

set the framework for the latest work in the school of "Slavery as Capitalism."

Beckert's *Empire of Cotton: A Global History* (2014) offered a history of capitalism's role in enslavement.[40] Walter Johnson, *River of Dark Dreams: Slavery and Empire in the Cotton Kingdom* (2013), examined the world-wide capitalism that hungered for land and profit and thirsted for exploited labor.[41] Baptist's *The Half Has Never Been Told: Slavery and the Making of American Capitalism* (2014) examined the growth of slavery alongside the growth of the South in the first 80 years of America's independence.[42]

These new scholars were less interested in defining what is and what is not the capitalist economic system. They emphasized the cruelty of slavery as part of economic and market forces. Calvin Schermerhorn, in *Money over Mastery, Family over Freedom: Slavery in the Antebellum Upper South* (2011) and *The Business of Slavery and the Rise of American Capitalism, 1815-1860* (2015), wrote of the efforts to keep family members off the auction block and then of the entrepreneurial work of slavery and the slave trade, as well as the federal policies that aided the business.[43] Baptist used a new rhetoric to awaken those who seemed to forget that plantations were "forced labor camps." In 2016 Rockman and Beckert published the edited collection from their conference, and

---

40 Sven Beckert, *Empire of Cotton: A Global History* (London: Penguin Books, 2014).

41 Johnson, *River of Dark Dreams: Slavery and Empire in the Cotton Kingdom* (Cambridge: Belknap Press, 2013).

42 Edward E, Baptist, *The Half Has Never Been Told: Slavery and the Making of American Capitalism* (New York: Basic Books, 2014).

43 Calvin Schermerhorn, *Money over Mastery, Family over Freedom: Slavery in the Antebellum Upper South* (Baltimore: Johns Hopkins Press, 2011) and *The Business of Slavery and the Rise of American Capitalism, 1815-1860* (New Haven: Yale University Press, 2015).

the introduction to *Slavery's Capitalism* declared that slavery was "the foundational American institution, organizing the nation's politics, legal structures, and cultural practices."[44] These scholars turned the conversation about slavery as a form of capitalism to the brutality of capitalism itself.

Critics pounced. Christopher Morris, in "With 'the Economics-of-Slavery Culture Wars' It's Déjà vu All Over Again," had much to say against their arguments. For one thing, they did not admit the lengthy historiography that preceded them on their subject. For another, they did not define their terms. Morris pointed out the complications between capitalism and slavery when the enslaved people were "investments, laborers, and producers who were commoditized, monetized, and exchanged all at once."[45]

Economic historian Richard Sutch in a 2018 essay surveyed the central issues of slavery and economics and how economists believe they have changed over time, as well as how some of the issues have been resolved. Sutch looks first at profitability, and asks did slave owners make money and would the system have survived? He argues there is now a consensus in favor of positive answers. Secondly, he asks, was slave labor productive, what Fogel and Engerman had called "efficiency"? Here too Sutch finds a consensus in favor of a positive answer, though economists differ over the sources of efficiency (work pace vs. resource allocation). Thirdly, how was slave labor treated: enlightened long-term paternalism vs. short-sighted brutal driving? Here the evidence now favors

---

44 Sven Beckert and Seth Rothman, eds., *Slavery's Capitalism: A New History of American Economic Development* (Philadelphia: University of Pennsylvania Press, 2016), 1.

45 Christopher Morris, "With 'the Economics-of-Slavery Culture Wars' It's Déjà vu All Over Again," *The Journal of the Civil War Era* 10, no. 4 (December 2020): 524-557. See also, Scott Reynolds Nelson, "Who Put Their Capitalism in My Slavery," *Journal of the Civil War Era* 5, no. 2 (June 2015): 289-310.

the latter, including much more use of the slave trade and rates of family separation than was previously known. Finally, was slavery vital for accelerated US growth? This question was largely neglected by earlier generations, but it is key for the New Historians of Capitalism. Economists complain that New Historians have weak evidence, and they tend to conflate complicity with economic impact.[46]

The historiography of slavery as capitalism is on-going. Some declare that slavery was commercial but not capitalist. Or perhaps slavery was capitalist, but qualitatively different from merchant or industrial capitalism. Most historians agree that by the late antebellum period a vast amount of southern social, intellectual, and political capital was invested in slavery, and that in the decade proceeding the Civil War, with high cotton prices, slavery was profitable. But just as certainly American slavery was more than an economic system.

Scholars analyzing slavery as part of the U.S. economic system insisted that slavery was all-American and not just southern. Wendy Warren, in *New England Bound: Slavery and Colonization in Early America* (2016), showed the importance of slavery to the economy of the Puritan colonies.[47] Christy Clark-Pujara presented a detailed history of one northern state's involvement in the business of slavery, Rhode Island, *Dark Work: The Business of Slavery in Rhode Island* (2016).[48]

---

46 Richard C. Sutch, "The Economics of African American Slavery: The Cliometrics Debate," Working Paper 25197, National Bureau of Economic Research, October 2018 (http://www.nber.org/papers/w25197); see also the older Paul A. David et al, *Reckoning with Slavery*: A Critical Study in the Quantitative History of American Negro Slavery (New York: Oxford University Press, 1976).

47 Wendy Warren, *New England Bound: Slavery and Colonization in Early America* (New York: Liveright, 2016).

48 Christy Clark-Pujara, *Dark Work: The Business of Slavery in Rhode Island* (New York: NYU Press, 2016).

SLAVERY AS THE FABRIC OF SOUTHERN LIFE

Slavery, of course, entailed so much more than economic exploitation. Beyond its place in the theory of capitalist development, slavery was the southern milieu that touched every aspect of life.

Once again Ulrich B. Phillips's 1918 *American Negro Slavery* was considered the standard work on the subject until the 1950s. In that book Phillips made two arguments that enslavers themselves had clung to: that Black people were inferior by nature; that slavery was a relatively mild form of coerced labor.

Phillips was ambivalent regarding the influence of Africa on African Americans. Occasionally he seemed to believe in African cultural continuity among enslaved people. "His nature was an African's profoundly modified but hardly transformed by the requirements of European civilization." Yet only a few sentences later Phillips emphasized discontinuity between Africa and African Americans. On the slave plantation, Phillips wrote, the enslaved person left Africa behind: "Ceasing to be Foulah, Coramantee, Ebo or Angola, he became instead the American negro."

In any event, Phillips's view of Africa was ignorant and terribly negative. "No people is without its philosophy and religion," he admitted, but "of all regions of extensive habitation equatorial Africa is the worst." Any such African continuities as he was willing to acknowledge he deplored. In the opinion of Phillips and of his students and followers, as well as many white historians and the white American public, slavery was necessary and successful for civilizing savages.[49]

---

49 Phillips, *American Negro Slavery*, 291, 35, 4244, 342.

The reaction to Phillips's interpretation included a scrutiny of the relationship between slavery and racism. One area of inquiry centered around the question of whether slavery caused racism, or racism caused slavery. Oscar and Mary Handlin in 1950 contended that the first Africans in America were gradually enslaved; thus, slavery was the cause of racism.[50] On the other hand, Carl Degler in 1959 argued that a pre-existing white racism was a major cause of the enslavement of Africans.[51]

In 1967, David Brion Davis published the first of his important multivolume scholarly studies on slavery, *The Problem of Slavery in Western Culture*. He argued that an anti-slavery or abolitionist movement could not develop until people could break away from Christian and classical theories of servitude that tended to rationalize human bondage. According to Davis there had to be a revolution in attitudes toward sin, toward human nature, and toward the possibilities of moral and human progress, which began with the enlightenment.[52]

In 1968 Winthrop Jordan argued in a massive study that the perception of difference constituted "the indispensable key to the degradation of Negroes in English America." He theorized that African attributes prompted pejorative emotions: "these qualities had for Englishmen added up to savagery; they were major components in that sense of difference which provided the mental margin absolutely requisite for placing the European on the deck of the slave ship and the Negro in the hold." At the end of his investigation, Jordan basically threw up his hands

50 Oscar and Mary Handlin, "Origins of the Southern Labor System," *William and Mary Quarterly* 7, no. 2 (Apr. 1950): 199-222.

51 Carl N. Degler, "Slavery and the Genesis of American Race Prejudice," *Comparative Studies in Society and History* 2, no. 1 (Nov. 1959): 49-66.

52 David Brion Davis, *The Problem of Slavery in Western Culture* (Ithaca: Cornell University Press, 1966).

and suggested that determining which came first, racism or slavery, is a chicken and egg problem.[53]

In 1975, Edmund Morgan published his *American Slavery, American Freedom: The Ordeal of Colonial Virginia* where he centered Bacon's Rebellion and argued that class conflict led to slavery as the lifetime status for people of African descent. One of the blatant ironies of American history was that the tradition of liberty grew side by side with slavery. Morgan noted the paradox of the slaveholding revolutionaries and slaveholding "republicanism"; generations of historians have followed Morgan's paradigm.[54]

This chicken and egg problem is not just academic but has real world and policy issue relevance. If the reaction of whites to encountering Africans was not just difference, but prejudice, then the dilemma of ridding the United States of racism is much more difficult.

The historiographical shift of slavery studies to the theme of slavery as a way of life brought many complications to the debate, and the debate between Phillips and Stampp continued until Stanley M. Elkins published *Slavery* in 1959. Building upon the research and insights of Stampp, and on an earlier work by Frank Tannenbaum, Elkins extended the comparison between slavery in the English colonies of North America and the Spanish colonies to the south.

He argued that in South America the Catholic Church served as an ameliorating institution between the enslaver and the enslaved, whereas in American culture when

---

53 Winthrop D. Jordan, *White Over Black: American Attitudes Toward the Negro, 1550-1812* (Chapel Hill: University of North Carolina Press, 1968), 91, 97.

54 Edmund Morgan, *American Slavery American Freedom: The Ordeal of Colonial Virginia* (New York: W.W. Norton & Co., 1975), 4.

capitalism was emerging, the United States offered no countervailing institutions. That part of the book has been undercut by those who knew more about South American culture than Elkins did.[55]

Elkins also focused more directly upon the personality of the enslaved people themselves than any earlier scholar had done. He used psychological data on survivors of the Nazi death camps to draw a parallel between the experience of the prisoners and that of enslaved people. The personality patterns of the death camp prisoners, he wrote, were completely reshaped under the power of guards who functioned as perverse "father figures" (the arbiters of life, death, and sustenance). According to Elkins, the dehumanization of Jewish prisoners was analogous to the shock of the enslaved's capture, removal to an alien culture, and "seasoning" on the slave plantation. The "sanctions of the system," he assumed, "were in themselves sufficient to produce a recognizable personality type."[56] (This idea of a personality change in concentration camps has been widely challenged.)

Elkins admitted that the "seasoning" system worked less well in practice than in theory. He acknowledged a space where enslaved workers could "escape the full impact of the system and its coercion upon personality," where "the system's authority-structure claimed their bodies but not their souls."

Nevertheless, the "Elkins Thesis" depicted "Sambo" as the typical slave, made inferior by the environment of slavery. This proved highly controversial. In response, other scholars,

---

55 Frank Tannenbaum, *Slave and Citizen: The Negro in the Americas* (New York: Vintage Books, 1946). Stanley M. Elkins, *Slavery: A Problem in American Institutional and Intellectual Life* (Chicago: University of Chicago Press, 1959), 86.

56 Elkins, *Slavery*, 139.

particularly in later years, showed how enslaved people could sometimes use the white designation of "Sambo" to their own advantage.

For example, African American historian John Blassingame presented examples of enslaved people's pretending and using "Sambo" to deter some of the horrors of slavery.[57] Leslie Howard Owens, *This Species of Property: Slave Life and Culture in the Old South* (1976), examined personalities and power dynamics in the enslaved community.[58] Moreover, abundant evidence, including scholarship prior to Elkins's book, showed that many enslaved workers chose instead the path of escape, rebellion, or "day to day resistance."

Until the 1970s the question of the nature and origin of the culture of enslaved workers had been addressed only sporadically. One of the most controversial topics in the literature of Southern history at that time was whether the folk culture of the enslaved retained any African sources.

If Phillips, who had at least studied the primary plantation documents, straddled both sides of the African cultural continuity issue, social scientists who were not encumbered by such impedimenta came down more firmly on one side or the other. The major school of thought emphasized the influence of European culture upon enslaved Africans. According to what has been called the "catastrophist school" of American sociological thought: African Americans—alone among all the peoples that made up the United States—had lost their entire native culture.

---

57 John W. Blassingame, *The Slave Community: Plantation Life in the Antebellum South* (New York: Oxford University Press, 1972).

58 Leslie Howard Owens, *This Species of Property: Slave Life and Culture in the Old South* (New York: Oxford University Press, 1976). See also, Raymond A. Bauer and Alice H. Bauer, "Day to Day Resistance to Slavery," *Journal of Negro History* 27 (1942): 388-419.

Following the position enunciated in 1919 by the University of Chicago sociologist Robert E. Park, the catastrophists regarded Black folkways to be an imperfect acculturation to EuroAmerican culture. According to Park, "the Negro, when he landed in the United States, left behind him almost everything but his dark complexion and his tropical temperament. It is very difficult to find in the South today," he wrote in 1919, "anything that can be traced directly back to Africa."[59]

The foremost figure of the catastrophist school was the Black sociologist E. Franklin Frazier. "Probably never before in history," Frazier wrote in *The Negro Family in the United States* (1939), "has a people been so completely stripped of its social heritage as the Negroes who were brought to America." Frazier gave an added spin on losing their African heritage; they had "gradually taken over the more sophisticated American culture."

African Americans constituted, in Frazier's words, the one group "not distinguished by culture from the dominant group." Frazier's sophisticated restatements of part of Phillips's position suggest a certain embarrassment over the African past and what he seems to have regarded as the shameful experience of slavery.[60]

Others in the catastrophist interpretation of the 1930s also wrote about Black culture as a derivation of white

---

59 Robert E. Park, "The Conflict and Fusion of Cultures with Special Reference to the Negro," *Journal of Negro History* 4, no. 2 (Apr. 1919): 11618. It was many years later that Orlando Patterson gave his perspective on those conservative and radical manifestations of the sociological catastrophist school. Orlando Patterson, "Rethinking Black History," *Harvard Educational Review* 41, no. 3 (1971): 299304.

60 E. Franklin Frazier, *The Negro Family in the United States* (Chicago: University of Chicago Press, 1939), 2122, 479, and *The Negro in the United States* (revised ed., New York: Macmillan, 1957; orig. pub. 1949), 68081. See also his "Traditions and Patterns of Negro Family Life in the United States," in *Race and Culture Contacts*, ed. E. B. Reuter (New York: McGraw, 1934), 194; and *The Negro Church in America* (New York: Schocken Books, 1963).

culture and not as its own set of customs and values with roots in Africa. The classic sociological study of the South Carolina Sea Islands in 1930 was *Folk Culture on St. Helena Island* by Guy B. Johnson. He traced the genealogy of African American speech, songs, and folk beliefs mainly to white sources. "The Negro's almost complete loss of African language heritages is startling at first glance," he wrote, "but slavery as practiced in the United States made any other outcome impossible." Johnson even attributed songs developed in slavery as "borrowed from white folk music."[61]

Many others were of the same tradition: Guion Griffis Johnson and T.J. Woofter, Jr., Edward M. von Hornbostel, Newman Ivey White, Robert Winslow Gordon, and George Pullen Jackson.[62]

Black scholars disagreed. John Wesley Work, James Weldon Johnson, and N.G.J. Ballanta adamantly claimed African origins for the African American spirituals. One white scholar who shared that view was the music critic Edward Krehbiel.[63] Others

------

61 Guy B. Johnson, *Folk Culture on St Helena Island, South Carolina*, (Chapel Hill: University of North Carolina Press, 1930) 1011, 128, 171. For a discussion of Guy B. Johnson and his role in the St. Helena project, see Daniel Joseph Singal, *The War Within: From Victorian to Modernist Thought in the South, 19191945* (Chapel Hill: University of North Carolina Press, 1982), 31527, and Guy B. Johnson, "Reminiscences About Sea Island Research in 1928," in *Sea and Land: Cultural and Biographical Adaptations in the Southern Coastal Plain*, eds. James L. Peacock and James C. Sabella, *Southern Anthropological Society Proceedings*, no. 21 (Athens: University of Georgia Press, 1988), 3-12.

62 Guion Griffis Johnson, *A Social History of the Sea Islands* (Chapel Hill: University of North Carolina Press, 1930); T.J. Woofter, Jr., *Black Yeomanry: Life on St. Helena Island* (Chapel Hill: University of North Carolina Press, 1930); Edward M. von Hornbostel, "American Negro Music," *International Review of Missions*, 15 (1926), 74851; Newman Ivey White, *American Negro Folk Songs* (Cambridge: Harvard University Press, 1928); George Pullen Jackson, *White and Negro Spirituals: Their Life Span and Kinship* (New York: J. J. Augustin, 1943).

63 John Wesley Work, Introduction to *Folk Song of the American Negro*, ed. Frederick J. Work (Nashville: Fisk University Press, 1907); James Weldon Johnson and J. Rosamond Johnson, *The Book of American Negro Spirituals* (New York: The Viking Press, 1925); Nicholas George Julius Ballanta, *St Helena Island Spirituals* (New York: G. Schirmer, 1925); Edward Krehbiel, *AfroAmerican Folksongs: A Study in Racial and National Music* (New York: G. Schirmer, 1914). For studies of the controversy over the spirituals, see Charles Joyner, "Music: Origins of the Spirituals," in *Encyclopedia of Black America*, ed. W. Augustus Low

soon followed in arguing the "Africanity" of slave culture.

By the 1930s, white anthropologist Melville J. Herskovits was beginning to ask if scholars might, upon close examination of African American culture, find "that there are some subtle elements left of what was ancestrally possessed." Herskovits had early in his career scorned the idea that there were even lingering traces of Africa among African Americans and had doubted that there was any separate African American culture. "That they have absorbed the culture of America," he wrote in 1925, "is too obvious, almost, to be mentioned."

But then, as he began to conduct comparative research in New World African American cultures, Herskovits began to question his earlier position. In 1941, following several years of fieldwork in the Caribbean, Brazil, and West Africa, Herskovits published his most significant work, *The Myth of the Negro Past*. In it he proposed a general theory of culture change that posited the persistence of African "survivals" in African American culture. Such survivals had already been available for study.[64]

The Savannah Unit of the Federal Writers Project had demonstrated the facts the previous year in *Drums and Shadows: Survival Studies Among the Georgia Coastal Negroes*. But *Drums and Shadows* was met with indifference. *The Myth*

and Virgil A. Clift (New York: McGraw-Hill, 1981): 59196; John David Smith, "The Unveiling of Slave Folk Culture, 18651920," *Journal of Folklore Research* 21, no. 1 (Apr. 1984), 4762; D.K. Wilgus, *AngloAmerican Folksong Scholarship Since 1898* (New Brunswick: Rutgers University Press, 1959), 34564.

64 Melville J. Herskovits, "The Negro in the New World: The Statement of a Problem," *American Anthropologist* 32, no. 1 (Jan.-Mar., 1930), 14155; Herskovits, "The Negro's Americanism," in *The New Negro: An Interpretation*, ed. Alain Locke (New York: Atheneum, 1925), 35960. As late as 1937, when he published *Life in a Haitian Valley*, Herskovits still believed that "going native" (that is, being a participant observer) was "neither possible nor of benefit among West African Negroes and their New World descendants." Herskovits, *Life in a Haitian Valley*, (New York: A. A. Knopf, 1937), 32627.

of the Negro Past, however, was immediately noticed—and was immediately controversial.[65]

Nearly all American intellectuals, Black scholars and white, denounced the Herskovits thesis as misguided and exaggerated. Racial egalitarians such as E. Franklin Frazier and Guy B. Johnson were concerned that segregation-ists might use Herskovits's arguments to build a case that African Americans were unable to assimilate. Herskovits was no supporter of segregation (even though much of *Myth of the Negro Past* was built upon the scholarship of Ulrich B. Phillips, whom he quoted approvingly a dozen times). But few Americans, other than ardent white supremacists, were prepared to accept his thesis of African survivals in the New World.

The Black folklorist Zora Neale Hurston, on the other hand, suggested in *Mules and Men* (1935) a more complex relationship between African and European elements under-lying African American folklore.[66] Like Herskovits, Hurston had studied with Franz Boas at Columbia University, and she did not agree with all his ideas either.

Boas, eager to combat the tradition in anthropology that considered Black people to be at an earlier, less advanced level of civilization than whites, insisted on denying any enduring influence of African culture. At the same time, in a prolific series of books, articles, and platform addresses, Boas inaugurated what would ultimately become a massive

---

65 Herskovits, *The Myth of the Negro Past* (New York: Harper & Brothers, 1941; Boston: Beacon Press, 1958), 8, 25, 37, 40, 41, 45, 88, 118, 120n, 126, 127, 304; Georgia Writers Project, *Drums and Shadows: Survival Studies Among the Georgia Coastal Negroes* (Athens: UGA Press, 1940). See Guy B. Johnson's review of Herskovits in *American Sociological Review* 7, no. 2 (Apr. 1942): 289-290. Cf. John F. Szwed, "An American Anthropological Dilemma: The Politics of AfroAmerican Culture," in *Reinventing Anthropology*, ed. Dell Hymes (New York: Vintage Books, 1972), 15381.

66 Zora Neale Hurston, *Mules and Men* (Philadelphia: J. B. Lippincott Co., 1935).

campaign for the recognition that culture is not racial that is to say, not biological but social.[67]

Another Boas student was Ruth Benedict. Her book, *Race: Science and Politics* (1940), was an indictment of racism as a faulty and dangerous way to classify people. Yet, Benedict agreed with the catastrophic version of history: "Their patterns of political, economic, and artistic behavior were forgotten even the languages they had spoken in Africa." She accounted for this loss in the same way that E. Franklin Frazier and Guy B. Johnson had: "Conditions of slavery in America were so drastic that this loss is not to be wondered at."[68]

Gunnar Myrdal's 1944 publication of *An American Dilemma*, while calling attention to the problem of racial prejudice in a supposedly democratic, egalitarian society, also took the catastrophist position and again misunderstood Black culture. He wrote that African American culture "is a distorted development, or a pathological condition, of the general American culture."[69]

The catastrophist interpretation continued to dominate the historiography as late as 1963 when Nathan Glazer and Daniel Patrick Moynihan echoed that interpretation in their

---

67 With the publication of *The Mind of Primitive Man* (New York: MacMillan, 1911), Franz Boas set the tone for all subsequent serious work in anthropology. According to Boas, the traits of the American Negroes are adequately explained on the basis of history and social status, the tearing away from the African soil and the consequent complete loss of the old standards of life. See also Boas, *Race and Nationality* (New York: Frank Boas, 1915), 140; and *Race and Democratic Society* (New York: J. J. Augustin, 1945).

68 Ruth Benedict, *Race: Science and Politics* (New York: Penguin Books, 1940, 1959), 8687. See the following by Elsie Clews Parsons: *Folk Tales from the Sea Islands, South Carolina* (Cambridge: Harvard University Press, 1923); *Folk Tales of the Andros Islands* (Cambridge: Harvard University Press, 1918); *Folk Lore from the Cape Verde Islands* (Cambridge: Harvard University Press, 1923); *Folk Lore of the Antilles, French and English*, vols. 13 (Cambridge: Harvard University Press, 193335, 1943). See also Newbell Niles Puckett, *Folk Beliefs of the Southern Negro* (Chapel Hill: University of North Carolina Press, 1926).

69 Gunnar Myrdal, *An American Dilemma: The Negro Problem* (New York: Harper & Brothers, 1944), 92829.

Beyond the Melting Pot (1963). "The Negro," they wrote, "is only an American and nothing else. He has no culture and values to guard and protect."[70]

In 1977 the catastrophic school of thought ended (or so scholars believed) with *Black Culture and Black Consciousness: Afro-American Folk Thought from Slavery to Freedom* by Lawrence W. Levine. Levine, having researched a treasure trove of oral tradition, songs, tales, and poems, insisted on the value of Black culture. Levine changed the historical analysis. After him, no major scholar has embraced the catastrophic school in an overall sense, although some have emphasized white influence in specific fields, such as language or religion.[71]

Writing in the 1980s, both John Boles and John Blassingame, for instance, thought that religion, which they described as the principal channel through which culture reached enslaved people, embodied mostly European culture. Even so, they acknowledged African influence. While imprecise on the proportions or the process, neither argued exclusively British or European sources in the formation of culture within the enslaved community.[72]

Acknowledging African roots was important to Sterling Stuckey. He looked at Africa as a continent, not a country, a continent populated by a multiplicity of ethnic groups. He argued in *Slave Culture: Nationalist Theory and the Foundations of Black America* (1987) that enslaved people

---

70 Nathan Glazer and Daniel Patrick Moynihan, *Beyond the Melting Pot: The Negroes, Puerto Ricans, Jews, Italians, and Irish of New York City* (Cambridge: Harvard University Press, 1963), 53.

71 Lawrence W. Levine, *Black Culture and Black Consciousness: Afro-American Folk Thought from Slavery to Freedom* (New York: Oxford University Press, 1977).

72 Boles writes in *Black Southerners, 16191869* (Lexington: University of Kentucky Press, 1983), "In no other aspect of black cultural life than religion, had the values and practices of whites so deeply penetrated," 165. Blassingame, *The Slave Community*, 98. See also John Boles, ed., *Masters and Slaves in the House of the Lord: Race and Religion in the American South, 1740-1870* (Lexington: University of Kentucky Press, 1988).

created their own new culture based on religion: "Christianity provided a protective exterior beneath which more complex, less familiar (to outsiders) religious principles and practices were operative."

Although the great African American mystic theologian, Howard Thurman, was a member of the catastrophist school, he thought the question of continuity vs. non-continuity was less important than the fact that enslaved people created their culture and the spirituals in the New World out of the circumstances they found themselves in and fashioned from the materials at hand. Thurman's approach is represented in Nathan Huggins's *Black Odyssey: The African-American Ordeal in Slavery* (1977), which detailed the trauma of the middle passage.[73]

Stuckey described the usefulness of an African American Christianity that reflected "a religious outlook toward which the master class might otherwise be hostile." Most important, according to Stuckey, "by operating under cover of Christianity, vital aspects of Africanity, which were considered eccentric in movement, sound, or symbolism, could more easily be practiced openly." Stuckey wrote from an Afrocentric perspective, using African rather than European ideals as a standpoint from which to understand the culture of the African diaspora.

Christianity, as he saw it, was "shot through with African values." What Blassingame described as "the 'Americanization' of the bondsman" Stuckey called the "Africanization of Christianity."[74] Religion was once considered taboo for historians to

---

73 Nathan Irvin Huggins, *Black Odyssey: The African American Ordeal in Slavery* (New York: Knopf Doubleday, 1990). On Howard Thurman, see Peter Eisenstadt, *Against the Hounds of Hell: A Life of Howard Thurman* (Charlottesville: University of Virginia Press, 2021)

74 Sterling Stuckey, *Slave Culture: Nationalist Theory and the Foundations of Black America* (New York: Oxford University Press, 1987), 3536, 57, 54. See also, Molefi Kete Asante, *The Afrocentric Idea* (Philadelphia: Temple University Press, 1987); Joseph E. Holloway, *Africanisms in American Culture* (Bloomington: Indiana University Press, 1990).

write about, but Albert J. Raboteau, *Slave Religion: The "Invisible Institution" in the Ante-Bellum South* (1978) inspired other scholars and helped make the study of religion a hot topic in the history profession.[75]

African ethnicity was the focus in a classic work by Daniel Littlefield. In *Rice and Slaves: Ethnicity and the Slave Trade in Colonial South Carolina* (1983), Littlefield examined the influence of African ethnicity and showed, for example, that Africans from certain particular regions and ethnic backgrounds were sought after because of their knowledge and skill in the agriculture of rice.

Ethnicity in colonial and early American slavery studies, such as the pioneering work of Littlefield, has developed into a robust subfield of the larger historiography.[76] Philip D. Morgan, in *Slave Counterpoint: Black Culture in the Eighteenth-Century Chesapeake & Lowcountry*, (1998), noted ethnicity in this 1998 study of colonial Virginia and South Carolina, as did geographer Judith Carney in *Black Rice: The African Origins of Rice Cultivation in the Americas* (2001).[77] A lively debate has emerged since Littlefield's pioneering work on African ethnicity as the criteria of skills needed in the New World, but instead of seeing Africa as one country, all scholars now understand that there were and are various ethnicities, groupings, regional differences

---

75 Albert J. Raboteau, *Slave Religion: The "Invisible Institution" in the Antebellum South* (New York: Oxford University Press, 2004).

76 Daniel C. Littlefield, *Rice and Slaves: Ethnicity and the Slave Trade in Colonial South Carolina* (Champaign: University of Illinois, 1991; orig. pub., 1983).

77 Philip D. Morgan, *Slave Counterpoint: Black Culture in the Eighteenth-Century Chesapeake and Lowcountry* (Chapel Hill: University of North Carolina Press, 1998). Morgan's examination of these two areas, in which three-fourths of all enslaved people in the new United States lived at the time of the America Revolution, emphasized the oppressive nature of slavery but also showed the enslaved people's ability to shape their lives. Judith Carney, *Black Rice: The African Origins of Rice Cultivation in the Americas* (Cambridge: Harvard University Press, 2001).

and countries among Africans who shared a continent.[78] In *Undercurrents of Power: Aquatic Culture in the African Diaspora* (2018), Kevin Dawson looked at ethnicity in his examination of the maritime skills that captured Africans brought across the Atlantic.[79]

Given the ideologies of our own time, it is not easy to understand the widespread aversion to Africa among those most strongly committed to racial equality. Why were most Black intellectuals reluctant to acknowledge their African heritage? The answer lies in their understanding of the place Africa held in white racism. In the first half of the twentieth century, for African Americans to acknowledge a continuing African heritage seemed tantamount to acknowledging that they had a very tenuous hold on "civilization."[80]

Moving beyond the decision of either/or on African influence, white South Carolina theologian James McBride Dabbs, in *Southern Heritage* (1958), wrote, "not only has the Negro adopted our culture, he has helped to create it."[81] This interpretation is identified with Mechal Sobel's *The World They Made Together: Black and White Values in Eighteenth-Century Virginia* (1987). Sobel asserted a convergence of African and European elements in both African American culture and

---

78 The first sustained attack on the idea of skills and ethnicity was from David Eltis, Philip Morgan, and David Richardson, "Agency and Diaspora in Atlantic History: Reassessing the African Contribution to Rice Cultivation in the Americas," *American Historical Review* 12, no. 5 (December 2007): 1329-1358. The best debate on this is the *AHR* forum, S. Max Edelson, Gwendolyn Mildo Hall, Walter Hawthorne, David Eltis, Philip Morgan, and David Richardson, "AHR Exchange: The Question of 'Black Rice,'" *American Historical Review* 115, no. 1 (February 2010): 123-171.

79 Kevin Dawson, *Undercurrents of Power: Aquatic Culture in the African Diaspora* (Philadelphia: University of Pennsylvania Press, 2018).

80 Joel Williamson discusses the phenomenon in *The Crucible of Race: Black-White Relations in the American South since Emancipation* (New York: Oxford University Press, 1984).

81 James McBride Dabbs, *The Southern Heritage* (New York: Knopf, 1958), 72, 26061, 26364.

EuroAmerican culture, but the degree of such convergence depended on time and place.[82]

Scholarship on some of the cultural aspects of slavery began to include how enslaved people shaped American culture. Looking at Southern food traditions, for example, Kevin Mitchell and David Shields, *Taste of the State: South Carolina's Signature Foods, Recipes, and Their Stories*, examine the cultural depth and evolution of specific foods.[83]

Folklorists get the credit for noticing another cultural phenomenon in U.S. slavery studies. Whether Fullah or Fante, or Gola or Guinea, or another African ethnic group, on any given morning in a low country rice field, an enslaved African would meet more Africans from more ethnic groups than he or she would have encountered in a lifetime in Africa. Similarly, the varied African cultures were increasingly fused in combinations that did not exist in Africa.

A new culture, predominantly African in origin, but different from any particular African culture, took shape. Herded together with others with whom they shared only a common condition of enslavement and some degree of cultural overlap, Africans in the U.S. created a new language, a new religion, and a new culture.[84]

The work on folklore, and the effort to understand how the Black community survived the horrors of bondage, became part of the historiography of slavery, and it greatly influenced

---

82 Mechal Sobel, *The World They Made Together: Black and White Values in Eighteenth-Century Virginia* (Princeton: Princeton University Press, 1989).

83 Kevin Mitchell and David Shields, *Taste of the State: South Carolina's Signature Foods, Recipes, and Their Stories* (Columbia: University of South Carolina Press, 2021).

84 Joyner, *Down by the Riverside: A South Carolina Slave Community* (Champaign: University of Illinois Press, 1984), esp. xxxxii, 196240. See also Joyner, *Remember Me: Slave Life in Coastal Georgia* (Athens: University of Georgia Press, 1989).

another major interpretation of American slavery. In 1969 Orlando Patterson, in *The Sociology of Slavery: An Analysis of the Origins, Development, and Structure of Negro Slave Society in Jamaica*, suggested that some areas of life were not under the control of enslavers, areas where enslaved people had psychological room in which to move around and create their own culture.[85] This opened a new school of inquiry, the "slave community," or perhaps better labeled the "community and culture" school, which forcefully announced itself in 1972 with the almost simultaneous publication of John Blassingame's *The Slave Community: Plantation Life in the Antebellum South* and sociologist George P. Rawick's *From Sundown to Sunup: The Making of the Black Community*.[86]

Both books were based on exhaustive research in primary sources emanating from enslaved people themselves. Rawick worked with the Federal Writers Project's 1930s interviews with people who had been enslaved. His book was published as the first volume of a forty-one-volume series of facsimile reprints of the typescripts of those interviews. Blassingame researched the nineteenth-century autobiographies of people who escaped from slavery. Felicitously written and published by a major press, Blassingame's book received the most attention.

These works addressed a void, and they were soon followed by others. Eugene D. Genovese's *Roll, Jordan, Roll: The World the Slaves Made* (1974) examined the slave community's perseverance under oppression. The book was greeted initially with almost universal acclaim. Lawrence McDonnell, for

---

85 Patterson, *The Sociology of Slavery: An Analysis of the Origins, Development, and Structure Negro Slave Society in Jamaica* (Plainsboro: AUP, 1969).

86 Blassingame, *The Slave Community*; George P. Rawick, *From Sundown to Sunup: The Making of the Black Community* (Westport: Greenwood, 1972).

instance, advanced Genovese's central arguments in a series of essays that explored the struggle between enslavers and enslaved workers in terms of violence within the slave community, the internal economy of slavery, and the political contradictions of fugitivism, sexuality, and corporal punishment.[87]

Genovese had very few early critics. One was African American Historian of Education James D. Anderson. His review essay, "Aunt Jemima in Dialectics," found problems with the implications of Genovese's arguments, and presaged later criticism.[88] Various reactions to Genovese's work also looked at his idea of paternalism, that enslavers saw their best interests were served by being less brutal toward their enslaved workers. Whereas Charles Grier Sellers Jr. had argued that white southerners' religious guilt abounded in the 1850s and lay behind the efforts to humanize the institution, Genovese rejected the idea that slaveholders felt any guilt. Where Genovese considered paternalism as an ideology, Lacy Ford, *Deliver Us from Evil: The Slavery Question in the Old South* (2009), analyzed its purposes and related changes in white attitudes toward slavery as a political weapon.[89]

---

87 Genovese, *Roll, Jordan, Roll: The World the Slaves Made* (New York: Vintage, 1974); Lawrence McDonnell, "Slavery and Identity," *Canadian Review of American Studies* 15, no.2 (Summer 1984): 167-183; "Work, Culture, and Society in the Slave South, 1790-1865" in *Black and White Cultural Interaction in the Antebellum South,* ed. Ted Ownby (Jackson: University Press of Mississippi, 1993), 125-149; "Money Knows No Master: Market Relations and the American Slave Community" in *Developing Dixie: Modernization in a Traditional Culture,* eds. Winifred B. Moore, Jr., Joseph F. Tripp, and Lyon G. Tyler (Westport: Greenwood Press, 1988), 31-44; (with Troy Smith, and Orville Vernon Burton) "The Transnational War Against Slavery: Rethinking Abolition and its Opponents through the *Slavery and Anti-Slavery* Archive" in *The Abolition of Slavery in Britain, 1787-1840: Debate and Dissension,* ed. Susan Finding (Paris: Armand Colin, 2009), 121-126; "Ambiguities of the Upcountry Slaves' Economy" in *The Old South,* ed. Mark M. Smith (Malden: Basil Blackwell, 2001), 188-197.

88 James D. Anderson, "Aunt Jemima in Dialectics: Genovese on Slave Culture," *The Journal of Negro History* 61, no. 1 (January 1975): 99-114. See also, J. William Harris, "Eugene Genovese's Old South: A review Essay," *The Journal of Southern History* 80, no. 2 (May 2014): 327-372.

89 Charles Grier Sellers, Jr., "The Travail of Slavery," in *The Southerner as American,* ed. Sellers (Chapel Hill: University of North Carolina Press, 1960), 40-71; Lacy K. Ford, *Deliver Us from Evil: The Slavery Question in the Old South* (New York: Oxford University Press, 2009).

Historical work in the 1970s continued the investigation of slavery as the fabric of southern society or slavery as a way of life. With her award-winning *Rehearsal for Reconstruction: The Port Royal Experiment* (1964), Willie Lee Rose also realized that any understanding of Reconstruction required the study of slavery specifically. In 1976, she published *A Documentary History of Slavery in North America* with an insightful introductory essay and commentaries on each primary source. Rose showed that slavery evolved and changed over time, but she also argued that violence and trauma never ceased to be its basis.[90]

Scholars studying slavery in its day-to-day living found that warm human relationships were possible, depending on the locale and the character of the enslaver. Records and personal narratives set down by formerly enslaved people showed a picture of a social system in which there was some room for Black autonomy and some opportunity to fulfill many roles: father, mother, lover, parent, laborer, servant, skilled craftsman, rogue, supervisor, entertainer, revolutionary, teacher, preacher, and more.

Herbert G. Gutman's *The Black Family in Slavery and Freedom, 1750-1925* (1976) portrayed the slave community with the strength and courage needed when they became free people.[91] These "community and culture" historians held that, despite the power of the enslaver class, enslaved people were able to find space for themselves and create a syncretic African American culture and community rooted in the family, religion, and a folk-culture of resistance. This was a powerful new trend in slavery studies. The English historian

90 Willie Lee Rose, *Rehearsal for Reconstruction: The Port Royal Experiment* (New York: Oxford University Press, 1976) and *A Documentary History of Slavery in North America* (New York: Oxford University Press, 1976).

91 Herbert G. Gutman, *The Black Family in Slavery and Freedom, 1750-1925* (New York: Vintage, 1976).

Peter Parish, in *Slavery: History and Historians*, (1989), dubbed Blassingame, Genovese, Gutman, and Levine powerful contributors to the modern debate about Southern slavery.[92]

Because the culture of an enslaved group of people has so much variety, historian James C. Bonner called for more scholarly attention to specific communities to understand slavery. In 1965, he insisted that local communities offered "a fertile and unworked field" for professional scholars.[93] In 1974, Elinor Miller and Eugene D. Genovese edited *Plantation, Town, and Country* to demonstrate how far the local approach had developed and to suggest opportunities for further study.[94]

Charles Joyner advocated the study of culture and community in specific localities, examining, in his words, "large questions in small places." Joyner, who held Ph.Ds. in both history and folklore (which his wife explained was the only Ph.D. field that paid less than history), put both degrees to good use in *Down By the Riverside: A South Carolina Slave Community* (1984).[95]

The next year, another very well-received local study was Orville Vernon Burton's *In My Father's House Are Many Mansions: Family and Community in Edgefield, South Carolina* (1985).[96] Using one South Carolina county, it compared not just structure of families between white and Black households, but values such as religion and community. For those

---

92 Parish, *Slavery*, 6.

93 James C. Bonner, "Profile of a Late Ante-bellum Community," *American Historical Review* 49, no. 4 (July 1944): 663-80.

94 Elinor Miller and Eugene D. Genovese, eds., *Plantation, Town, and Country: Essays on the Local History of American Slave Society* (Champaign: University of Illinois Press, 1974).

95 Joyner, *Down by the Riverside*.

96 Orville Vernon Burton, *In My Father's House Are Many Mansions: Family and Community in Edgefield, South Carolina* (Chapel Hill: University of North Carolina Press, 1985).

comparisons, I created a vast database and used quantitative techniques for analysis.

Today, every humanities project works at least in some way within a digital, internet environment.[97] Even further into the digital world are discussions of the books on Twitter and other social media, no longer nice, long reviews in daily newspapers.

Local studies tended to fill in crucial details and point out exceptions. In the process, community studies gave clear examples of slave resistance and the power to survive, offering details of loss, struggle, and resilience. They added the awareness of how place and specific situation mattered. Age, gender, location, size of the enslaved populace, what crops they grew (for the plantation and for themselves), their specific jobs, who their enslavers were, their time in history, all powerfully influenced the lives of the people held in bondage.[98]

The local or community studies were a precursor of what we call microhistory now. The monumental study some forty years in the making by Sydney Nathans, *A Mind to Stay: White Plantations, Black Homeland* (2018) of the people owned by the white Duncan Cameron in North Carolina and the 144 enslaved humans taken by Cameron's sib to

---

97 For example, the Gale database, *Slavery and Anti-Slavery: A Transnational Archive*, contains more than five million cross-searchable pages sourced from books, pamphlets, newspapers, periodicals, legal documents, court records, monographs, manuscripts, and maps from many different countries. The Hathi Trust, with more than a million digitized books, keeps growing. This does not even address the multitudinous entries in Twitter and Facebook feeds. Even more exciting are databases that exist and are being created to allow historians to move forward the frontiers of the knowledge we currently have about slavery. The Trans-Atlantic Slave Trade Database, at Emory University is changing our understanding of the forced migration of Africans to the new world, and the horrible Middle Passage. See, https://www.slavevoyages.org/voyage/database and see http://justice-deferred.clemson.edu

98 In addition to Bonner, "Profile of a Late Ante-bellum Community," among the pioneering local studies was Edward W. Phifer, "Slavery in Microcosm: Burke County, North Carolina," *Journal of Southern History* 28, no. 2 (May 1962): 137-65.

Alabama illustrates how essential these studies of plantations and communities are.[99]

In 1985 Deborah Gray White added another dimension to slavery studies. In *Ar'n't I A Woman* she argued that slavery was qualitatively different for enslaved women. Among other issues, White explored sexual violence against enslaved women. She noted that much of the historical discussion had a mistaken over-reliance on patriarchy as an explanatory factor in the context of the slave community.

White opened up the concept of "intersectionality," and historians of slavery since then have felt the need to write about class and gender.[100] And, Wilma King expanded this idea of intersectionality to children in *Stolen Childhood: Slave Youth in Nineteenth Century America* (1995). Daina Berry and Leslie Harris drew upon the importance of intersectionality in their edited volume *Sexuality and Slavery: Reclaiming Intimate Histories in the Americas* (2018).[101]

The investigation of particular localities had always included women. In 1996 Brenda Stevenson examined slave communities in *Life in Black and White: Family and Community in the Slave South*.[102] Her work on Loudoun County, Virginia, pointed to the importance of women in larger kin networks.

The emphasis on women in the studies of slavery has opened the field in remarkable new ways, with works such as

---

99 Sydney Nathans, *A Mind to Stay: White Plantations, Black Homeland* (Cambridge, Massachusetts: Harvard University Press, 2017).

100 Deborah Gray White, *Ar'n't I A Woman: Female Slaves in the Plantation South* (New York: W. W. Norton & Co., 1985).

101 Wilma King, *Stolen Childhood: Slave Youth in Nineteenth Century America* (Bloomington: Indiana University Press, 1995); Ramey Berry and Leslie M. Harris, eds., *Slavery and Sexuality: Reclaiming Intimate Histories in the Americas* (Athens: UGA Press, 2018).

102 Brenda E. Stevenson, *Life in Black and White: Family and Community in the Slave South* (New York: Oxford University Press, 1996).

Tera Hunter's *Bound in Wedlock: Slave and Free Black Marriage in the Nineteenth Century* (2017) and Jennifer Morgan's *Laboring Women: Reproduction and Gender in New World Slavery* (2004).[103] Tamika Nunley, *At the Threshold of Liberty* (2021) investigated the shifting identities of enslaved women.[104] Jessica Marie Johnson, *Wicked Flesh: Black Women, Intimacy, and Freedom in the Atlantic World* (2020) examined some of the immense complexities.[105]

On one hand, it is hard to imagine how scholars neglected women until the 1980s. On the other, the topic remains controversial; the relationship between white and Black women, for instance, is fraught with contention. Thavolia Glymph's *Out of the House of Bondage: The Transformation of the Plantation Household* (2008) and *The Women's Fight: The Civil War's Battles for Home, Freedom, and Nation* (2019), comprehensive in examining gender and family issues, highlighted some promising new directions in this branch of historiography.[106] The lens of gender now includes masculinity and also gay and lesbian relationships.

Because the plethora of local studies tended to reinforce an interpretation of agency within the enslaved community, they may have given less emphasis to the systematic total oppression of slavery. Consequently, the community school certainly had its detractors.

---

103 Tera W. Hunter, *Bound in Wedlock: Slave and Free Black Marriage in the Nineteenth Century* (Cambridge: Harvard University Press, 2017); Jennifer L. Morgan, *Laboring Women: Labor and Reproduction in New World Slavery* (Philadelphia: University of Pennsylvania Press, 2004).

104 Tamika Y. Nunley, *At the Threshold of Liberty: Women, Slavery, and Shifting Identities in Washington, D. C.* (Chapel Hill: University of North Carolina Press, 2021).

105 Jessica Marie Johnson, *Wicked Flesh: Black Women, Intimacy, Freedom, and Freedom in the Atlantic World* (Philadelphia: University of Pennsylvania Press, 2020).

106 Thavolia Glymph, *Out of the House of Bondage: The Transformation of the Plantation Household* (Cambridge: Cambridge University Press, 2008) and *The Women's Fight: The Civil War's Battles for Home, Freedom, and Nation* (Chapel Hill: University of North Carolina Press, 2019).

SLAVERY AND ITS CONSEQUENCES

Leading Black sociologist Orlando Patterson, who had helped inspire the "culture and community" school of slavery studies in 1969, revisited the issue in 1998, but then asserted that revisionist arguments about slavery were "an intellectual disgrace, the single greatest disservice that the American historical profession has ever done to those who turn to it for guidance about the past and the etiology of present problems." In particular, Patterson looked at the Black family, warned of its sorry state, declared there was a "Black Matriarchy," and looked to slavery as the origin of that matriarchy.

Patterson agreed that enslaved fathers had children "whom they loved and by whom they were loved" (a point brought out in the 1970s and 1980s by community studies), but he found this incidental to the point that enslaved fathers had no legal or civic rights and responsibilities for their families.[107] In fact, both points are true. The debate about whether the Black enslaved family was matriarchal is on-going.[108]

Sociologist Patterson was not the only detractor. Historian Peter Kolchin earlier had leveled very severe criticisms. In *Unfree Labor: American Slavery and Russian Serfdom* (1987) and *American Slavery, 1619-1877* (1993), Kolchin argued, partly on the basis of his comparative work with Russian serfdom,

---

107 Patterson, *Rituals of Blood: Consequences of Slavery in Two American Centuries* (Washington, D.C.: Civitas/Counterpoint, 1998), xiii, 27.

108 Burton, "Revisiting the Myth of the Black Matriarchy," in *Dixie Redux: Essays in Honor of F. Sheldon Hackney*, eds. Orville Vernon Burton and Ray Arsenault (Montgomery: New South Books, 2013), 119-65. Daryl Michael Scott, *Contempt and Pity: Social Policy and the Image of the Damaged Black Psyche, 1880-1996* (Chapel Hill: University of North Carolina Press, 1997). For this article, chapter 3 is most relevant. Other scholars early on also explored images and stereotypes of black women. For example, Patricia Hill Collins, *Black Feminist Thought: Knowledge, Consciousness, and the Politics of Empowerment* (Oxfordshire: Routledge, 1991), chapter 4, "Mammies, Matriarchs, and Other Controlling Images," is especially relevant to this argument, esp. her analysis on pp 73-76; and Nell Irvin Painter, *Creating Black Americans: African American History and Its Meanings, 1619-Present* (New York: Oxford University Press, 2006), 94-95, 348, discusses primarily Black artists and depictions of African Americans over time, and argued that the "trauma" of slavery influenced African Americans culturally and strengthened Black community bonds.

that the close proximity in which southern enslavers and their enslaved workers lived dramatically stifled the slave's opportunity for cultural autonomy and self-expression. He even contended in *American Slavery* that there was no such thing as a "slave community," but only a shared sense of identification with fellow sufferers. He admitted some chances for slave autonomy, but very, very few.[109]

Nell Irvin Painter, *Soul Murder and Slavery* (1995) captured some of the difficulties. She noted that in many of the slavery and community studies, "Slaves emerged from historians' computers in the pose of lofty transcendence over racist adversity." That, she stated, is not acceptable history. And yet, "to acknowledge psychological trauma as a result of the vicious physical and emotional practices that slavery entailed has seemed tantamount to recapitulating Elkins." That also, she stated, is unacceptable.[110]

Another line of revision was put forth in William Dusinberre's *Them Dark Days: Slavery in the American Rice Swamps* (1996). Dusinberre argued that slavery on the South Carolina rice plantations was far harsher than generally assumed. The child mortality rate for those under age fifteen was twenty-eight percent for the general population and forty-six percent for enslaved children in general, but it was sixty-six percent for the children of enslaved parents working on rice plantations. These figures continue to underline the importance of place.

On the other hand, Dusinberre argued, contrary to Kolchin, there was indeed a form of slave community, albeit one of

---

109 Peter Kolchin, *Unfree Labor: American Slavery and Russian Serfdom* (Cambridge: Harvard University Press, 1987) and *American Slavery, 1619-1877* (New York: Farrar, Straus, Giroux, 1994).

110 Painter, *Soul Murder and Slavery* (Waco: Baylor University Press, 1995), 11.

endurance rather than mere autonomy.[111] Kathleen Hilliard agreed with Kolchin. In *Masters, Slaves, and Exchange: Power's Purchase in the Old South* (2013), Hilliard examined human relationships amid the economic and political commodification of human chattel.[112]

Also agreeing with Kolchin was his student, Jeff Forret, who challenged the Slave Community School most specifically in *Slave against Slave: Plantation Violence in the Old South* (2015). Forret's work complicated the paradigm of the harmonious slave community.[113]

Forret's research included court records, which have been a rich source in slavery studies. Slavery could not survive without a legal foundation. In 1978 A. Leon Higginbotham, Jr., an African American Judge, showed the foundational relationship between race and injustice under the law *In the Matter of Color: Race & the American Legal Process: The Colonial Period* (1978).[114] In 1996 Thomas D. Morris, *Southern Slavery and the Law, 1610-1860* (1996), presented an overview of the history done on this topic.[115] Since then, a plethora of studies of slavery and the law shows its importance.

Lee Wilson, *Bonds of Empire: The English Origins of Slave Law in South Carolina and British Plantation America, 1660-1783* (2021) outlined how the law from England defined slavery as a

111 William Dusinberre, *Them Dark Days: Slavery in the American Rice Swamps* (Athens: University of Georgia Press, 1996).

112 Kathleen M. Hilliard, *Masters, Slaves, and Exchange: Powers Purchase in the Old South* (Cambridge: Cambridge University Press, 2014).

113 Jeff Forret, *Slave against Slave: Plantation Violence in the Old South* (Baton Rouge: LSU Press, 2015).

114 A. Leon Higginbotham, Jr., *In the Matter of Color: Race & the American Legal Process: The Colonial Period* (New York: Oxford University Press, 1978).

115 Thomas D. Morris, *Southern Slavery and Law, 1610-1860* (Chapel Hill: University of North Carolina Press, 1996).

right of property.[116] The manifestation of British law created a legal system that protected enslavers from societal questioning of the immorality of enslaving other people.

Christopher Waldrep in *Roots of Disorder: Race and Criminal Justice in the American South* (1998) illustrated how a careful local study of lower court records in Warren County, Mississippi (Vicksburg) showed both how whites and enslaved people used the courts to their advantage.[117] Waldrep argued that the use of courts by Black people who believed in "constitutionalism" also fostered white vigilantism and extralegal solutions.

Ariela Gross used southern courtrooms to show details in legal disputes, which were often cultural, *Double Character: Slavery and Mastery in the Antebellum Southern Courtroom* (2006).[118] Gross teamed up with Alejandro de la Fuente, in *Becoming Free, Becoming Black: Race, Freedom and Law in Cuba, Virginia, and Louisiana* (2020), to study how enslaved people, as well as free people of color, used the legal system to petition for their freedom.[119]

Kelly Kennington looked at more than 300 cases where enslaved people sued for freedom, *In the Shadow of Dred Scott: St. Louis Freedom Suits and the Legal Culture of Slavery in Antebellum America* (2019).[120]

Sophie White, *Voices of the Enslaved: Love, Labor, and*

116 Lee Wilson, *Bonds of Empire: The English Origins of Slave Law in South Carolina and British Plantation America, 1660-1783* (Cambridge: Cambridge University Press, 2021).

117 Christopher Waldrep, *Roots of Disorder: Race and Criminal Justice in the American South* (Champaign: University of Illinois Press, 1998).

118 Ariela Gross, *Double Character: Slavery and Mastery in the Antebellum Southern Courtroom* (Athens: University of Georgia Press, 2006).

119 Ariela Gross and Alejandro de la Fuente, *Becoming Free, Becoming Black: Race, Freedom and Law in Cuba, Virginia, and Louisiana* (New York: Cambridge University Press, 2020).

120 Kelly Kennington, *In the Shadow of Dred Scott: St. Louis Freedom Suits and the Legal Culture of Slavery in Antebellum America* (Athens: University of Georgia Press, 2019).

Longing in French Louisiana (2019), used court records to show the experience and the values of enslaved women.[121] Also analyzing court documents, Christian Pinnen, *Complexion of Empire in Natchez: Race and Slavery in the Mississippi Borderlands* discussed agency in manumission cases and their far-reaching repercussions.[122]

The justice system was not usually effective for the resistance movement. Another potential recourse for enslaved people involved other forms of resistance, rebellion and attempted escape. An examination of the resistance of enslaved people, not a local community study but a far-reaching synthesis, was W. E. B. Du Bois's *Black Reconstruction in America: An Essay Toward a History of the Part Which Black Folk Played in the Attempt to Construct Democracy in America, 1860-1880* (1935).[123]

Du Bois claimed that the final collapse of the Confederacy was in large part a consequence of a general strike by enslaved persons, their refusal to work, or their leaving work to move behind U. S. Army lines, and even fighting in the U. S. Army. In 1999, John Hope Franklin and Loren Schweninger, *Runaway Slaves: Rebels on the Plantation*, offered an analysis of resistance and escape in a sweeping overview rather than a local study.[124]

Steven Hahn, *A Nation under Our Feet: Black Political Struggles in the Rural South from Slavery to the Great Migration* (2003) connected resistance during slavery with the post-Civil

---

121 Sophie White, *Voices of the Enslaved: Love, Labor, and Longing in French Louisiana* (Chapel Hill: Omohundro Institute and the University of North Carolina Press, 2019).

122 Christian Pennen, *Complexion of Empire in Natchez: Race and Slavery in the Mississippi Borderlands* (Athens: University of Georgia Press, 2019).

123 Du Bois, *Black Reconstruction in America: An Essay Toward a History of the Part Which Black Folk Played in the Attempt to Construct Democracy in America, 1860-1880* (Philadelphia: Albert Saifer, 1935).

124 John Hope Franklin and Loren Schweninger, *Runaway Slaves: Rebels on the Plantation* (New York: Oxford University Press, 1999).

War grassroots Black mobilization for political power.[125] Recent work on resistance and escaping to freedom includes Erica Dunbar, *Never Caught: The Washingtons' Relentless Pursuit of Their Runaway Slave, Ona Judge* (2017), Alice Baumgartner, *South to Freedom: Runaway Slaves to Mexico and the Road to the Civil War* (2020), and Karen Cook Bell, *Running from Bondage: Enslaved Women and Their Remarkable Fight for Freedom in Revolutionary America* (2021).[126]

An examination of resistance to slavery still acknowledges the role of the enslaved community. Because of their deep dive into details, community studies persist. See, for example, recent community studies of Nat Turner's rebellion, especially Vanessa Holden's *Surviving Southampton: African American Women and Resistance in Nat Turner's Community* (2021).[127]

In reality, none of the "culture and community" scholars romanticized the slavery experience. They had read Stampp and Elkins and John Hope Franklin. They took slavery's brutality to be already convincingly established. But they were also influenced by what they considered the obvious neglect of Black culture and Black achievement inherent in any emphasis on slavery's traumatic and pathological effects. Not one of the historians in this school of thought portrayed slavery as an easy life nor contended that the cultural achievement of

---

125 Steven Hahn, *A Nation Under Our Feet: Black Political Struggles in the Rural South from Slavery to the Great Migration* (Cambridge: Belknap Press, 2003).

126 Erica Dunbar, *Never Caught: The Washingtons' Relentless Pursuit of Their Runaway Slave, Ona Judge* (New York: 37 Ink, 2017). Alice L. Baumgartner, *South to Freedom: Runaway Slaves to Mexico and the Road to Civil War* (New York: Basic Books, 2020); Karen Cook Bell, *Running from Bondage: Enslaved Women and Their Remarkable Fight for Freedom in Revolutionary America* (Cambridge: Cambridge University Press, 2021).

127 Vanessa Holden, *Surviving Southampton: African American Women and Resistance in Nat Turner's Community* (Champaign: University of Illinois Press, 2021). See also, Kenneth Greenberg, *Nat Turner: A Slave Rebellion in History and Memory* (New York: Oxford University Press, 2003); David F. Allmendinger, *Nat Turner and the Rising in Southampton County* (Baltimore: Johns Hopkins University Press, 2014).

enslaved people had been pain-free. It became obvious, however, that the impression conveyed by a series of studies may be different from that conveyed by any one of them separately.

The overarching theme of slavery studies over the last fifty years has been a balance--the horrors of slavery juxtaposed with agency, resistance, and survival. In 1998, Ira Berlin wrote *Many Thousands Gone: The First Two Centuries of Slavery in North America* and followed with *Generations of Captivity: A History of African-American Slaves* (2003).[128] Berlin delved into the constructions of race more broadly and also showed how these early years of enslaved labor in the U.S. gave a foundation to U.S. history. Berlin explored the complexities of slavery, ever evolving and ever at the center of American political, cultural, and economic history.

In 2006 James and Lois Horton summarized the history of slavery in *Slavery and the Making of America*.[129] Like any historian going forward, they grappled with the literature: the profitability of using enslaved labor alongside the moral repugnance of slavery, the valiant struggles for freedom.

Using biography can also describe slavery. Two notable examples are Annette Gordon-Reed's *The Hemingses of Monticello: An American Family* (2009) and David Blight's *Frederick Douglass: Prophet of Freedom* (2018).[130] Fiction is not the topic of this article, but please note that works of fiction can be historical, and good fiction can pack an emotional

---

128 Ira Berlin, *Many Thousands Gone: The First Two Centuries of Slavery in North America* (Cambridge: Belknap Press, 1998) and *Generations of Captivity: A History of African American Slaves* (Cambridge: Belknap Press, 2003).

129 James Oliver Horton and Lois E. Horton, *Slavery and the Making of America* (New York: Oxford University Press, 2006).

130 Annette Gordon-Reed, *The Hemingses of Monticello: An American Family* (New York: W. W. Norton & Co., 2008); David W. Blight, *Frederick Douglass: Prophet of Freedom* (New York: Simon and Schuster, 2018).

punch that is denied to scholarly endeavors. Works by Toni Morrison and Colson Whitehead are two important examples among so very many.

Many of the more recent works on slavery, whatever else animates the research, look to a transnational basis. Throughout his career, Randy J. Sparks has championed in books and essays how important it is to place slavery in the American South in the context and in relationship to the Atlantic World, see especially *The Two Princes of Calabar: An Eighteenth Century Atlantic Odyssey* (2004), and *Africans in the Old South: Mapping Exceptional Lives Across the Atlantic World* (2016).[131] Susan Dwyer Amussen's *Caribbean Exchanges: Slavery and the Transformation of English Society, 1640-1700* (2007) showed the importance of slavery in the development of law and culture in Barbados and Jamaica.[132]

With a focus on the slave trade rather than slavery itself, transnational work includes Kevin McDonald, *Pirates, Merchants, Settlers, and Slaves: Colonial America and the Indo-Atlantic World* (2015).[133] He connected the Atlantic Ocean with the Indian Ocean, New York with Madagascar. Simon Newman looked to Barbados in the 1600s to show how the development of racial slavery transformed the New World, *A New World of Labor: The Development of Plantation Slavery in the British Atlantic* (2013).[134] John Harris's book on New York

---

131 Randy J. Sparks, *The Two Princes of Calabar: An Eighteenth Century Atlantic Odyssey* (Cambridge: Harvard University Press, 2004) and *Africans in the Old South: Mapping Exceptional Lives Across the Atlantic World* (Cambridge: Harvard University Press, 2016).

132 Susan Dwyer Amussen, *Caribbean Exchanges: Slavery and the Transformation of English Society, 1640-1700* (Chapel Hill: University of North Carolina Press, 2007).

133 Kevin P. McDonald, *Pirate, Merchants, Settlers, and Slaves: Colonial America and the Indo-Atlantic World* (Berkeley: University of California Press, 2015).

134 Simon P. Newman, *A New World of Labor: The Development of Plantation Slavery in the British Atlantic* (Philadelphia: University of Pennsylvania Press, 2013).

and the slave trade, *The Last Slave Ships: New York and the End of the Middle Passage* (2020), focused attention on slavery to the northern part of the US.[135] Looking even farther north, Harvey Whitfield wrote about slavery in Canada, *North to Bondage: Loyalist Slavery in the Maritimes* (2016).[136]

A resurgence of books on resistance in slavery studies looks at transnational movements and events. Vincent Brown's *Tacky's Revolt: The Story of an Atlantic Slave War (2020)* covered the slave rebellions in Jamaica in the 1760s.[137] Greg Grandin, *The Empire of Necessity: Slavery, Freedom, and Deception in the New World* (2014), included four continents to tell of the slave rebellion in 1805 off a remote island in the South Pacific.[138] Also with a focus on transnational information networks, scholarship examining the intellectual history and political ideology, including pro-slavery theory and values of the U.S., includes international thought on slavery.[139]

---

135 John Harris, *The Last Slave Ships: New York and the End of the Middle Passage* (New Haven: Yale University Press, 2020).

136 Harvey Amani Whitfield, *North to Bondage: Loyalist Slavery in the Maritimes* (Vancouver: UBC Press, 2016).

137 Vincent Brown, *Tacky's Revolt: The Story of an Atlantic Slave War* (Cambridge: Belknap Press, 2020).

138 Greg Grandin, *The Empire of Necessity: Slavery, Freedom, and Deception in the New World* (New York: Henry Holt and Co, 2014).

139 See for example, Linda M. Heywood and John K. Thornton, *Central Africans, Atlantic Creoles, and the Foundation of the Americas, 1585-1660* (New York: Cambridge University Press, 2007). See also, Gardner and Moltke-Hansen, "Transformation of Southern Intellectual History."

SLAVERY IN PUBLIC HISTORY AND MEMORY

Memory studies of slavery analyze the popular understanding of slavery's past. Ana Lucia Araujo's *Slavery in the Age of Memory: Engaging the Past* (2020) discussed these issues as well as how historians think about and write about and use history in political debates.[140] Clint Smith, *How the Word is Passed: A Reckoning with the History of Slavery Across America* (2021), explored the legacy of slavery and the stories told and untold.[141] Memory is also the basis for Ethan Kytle and Blain Roberts in their book, *Denmark Vesey's Garden: Slavery and Memory in the Cradle of the Confederacy* (New Press, 2018).[142] Appealing to the general reading public, they used the usual history sources, and also music, sports, tourist guidebooks.

Because many people learn history through public sites and museums, public history has taken on a renewed emphasis in the historiography. Returning to one of the aims of the 1619 Project, that slavery applies to all of American history, I note that the public reaction to that project shows that people remain very interested in U.S. History.

Unfortunately, what the public knows about history is vastly different from what historians know about it. And emotions can run high, as in deciding how to handle historical monuments. Because so many of the historical sites that portray U.S. history have been lacking in the newer studies, the

---

140 Ana Lucia, *Slavery in the Age of Memory: Engaging the Past* (New York: Bloomsbury Academic, 2020).

141 Clint Smith, *How the Word is Passed: A Reckoning with the History of Slavery Across America* (Boston: Little, Brown and Co., 2021).

142 Ethan Kytle and Blain Roberts, *Denmark Vesey's Garden: Slavery and Memory in the Cradle of the* Confederacy (New York: New Press, 2018).

National Park Service asked the Organization of American Historians to examine issues. Historians answered the call.

Imperiled Promise: The State of History in the National Park Service (2011) presented a historical analysis of what has been done well and what is sorely lacking--the good, the bad, and the ugly.[143] This assessment opens the door for historians interested in public history.

Public history includes tourism of historical sites, and Antoinette Jackson warns that historians must be very careful in piecing together the stories they tell. In *Speaking for the Enslaved: Heritage Interpretation at Antebellum Plantation Sites* (2012), she looked specifically at the agency of voices traditionally silenced.[144] She argued for the systematic recovery of knowledge that public history often ignores.

Much public history has to address the relationship between slavery and racism. Some of the current literature has analyzed that relationship, considering for instance the role of systemic racism. Black journalist and public intellectual Ta-Nehisi Coates, *Between the World and Me* (2015), talked to his son about the problems inherent in being an African American in the U.S. The book offered little hope, but it does have a determined outlook.[145]

Ibram X. Kendi, *Stamped from the Beginning: The Definitive*

---

143 Anne Mitchell Whisnant et. al., *Imperiled Promise: The State of History in the National Park Service* (Bloomington: Organization of American Historians, 2011), https://www.oah.org/files/imperiled-promise/. In 2014 the NPS reached out to me to write the administrative History of the Fort Sumter National Monument and the Charles Pinckney National Historic Site, and I agreed. The new ranger who headed that park attempted to have me removed from the project when I centered slavery, especially as the central cause of the Civil War. See Beatrice Burton, Megan Shockley, and Orville Vernon Burton, *Fort Sumter and Fort Moultrie National Historical Park, Charleston, SC Administrative History* (Washington, DC: The National Park Service, November, 2020).

144 Antoinette Jackson, *Speaking for the Enslaved: Heritage Interpretation at Antebellum Plantation Sites* (Oxfordshire: Routledge, 2012).

145 Ta-Nehisi Coates, *Between the World and Me* (New York: Spiegel & Grau, 2015).

History of Racist Ideas in America (2017), revised the story for some of American historical leaders.[146] His polemics were not always correct, but his analysis was path-breaking and worthwhile. Kendi's *How to be an Antiracist* (2019) is a self-help book for everyone, whether white or a person of color.[147]

Historians are increasingly forgoing nuance and stating explicitly why the history of slavery affects race relations and the political culture of the U.S. today. There may be a moral imperative to do so.

In conclusion, I remember a quote about historiography, attributed to Will Durant: "History proves that anything can be proved by history." And yet, history is the finest of endeavors. Because history entails all the past of all of humankind, historians will never be able to attain the whole Truth; some things are beyond knowing. Historians face the ambiguities of the past, but we are unable to resolve them. We simply try our best to interpret, to analyze, to see the patterns of the social, spiritual, relational, political, legal, economic, and other realities. Writing history is an act of faith. I believe we historians stand in solidarity as we research the mysteries of the past.

---

146 Ibram X. Kendi, *Stamped from the Beginning: The Definitive History of Racist Ideas in America* (New York: Nation Books, 2016).

147 Kendi, *How to be an Antiracist* (New York: One World, 2019).

RACIALIZING CAIN, DEMONIZING BLACKNESS & LEGALIZING DISCRIMINATION: PROPOSAL FOR RECEPTION OF CAIN AND AMERICA'S RACIAL CASTE SYSTEM[1]

Joel B. Kemp, *Candler School of Theology, Emory University, Atlanta GA 30322*

INTRODUCTION

The killings of Ahmaud Arbery, Breonna Taylor, and George Floyd ignited a renewed engagement with one of America's perennial failings—the denial of human rights and full citizenship to African American/Black American persons.[2] The

---

1 Originally published in *Perspectives in Religious Thought* 48, no. 4 (2021): 377-399. Reprinted by permission.

2 For purposes of this essay, I will use the terms "African Americans" and "Black Americans" interchangeably to identify individuals within the African diaspora who are (or were) living in the United States of America, except when quoting historical sources that use older, and occasionally more offensive, terminology. For a helpful conversation about the importance and significance of naming individuals counted among the peoples of Africa and the African diaspora within the realm of biblical scholarship, see Hugh R. Page Jr., "The Africana Bible: A Rationale," in *The Africana Bible: Reading Israel's Scriptures from Africa and the African Diaspora*, ed. Hugh R. Page Jr., et al. (Minneapolis: Fortress, 2010), 3–10.

murders of these individuals added "insult to injury" as many still grieved the deaths of Trayvon Martin, Sandra Bland, Tamir Rice, India Kager, Philando Castile, and others almost too numerous to name. For many, sadness was seasoned with anger as the legal system was slow (if not unwilling) to provide justice to the families whose loved ones died. Within some Black American communities and among others attuned to these issues, the sentiments of the prophet in Hab 1:2 could be heard: עַד־אָנָה יְהוָה שִׁוַּעְתִּי וְלֹא תִשְׁמָע אֶזְעַק אֵלֶיךָ חָמָס וְלֹא תוֹשִׁיעַ ("How long, O LORD, must I cry out for help and you will not hear? I call out to you, 'violence' yet you will not deliver?").[3] These and other incidents of legally sanctioned violence against Black and Brown bodies, coupled with the largely undisputed evidence about COVID-19's disproportionate negative effects upon the same communities, led many to ask one question— how did we get here?[4]

The painful poignancy of these twin plagues—racism and COVID-19—hit me with renewed force in the summer of 2020. During that summer, we relocated to Georgia and arrived shortly after the murder of another African American man: Rayshard Brooks. Joining a community still reeling from the killing of Ahmaud Arbery and attempting to process Rayshard's death, two memories from that time remain with me. First, I began encountering with increasing regularity the insidious efforts to portray Ahmaud Arbery as a dangerous, deviant criminal who somehow provoked the violence from his white assailants. The purpose (whether indicated

---

3 Unless otherwise noted, all translations of biblical texts are the author's.

4 For a recent article discussing the disproportionate impact of COVID-19 on minoritized communities in America, see Maggie Fox, "Study confirms pandemic hit Black Americans, Native Americans and Latinos harder than Whites," *CNN Health*, 4 October 2021, https://www.cnn.com/2021/10/04/health/pandemic-deaths-minorities/index.html.

explicitly or implicitly) was to exonerate his killers by trading in long-standing racial stereotypes that presume the inherent threat to civil order Black Americans represent and the necessity to protect the "citizenry" from such dangers.[5] Second, Chris Stewart—the attorney for the Brooks family—made a statement in a June 13th press conference that captured many individuals' sentiments:

> Other than that, it's just tiring. I'm sure everybody's tired of seeing it. We're so concerned about trying to find a vaccine for the coronavirus. The world is pitching in. We're pitching in millions and millions and millions of dollars. Scientists from around the world are trying to help find a vaccine. But nobody's trying to find a vaccine for civil rights abuses. It's something that we're told to wait for. It'll come. Nobody's trying to find a vaccine for why officers pull the trigger so quick on African Americans. There's no flood of money or scientists or the top experts or our leadership in this country trying to end that epidemic. But I guess that is because it doesn't hit close to home to the people that care.[6]

The fatigue and frustration Stewart embodied is analogous to the Hab 1:2 quotation at the beginning of this essay:

---

5 This trading in the tradition of Black dangerousness, particularly as it relates to Black men, was vividly displayed by Amy Cooper's 9-1-1 call in which she accused Christian Cooper—an African American man—of threatening her life. For an overview of this incident, see Amir Vera and Laura Ly, "White woman who called police on a black man bird watching in Central Park has been fired," CNN, 26 May 2020, https://www.cnn.com/ 2020/05/26/us/central-park-video-dog-video-african-american-trnd/index.html. As I will discuss, this theme of Black dangerousness is rooted deeply in American racial ideologies in part because of the racialized reception of Cain and its expressions in America's legal system.

6 For a complete transcript of the press conference, see https://www.rev.com/blog/transcripts/attorneys-of-rayshard-brooks-family-hold-press-conference-brooks-shot-by-police-in-atlanta.

How long must we wait for justice? Why does injustice seem so pervasive?

Drawing upon my professional and academic training, I sought answers in two disciplines: law and biblical studies.[7] I considered how the reception and (mis-) interpretation of biblical texts contributed to constructing and perpetuating America's racial caste system through its legal and criminal justice systems.[8] In this essay, I explore how the racialized interpretation of Cain and the mark God gave him (Gen 4:15) contributed to defining what I call the "3Ds of Blackness:" dangerousness, deviance, and depravity.[9] As I will argue, the villainy associated with Cain throughout biblical, early Jewish, and Christian traditions becomes racialized in America to help construct these 3Ds of Blackness ("3Ds") and ultimately to demonize Black people.[10] America's laws, legal decisions, and praxis (especially in the realm of criminal law) are a repository for the racialized reception of biblical texts serving to reinforce and further legitimate America's racialized hierarchy. Biblical interpretation provides an ideological foundation for America's racial systems, and the law gives these racial ideas their structure and force.

---

7 Prior to earning my PhD, I served as a minister in several churches and practiced law for over a decade.

8 The language of racial caste system to describe American racial realities is consistent with recent scholarship on the matter. See Isabel Wilkerson, *Caste: The Origins of Our Discontents* (New York: Random House, 2020).

9 Though this essay focuses on Genesis 4, I am exploring in another, larger work how the racialized reception of Genesis 4 ("Mark of Cain"), Genesis 9 ("Curse of Ham"), and Genesis 10 ("Table of Nations") contributed to inventing the 3Ds historically, as well as the continuing impact of these racialized interpretations upon current racial realities in America. In short, I am arguing in the larger work that the racialized reception of these three chapters from the Primeval History are indispensable components to the theological foundations upon which America's racial caste system rests.

10 My focus on the reception of biblical traditions in law is not intended to suggest that *only* these two traditions are responsible for the construction of America's racial hierarchy. Like most scholars investigating questions of race in America, I recognize the complexity of inter-relations among various components of society that contribute to current realities.

To structure this exploration, I have divided the essay into three sections. In the first section, I review scholars' conclusions about the meaning and function of Cain's story and the mark in Genesis 4. This section also investigates how Cain is received within later biblical traditions, as well as in Jewish and Christian traditions. My primary aim in this section is to demonstrate how the interpretive traditions of Cain began to coalesce around the 3Ds. The second section focuses on the racialization of Cain and the Mark of Cain within American contexts. Specifically, I outline how Black Americans were deemed to be descendants of Cain and, as a result, how black skin signaled God's verdict that black people are dangerous, deviant, and depraved. Additionally, I contend the legal restrictions placed upon black personhood, citizenship, and freedom were impacted by the ideologies contained in the 3Ds. The final section focuses on the impact of these 3Ds within the context of encounters with law enforcement officials in the late twentieth and early twenty-first century.[11] To illustrate how these 3Ds appear and contribute to these encounters, I will focus upon two events in the final section as case studies—Rodney King and Michael Brown.[12]

---

11 For this essay, discussing the presence of *racism* and the existence of *racist structures* does not mean that *every* person involved in the system is actively racist in overt ways. Therefore, it is neither my intention nor should a reader erroneously conclude that I am asserting that all people involved in America's legal and justice systems, including police officers, are racists as that term is stereotypically defined. Rather, a purpose of this essay is to sketch a framework for the pervasiveness of racist ideologies that are expressed in legal/judicial contexts and have their roots in biblical interpretation and theological construction.

12 Although I focus on the violence two black men suffered at the hands of police officers, it is critical to name the reality that black women continue to be recipients of violence in similar contexts. The #SayHerName movement is an attempt to remember and highlight the violence black women face in our society. For a brief overview of this movement, see Donna M. Owens, "Breonna Taylor and hundreds of Black women have died at the hands of police. The movement to say their names is growing," *USA Today*, 15 March 2021, https://www.usatoday.com/in-depth/news/investigations/2021/03/11/sayhername-movement black-women-police-violence/6921197002/. In addition, for a recent discussion of Black Women's encounters with violent law enforcement officials, see Michelle S. Jacobs, "The Violent State: Black Women's Invisible Struggle Against Police Violence,"*24 Wm. And Mary J. Women and L.* 39 (2017): 39–100.

CAIN AND HIS MARK: THE 3DS IN GENESIS AND BEYOND DEFINITIONS, CONTEXTS, AND METHODS

Before discussing the reception of Cain and the construction of his villainy within biblical and subsequent traditions, a brief comment on the 3Ds and the discipline of reception history is warranted. The "3Ds of Blackness" I will explore in this essay are the depictions of African Americans as dangerous, deviant, and depraved. The 3Ds are my terminology to capture a constellation of pejorative attributes assigned to Black Americans as part of the construction of racial castes in this nation. The "mythoracial" ideas of blackness and whiteness were created from biblical exegesis, as well as scientific inquiry that dominated the formative centuries of American life.[13] For this essay, the attribute of dangerousness describes the tactic of asserting that black persons are inherently criminal and thus a threat to the life, well-being, safety, and security of American citizenry. Consequently, the nation's legal systems are conscripted to regulate (often violently) black bodies to ensure this perpetual threat to American life is controlled.[14] The concept of deviance summarizes the claim

---

13 For a brief discussion of the terminology "mythoracial" and its connections to natural sciences, as well as biblical scholarship, see Paul Harvey, "'A Servant of Servants Shall He Be': The Construction of Race in American Religious Mythologies" in *Religion and the Creation of Race and Ethnicity: An Introduction*, ed. Craig R. Prentiss (New York: New York University Press, 2003), 13–27. While many texts discuss the relationship between race and biblical interpretation, two commonly cited texts are: (i) Cain Hope Felder, *Troubling Biblical Waters: Race, Class, and Family* (Maryknoll, NY: Orbis, 1989) and (ii) Randall C. Bailey and Tina Pippin, eds., *Race, Class, and the Politics of Biblical Translation*, Semeia 76 (Atlanta: SBL Press, 1998).

14 This thread connecting the mythology of black danger/criminality to America's legal and criminal justice system from slavery to modern day is well-explored among sociologists, historians, and legal scholars. Two treatments of these subjects are: (i) Michelle Alexander, *The New*

that Black Americans are inferior to and aberrant from the white norms of intelligence, morality, and other facets of personhood. This perceived moral deviance contributes to the insidious notion of inherent black savagery, heathenism, demonic nature, and barbarism—attributes that were invoked to justify exclusion of African Americans from full, legal equality.[15] The final component of the 3Ds—depravity—describes the perception of Black Americans as full of perverse, uncontrollable desires and impulses. This notion of depravity often focuses on the alleged hyper-sexuality, debauchery, and innately violent nature of Black Americans.[16] Collectively, I contend these 3Ds result in the demonization of African Americans—a process made "easier" by the biblical arguments connecting Cain, demons, and blackness that were influential within American society.

Given my analysis of biblical texts and the cultural effects of their interpretation, this project fits within the field of reception history (*Wirkungsgeschichte*).[17] Scholars in this area often point to Gadamer's *Wahrheit und Methode* (Truth and Method)

Jim Crow: Mass Incarceration in the Age of Colorblindness (New York: New Press, 2012) and (ii) Khalil Gibran Muhammad, *The Condemnation of Blackness: Race, Crime, and The Making of Modern Urban America* (Cambridge: Harvard University Press, 2019). See Muhammad, *Condemnation*, 6–8 for an example of the criminalizing of the myth of Black danger.

15 For a discussion of inferiority and its connection to America's legal structure, see A. Leon Higginbotham Jr., *In the Matter of Color: Race & The American Legal Process: The Colonial Period* (New York: Oxford University Press, 1978) and Higginbotham, *Shades of Freedom: Racial Politics and Presumptions of the American Legal Process* (Oxford: Oxford University Press, 1996).

16 See e.g., Muhammad, *Condemnation*, xiv and 35. See also David Whitford, "A Calvinist Heritage to the 'Curse of Ham': Assessing the Accuracy of a Claim about Racial Subordination," *Church History and Religious Culture* 90.1 (2010): 25–45, esp. 27–37 (discussing "Blackness as a Curse" and the "Hypersexual African").

17 Some scholars will also use *Rezeptionschichte* to describe this field. See Emma England and William Lyons, "Explorations in the Reception of the Bible," in *Reception His tory and Biblical Studies: Theory and Practice*, ed. Emma England and William Lyons, LHBOTS 6 (New York: T&T Clark, 2015), 4.

as a central text for defining this emerging field.[18] This discipline within biblical scholarship is primarily concerned "with the history of the reception of biblical texts, stories, images, and characters through the centuries in the form of citation, interpretation, reading, revision, adaptation, and influence."[19] Consequently, scholars are interested not only in what biblical texts meant in some original, historical context, but also (and perhaps primarily) how texts acquire meaning and function in different historical and cultural contexts.[20] Additionally, scholars are interested in analyzing how the Bible, and theological categories derived from it, shape ideas within larger political and cultural arenas.[21] For this essay, I am exploring how the reception of Genesis 4 defined blackness historically and contributes to the current treatment of Black Americans within America's judicial and criminal justice system. Since this project investigates the reception history of a biblical text and its impacts upon the lived experiences of Black Americans, this project also touches upon the discipline of African American /Africana Biblical Hermeneutics.[22] Within this discipline,

18 See, e.g., Brennan W. Breed, *Nomadic Text: A Theory of Biblical Reception History* (Bloomington: Indiana University Press, 2014), 8–11; Timothy Beal, "Reception History and Beyond: Toward the Cultural History of Scriptures," *BibInt* 19 (2011): 357–72, 362; and Mark Knight, "*Wirkingsgeschichte*, Reception History, Reception Theory," *JSOT* 33.2 (2010): 137–46, 137.

19 Beal, "Reception History," 359.

20 See, e.g., Mitzi J. Smith, *Insights from African American Interpretation* (Minneapolis: Fortress, 2017), 16; and Beal, "Reception History," 364. For a lengthier discussion, see Breed, *Nomadic Text*, 1–14.

21 See e.g., James G. Crossley, "The End of Reception History, a Grand Narrative for Biblical Studies and the Neoliberal Bible," in *Reception History*, 47; Smith, *Insights*, 2; and Knight, "*Wirkingsgeschichte*," 138.

22 For some classic studies within this discipline, see Brian K. Blount, *True to Our Native Land: An African American New Testament Commentary* (Minneapolis: Fortress, 2007); Randall C. Bailey, ed., *Yet With A Steady Beat: Contemporary U.S. Afrocentric Biblical Interpretation*, Semeia 42 (Atlanta: SBL Press, 2003); Gay L. Byron, *Symbolic Blackness and Ethnic Difference in Early Christian Literature* (London: Routledge, 2002); Vincent L. Wimbush, ed., *African Americans and the Bible: Sacred Texts and Social Textures* (New York: Continuum, 2000); and Cain Hope Felder, ed., *Stony the Road We Trod: African Amer ican Biblical Interpretation* (Minneapolis: Augsburg,

many scholars recognize African American approaches to reading scripture are a "dialectical process" in which "they read the Bible through their experience and their experience through the Bible."[23] Thus, like reception history, the range of authoritative interpreters and the media in which such biblical appropriations occur expands beyond the traditional categories venerated in historical-critical methodologies.[24] Second, as Mitzi Smith reminds readers, biblical interpretation is and "has always been political."[25] In this vein, many Africana scholars highlight how the "Christian Bible has been a source of disruption and instability in the lives of Africana people."[26]Additionally, some Africana scholars focus on how the Bible appears as a weapon to create, support, and legitimate colonial enterprises that dehumanize and oppress individuals.[27] In this project, I seek to join this conversation by investigating how certain racialized traditions regarding Cain effect African Americans' status before the law and encounters with law enforcement.[28]

1991). For a more complete list and a discussion of this discipline's connection to multiracial biblical studies, see Wongi Park, "Multiracial Biblical Studies," *JBL* 140.3 (2021): 435–59.

23 Demetrius K. Williams, "African American Approaches: Rehumanizing the Reader against Racism and Reading through Experience," in *Studying Paul's Letters: Contemporary Perspectives and Methods,* ed. Joseph A. Marchal (Minneapolis: Fortress, 2012), 168. For similar claims, see also Esau McCauley, *Reading While Black: African American Biblical Interpretation As An Exercise in Hope* (Downers Grove: InterVarsity, 2020), 17; and Carolyn Jones, "Yet With A Steady Beat: The Task of African American Biblical Hermeneutics," in *Steady Beat,* 164.

24 See Knight, "*Wirkingsgeschichte*," 138.

25 Smith, *Insights,* 1. For similar claims in reception history, see Nancy Klancher, "A Genealogy for Reception History," *BibInt* 21 (2013): 99–129, 101; and Beal, "Reception History," 364.

26 See Page, "Preface," in *Africana Bible,* xxvi.

27 See, e.g., Leslie R. James, "The African Diaspora as Construct and Lived Experience," in *Africana Bible,* 12.

28 For a recent discussion of the Bible, African Americans, and policing, see McCauley, *Reading,* 39.

CAIN IN GENESIS AND BIBLICAL TRADITIONS

Genesis 4 continues the story of the first family recorded in the Primeval History after the expulsion from the Garden of Eden (Gen 3:23–24). The narrative introduces the birth of Cain (וַיִּקַח) similarly to how other children are introduced throughout the biblical narrative—namely, a declaration of the woman's successful pregnancy and birth, followed by a quasi-etymology associated with the child's name (Gen 4:1).[29] After the birth of his brother Abel (הֶבֶל), their respective jobs are described, but no pejorative inference of their contrasting jobs is necessitated by the Hebrew text.[30] The first seeds of conflict and potential villainy for Cain emerge when the LORD rejects his offering (Gen 4:5). In response to this rejection, Cain becomes angry and is warned that sin is lurking/crouching (רֹבֵץ) at the door. Despite being warned of sin's presence and Cain's need to rule it (Gen 4:7b), Cain commits the first crime recorded in the Bible—fratricide (Gen 4:8).[31] As I will discuss, Cain's crime and its implications for his nature inform how he is received in later traditions and racialized in American contexts.[32]

---

29 For additional biblical examples, see Gen 4:25; 30:4–6; 30:22–24; and 1 Sam. 1:20. The author of Gen 4:1 connects Cain's name (וַיִּקַח) etymologically to the verb (קנה), which means to acquire. The precise connection between these words is tenuous and obscure, a conclusion that other scholars have noted. See, e.g., Gerhard von Rad, *Genesis: A Commentary*, trans. John H. Marks (Philadelphia: Westminster, 1961), 100; and E. A. Speiser, *Genesis: Introduction, Translation and Notes*, AB (Garden City: Doubleday, 1964), 30.

30 Although the biblical text reads descriptively, several interpreters insert an evaluative component to their respective jobs. Specifically, they argue Cain's occupation indicates the nefarious character and criminal actions that will follow in the narrative. See John Byron, *Cain and Abel in Text and Tradition: Jewish and Christian Interpretations of the First Sibling Rivalry* (Leiden: Brill, 2011), 36.

31 Several scholars identify the Cain-Abel relationship as a common, ancient motif the biblical writer is using (e.g., Romulus-Remus). See e.g., Claus Westermann, *Genesis 1–11: A Commentary*, trans. John J. Scullion, S. J. (Minneapolis: Augsburg, 1974), 286.

32 As I will discuss, Cain's violent action becomes imputed to Black Americans as "evidence"

After killing his brother, the LORD confronts Cain by noting Abel's blood is "crying to" or "petitioning" (יִמְקָעֹצ) the LORD from the ground (Gen 4:10). The LORD then announces a curse that includes the familiar refrain about the difficulty of agricultural labor and an announcement of Cain's imminent expulsion (Gen 4:11–12).[33] Several scholars conclude the reiteration of the curse upon the land and subsequent expulsion are the actual punishments Cain receives, rather than the mark itself.[34] Von Rad extends this position to claim the shedding of blood, the earth's response, and God's face being hidden from Cain add cultic significance to this episode.[35]

By Gen 4:11, the Hebrew term for curse (רוּרָאָ) has appeared twice already, in Gen 3:14 and Gen 3:17. In Gen 3:14 and 4:11, the author uses the same construction (הָתָא רוּרָאָ)to announce a curse upon two characters: the serpent and Cain. According to Westermann, this construction is intentional and further distinguishes Cain from the other human beings Genesis describes.[36] Additionally, because the serpent in Genesis becomes associated with the devil in later biblical traditions (e.g., Rev 20:2), the connections between Cain and the devil begin to materialize. A further connection between these two characters emerges from the term (בֿ,ֵ). Both Speiser and Westermann argue this root is related to an Akkadian

---

of a fundamentally violent and dangerous nature.

33 The parallels between the quasi-judicial setting of Genesis 3 and 4 appear regularly in the secondary literature on Genesis. See Westermann, *Genesis*, 286.

34 See Westermann, *Genesis*, 311, and von Rad, *Genesis*, 103.

35 Von Rad, *Genesis*, 103. Although I have not yet discovered a specific reference to this in the history of the racialized reception history of Cain, I want to investigate if this cultic understanding affected notions of Black Americans' alleged heathenism and isolation/distance from God.

36 Westermann, *Genesis*, 306–7.

term meaning evil or demon.[37] Consequently, what is lurking/ crouching at Cain's door should be understood in this light (Gen 4:7). As I will discuss, the associations between Cain and the devil intensify throughout the reception of the Cain story and ultimately contribute to the description of Blacks as devilish or demonic.

In response to the verdict, Cain requests a more lenient sentence because he fears the punishment is too harsh (Gen 4:14). The LORD hears this request and places a mark (תוֹא) upon Cain, seemingly for the purpose of protecting him (Gen 4:15). As will be discussed, the nature of this mark and its function becomes foundational for the racialization of this text in American contexts.[38] In light of the later reception of the mark and its purpose, two questions require consideration: (i) what was the mark? and (ii) what was its purpose? Within the biblical tradition, the term often translated as mark (תוֹא) in Gen 4:15 has a wide array of usages.[39] Since the biblical text does not describe the mark, scholars do not agree on its form.[40] In contrast to this lack of scholarly consensus, most agree that the function of the sign/mark (תוֹא) is clear: the mark is for Cain's protection.[41] Despite this scholarly clarity, the racialized reception of this sign consistently characterizes the sign as a mark of degradation, depravity, and deviance.

The reception of Cain and the construction of his villainy

---

37 See Speiser, *Genesis*, 33, and Westermann, *Genesis*, 299.

38 For a recent investigation, see Nyasha Junior, "The Mark of Cain and White Violence," *JBL* 139.4 (2020): 661–673.

39 For a recent survey of the biblical usages of this term, see Junior, *White Violence*, 662.

40 ⁹For a range of proposals, see Joel N. Lohr, "So YHWH established a sign for Cain: Rethinking Genesis 4,15," *ZAW* 121 (2009): 101–3; R. W. L. Moberly, "The Mark of Cain—Revealed at Last?" *HTR* 100 (2007): 11–28; and von Rad, *Genesis*, 103.

41 See e.g., Westermann, *Genesis*, 313; von Rad, *Genesis*, 103; and Lohr, "Rethinking," 101.

begin within the biblical tradition. New Testament writers mention Cain by name on three occasions: Heb 11:4; 1 John 3:12; and Jude 11.[42] In Heb 11:4, the author invokes Cain to prove the author's point about God's assessment of Abel and the reasons for it. In Heb 11:2, the author argues faith ($\pi\iota\sigma\tau\iota\varsigma$) is the reason God approved of the ancestors/elders. So, according to this author, Abel's faith is the reason his offering is more acceptable than Cain's. Moreover, Abel's faith is why God "testified" or "bore witness" ($\dot{\epsilon}\mu\alpha\rho\tau\upsilon\rho\dot{\eta}\theta\eta$) to the righteousness ($\delta\dot{\iota}\kappa\alpha\iota\sigma\varsigma$) of Abel. In this passage, Cain's villainy is implied as a result of the comparison with his brother, who emerges as a prototype for martyrs in later traditions.[43]

In contrast, the author of 1 John 3:12 explicitly paints Cain as the villain of the author's stories.[44] Cain appears in 1 John 3 after the author describes the characteristics of two categories of people: those who are righteous/children of God vs. those who commit sin/children of the devil (1 John 3:4–10). Immediately preceding the author's invocation of Cain, 1 John 3:11 concludes with a summary of a central message for this community: Ὅτι αὕτη ἐστὶν ἡ ἀγγελία ἣν ἠκούσατε ἀπ᾽ ἀρχῆς, ἵνα ἀγαπῶμεν ἀλλήλους ("So this is the message which you heard from the beginning: that we should love one another"). Against this backdrop of the children of God v. children of the devil and the central commandment to love one another, 1 John 3:12 introduces Cain: οὐ καθὼς Κάϊν ἐκ τοῦ πονηροῦ ἦν καὶ

---

42 The following analysis will focus on Heb 11:4 and 1 John 3:12.

43 See Byron, *Cain and Abel*, 196, discussing the tradition of Abel as the first martyr. For a similar observation on Abel's reception history, see Westermann, *Genesis*, 319.

44 Jude 11 invokes Cain's story in the following phrase: ὅτι τῇ ὁδῷ τοῦ Κάϊν ἐπορεύθησαν ("For they walked in the way of Cain"). The author then links those individuals who followed in the way of Cain to individuals who abandoned God to follow "Balaam's error" and "perish in Korah's rebellion" (NRSV). This notion of godless individuals who perish is similar to what is captured in the earlier definition of deviance—one of the 3Ds of Blackness.

ἔσφαξεν τὸν ἀδελφὸν αὐτοῦ· καὶ χάριν τίνος ἔσφαξεν αὐτόν; ὅτι τὰ ἔργα αὐτοῦ πονηρὰ ἦν τὰ δὲ τοῦ ἀδελφοῦ αὐτοῦ δίκαια. ("We should not be like Cain, who was of the wicked one and killed his brother. And why did he kill him? Because his deeds were evil, but his brother's (were) righteous.")

This invocation of Cain contains several elements that will blossom into the 3Ds within later traditions, including America's racialized contexts. First, Cain is immediately identified as an individual not to be emulated (οὐ καθὼς Κάϊν). This characterization and subsequent justification of his exclusion contributes to the "othering" of Cain within biblical and later traditions. The connections among othering, exclusion, and African American experiences (past and present) have become increasingly evident to a wider cross-section of the populace.[45]Second, Cain's origins are associated with the evil one (ἐκ τοῦ πονηροῦ). First John 3:9–10 describes the attributes of those individuals who are τὰ τέκνα τοῦ διαβόλου ("the children of the devil.") Though the specific language of the devil is lacking in 1 John 3:11, most English translators translate (ἐκ τοῦ πονηροῦ) as a parallel construction to (τὰ τέκνα τοῦ διαβόλου). While the author of 1 John 3 is not necessarily making a genealogical or biological claim about Cain's origins (as later authors will), the author is assessing the nature and behavior of Cain. In 1 John 3 and subsequent traditions, Cain and his descendants emerge not only as individuals who commit bad acts, but also corrupt and evil persons (i.e., "depraved") whose actions reflect their degenerate nature.[46]

---

45 For a brief discussion of the use of scripture in othering, see Rodney S. Sadler Jr., "Genesis," in *Africana Bible*, 73.

46 As will be illustrated later in this essay, many of the defenses of American chattel slavery and the repressive/oppressive laws that enforced this system appealed to theological and scientific evidence demonstrating the alleged inherent depravity and irredeemably degenerate nature of enslaved Africans and their children.

Third, Cain is portrayed as a dangerous, violent man—i.e., a murderer. His danger is underscored because Cain murdered his brother, rather than loving his brother as the author admonishes this community to do (1 John 2:10; 4:20– 21). Consequently, Cain's murderous actions and devilish nature render him a threat to the community and unfit to participate fully in it. Fourth, and finally, the pattern of portraying Abel as righteous and Cain as wicked or evil present in Hebrews 11 continues in 1 John 3. First John 3 intensifies this "anti-Abel distinction" by directly connecting Cain to the devil/thief, who "comes only to steal and kill and destroy" (John 10:9 NRSV). As discussed later, racializing these attributes and ascribing them to African Americans becomes a justification for the legal logic deeming black persons as threats to the civil order who require violent regulation and constant surveillance.

The interpretive trajectory "villainizing" Cain outlined within the biblical narrative continues in early Jewish and Christian traditions and reflects what Byron identifies as "an exegetical campaign to defame him beyond what is found in Genesis."[47] This defamatory campaign culminates in efforts to demonize Cain in certain Jewish and Christian traditions by asserting three key elements: (a) Cain was the offspring of the devil or some fallen angel;[48] (b) Cain was a prototype for "anti-God" individuals;[49] and (c) Cain and his descendants are responsible for the increasing presence of evil in the world.[50] Cain's alleged demonic origins served as the roots out of which the 3Ds (dangerousness, deviance, depravity) sprung. For example, Cain's presumed demonic origins and

---

47 Byron, *Cain and Abel*, 37.

48 See Byron, *Cain and Abel*, 17.

49 See Byron, *Cain and Abel*, 66 (referencing Philo)

50 See Byron, *Cain and Abel*, 165 and 207–8.

inherently wicked nature are consistent with my categories of deviance and depravity. Cain's murderous episode of Abel evinces his dangerous nature. Moreover, Byron describes how certain interpreters connected Cain and his descendants to myths of savagery and sexual perversion, including comparing them to beasts.[51] While the racialization of Cain as it appears in American society is absent in the examples Byron offers, associations among Cain, blackness, and the 3Ds are present.[52] In America's appropriation of Cain's darkness, this symbolic darkness becomes a phenotypical characteristic—a divine marker reflecting God's determination that all such individuals with black skin are separate from and unequal to white people.

In summation, the seeds of the 3Ds of Cain and his association with darkness were planted in the earliest receptions of his story. These seeds flowered within early Jewish and later Christian interpreters to create a Cain ripe for American racialization. The next section explores briefly how Cain and his mark appear in racialized contexts within America, including how this racialized reception left its imprint upon America's legal system.

---

51 See Byron, *Cain and Abel*, 155. In the next section, I will discuss how this claim of sexual perversity is racialized and attached to definitions of blackness in America.

52 See Byron, *Cain and Abel*, 152.

RACIALIZING CAIN AND AMERICAN LEGAL RECEPTION

In light of the villainy Cain accrued throughout earlier traditions, how did these traditions become racialized in American contexts to influence theological constructions of blackness?[53] One link in this racialized chain is the way some Christian interpreters associated Cain and his mark with specific ethnic or racial groups, especially Jewish individuals.[54] According to Wistrich, the othering of Jewish individuals allowed some within the Christian tradition to assign to them "a universal, cosmic quality of evil, depicting them as children of the Devil."[55]

This strategy of "othering" by associating a targeted group (e.g., Jews) with Cain provided a convenient pattern and resource for white Americans to follow when constructing the ultimate racial other—enslaved Africans and their descendants in America.

Another significant factor affecting the "racing" of Cain in America was the tradition of associating blackness and black skin with evil, sin, and the devil. David Goldenberg

---

53 It is worth noting the prevalence of the so-called, "Curse of Ham" (Gen 9:18–29) in American discourse surrounding the biblical justification of American chattel slavery. While this passage was used widely to support the institution of slavery by asserting Ham (and Canaan) were the progenitors of African peoples, the Mark of Cain (Gen 4:15) provided biblical warrant to associate Black skin with divine condemnation and degradation. A frequently cited study on the centrality of Gen 9:18–25 to slavery is David M. Goldenberg, *The Curse of Ham: Race and Slavery in Early Judaism, Christianity, and Islam* (Princeton: Princeton University Press, 2003). For additional discussion of the centrality of the Curse of Ham and its connection to Mark of Cain, see Allen Dwight Callahan, *The Talking Book: African Americans and the Bible* (New Haven: Yale University Press, 2006), 28–30.

54 See Byron, *Cain and Abel*, 244.

55 Robert S. Wistrich, "Antisemitism," in *How Was It Possible? A Holocaust Reader*, ed. Peter Hayes (Nebraska: University of Nebraska Press, 2015), 6–17, 8.

locates the genesis of this tradition (partially) in Origen's discussion of Ethiopia and Ethiopians within biblical traditions, which exerted considerable influence within the patristic era.[56] Though the "blackness-as-evil" metaphor was applied consistently to Ethiopians, Goldenberg cautions against concluding these patristic interpreters had "an antipathy toward black Africans."[57] This patristic era linking of blackness with "otherness, sin, and danger" became an "enduring theme of medieval Western and Christian thought."[58] According to Jablonski, explaining phenotypical differences (especially skin color) theologically provided greater ammunition for justifying the enslavement of kidnapped Africans.[59] If black skin was not just a difference produced by climate or other biological factors, then Africans' dark skin could be explained as a *"degenerative process* from an original white or light condition."[60] The assertion of a "degenerative process" that accounts for Africans' skin color is consistent with my earlier description of deviance as a constituent element of the 3Ds of Blackness.[61] As

---

56 Goldenberg, *Curse of Ham*, 48–51. Goldenberg summarizes Origen's commentary on several Hebrew Bible passages, including Amos 9:7, Song 1:5, and Jeremiah 38:7 – 13.

57 Goldenberg, *Curse of Ham*, 74. Like Goldenberg, I am not arguing the church fathers were racist, as such term is used within modern, American contexts of racial discourse. Rather, the negative valences of blackness, including its associations with dark-skinned individuals, has a lengthy history preceding Americans' appropriation of it. As I argue in this essay, the presence of blackness within the Christian symbolic universe (as a vehicle to describe evil, sin, etc.) becomes racialized within American contexts to define Black Americans as embodiments of such attributes. This racializing process, in turn, is critical for the creation and maintenance of the racial caste system.

58 Nina G. Jablonski, *Living Color: The Biological and Social Meaning of Skin Color* (Los Angeles: University of California Press, 2012), 135.

59 See Jablonski, *Living Color*, 136, and Smith, *Insights*, 5.

60 Jablonski, *Living Color*, 137 (emphasis added).

61 The "degenerative process" also reflects the traditions that Cain was the biological product of a sexual encounter between Eve and the devil, which produced black offspring. See, e.g., Ricard J. Quinones, *The Changes of Cain: Violence and the Lost Brother in Cain and Abel Literature* (Princeton: Princeton University Press, 1991), 53. The false syllogism uniting Cain, the devil, and blackness/Black persons will be discussed later in this essay.

is true with each of the 3Ds, what could neutrally be described as a difference becomes loaded with moral judgments and legal restrictions to justify the subordination and dehumanization of African Americans. Moreover, several scholars observe the tendency among some biblical interpreters to associate not only black skin with Cain, but also the fuller range of phenotypical characteristics connected to Black Americans.[62] Cain's racialized reception in America appears in several contexts from the earliest years of this country until the twentieth century. Although a full accounting of each invocation of Cain is beyond the scope of this project, the following examples are representative to demonstrate the pervasiveness and persistence of the associations among Cain, black skin, slavery, and the 3Ds. An example from the first decades of the 1700s is found in the work of Elihu Coleman—an early abolitionist. According to Coleman, a common defense of slavery included that "a Mark set upon Cain, and they do believe that these Negroes are the Posterity of Cain, because of their hair, and their being so black."[63] His recounting of this defense exhibits the pattern among pro-slavery advocates of expanding the Mark of Cain beyond black skin to a description of the notable physical attributes distinguishing "Negroes" from whites in America. Phillis Wheatley (ca. 1753–1784) is considered by many historians to be the first African American poet to be published in this country. Perhaps her most famous poem, "On Being Brought from Africa to America," contains a reference to the Mark of Cain:

---

62 See Lewis M. Killian, "The Stigma of Race: Who Now Bears the Mark of Cain?" *Symbolic Interaction* 8 (1985): 1–14. Later in this essay, I will provide examples of this phenomenon.

63 Louis Ruchames, *Racial Thought in America* (Amherst: University of Massachusetts Press, 1969), 94.

Some view our sable race with scornful eye,
"Their colour is a diabolic die."
Remember, Christians, Negroes, black as Cain,
May be refin'd, and join th' angelic train.[64]

In this excerpt, Wheatley invokes the Mark of Cain and its effects on the meanings of blackness in a manner consistent with aspects of the earlier discussion. First, as a young girl brought from Africa to be sold into American chattel slavery, this poem reflects her familiarity with the use of Genesis 4 to justify black enslavement in this country. Second, her reference to the Cain narrative reflects both the theological and phenotypical function of this passage in early American history. From a theological standpoint, Wheatley demonstrates the prevalence of how "our sable race" was viewed, i.e., "their colour is a diabolic die." In this phrase, she elegantly links skin color with a theological or moral assessment of it—namely, skin color is the mark of a demonic (i.e., "diabolic") encounter. From a phenotypical perspective, the specific trait—black skin—is connected to the biblical character Cain and to the American racial caste system's label for those with black skin, i.e., "Negroes." By the mid-eighteenth century when this poem was written, the connections among Cain, the devil, black skin, and "Negroes" were so well-established Wheatley could simply state it without any need to explain these connections. Lastly, Wheatley's concluding admonition to Christians to remember Negroes "may be refin'd and join th' angelic train" may serve as a critique of the presumptive immutability of

---

64 For the full text of the poem, please see the following website: https://www.poetryfoundation.org/poems/45465/on-being-brought-from-africa-to-america

black nature, which could (or should) have implications for their place in America's racialized hierarchy.[65]

In addition to Wheatley's artistic appropriation of the racialized Cain, the Mormon church provides a uniquely American testimony to the prevalence and persistence of this story. The Mark of Cain (along with the Curse of Ham) played a central role in the nineteenth and twentieth century, defining a common Mormon understanding of race relations. According to Bingham, Joseph Smith concluded dark skin "marked people of African ancestry as cursed by God."[66] Smith further connected the biblical curses of Cain (Gen 4:15) and Canaan (Gen 9:24) as providing "a providential explanation for racial slavery."[67] Daniel Herman, commenting on Smith's use of the Cain story and its racialized character, concludes that Joseph Smith (and the Mormon church more broadly) was typical of other Americans who "adapted the myth of the curse to their own purposes."[68] One quintessential articulation of Cain's racialization exists in the writings of Brigham Young:

> You see some classes of the human family that are black, uncouth, uncomely, disagreeable and low in their habits, wild, and seemingly deprived of nearly all the blessings of the intelligence that is generally bestowed upon mankind. The first man that committed the odious crime of killing one of his brethren will be cursed the longest of

65 See Mary McAleer Balkun, "Phillis Wheatley's Construction of Otherness and the Rhetoric of Performed Ideology," *African American Review* 36 (2002): 121–35, 130.

66 Ryan Stuart Bingham, "Curses and Marks: Dispensations of Race in Joseph Smith's Bible Revision and the Book of Abraham," *Journal of Mormon History* 41.3 (2015): 22–57, 27.

67 Bingham, "Curses and Marks," 27.

68 Daniel Justin Herman, *Hell on the Range: A Story of Honor, Conscience, and the American West* (New Haven: Yale University Press, 2010), 74.

any one of the children of Adam. Cain slew his brother. Cain might have been killed, and that would have put a termination to that line of human beings. This was not to be, and the Lord put a mark upon him, which is the flat nose and black skin . . . .[69]

While striking in its assertions, this quotation is neither unique nor unprecedented in its use of Genesis 4. In this excerpt, elements of the 3Ds are clearly present. Words and phrases like "uncouth," "uncomely," "wild," "deprived of all the blessings of intelligence that is generally bestowed upon mankind" highlight the ways Cain's villainy was racialized to define Black Americans as the ultimate racial other—barely to be regarded as members of the "human family."[70]

In addition to these explicit references to Cain and the 3Ds, some antebellum commentators on enslaved Africans did not base overtly their assessment in biblical traditions. Rather, they alluded to the 3Ds that emerged from the racialization of Cain to either justify continued enslavement or oppose emancipation. Although many examples exist, I will limit the discussion to one sample from this literature. George Williams's work, *History of the Negro Race in America from 1619 to 1880*, is his attempt "to write a thoroughly trustworthy history" without being "the blind panegyrist of my race, nor as the partisan

---

69 See Speech delivered by Brigham Young, October 9, 1859, *Journal of Discourses* 7:282. https://www.mormonstories.org/top10toughissues/blacks.html

70 This tenuous, if not non-existent, membership in the human family has implications for how African Americans' legal standing is defined within various statutes and court decisions. As I will argue, the infamous decision in *Dred Scott v. Sanford* states explicitly in legal terms the implications of the 3Ds of blackness. In short, the definition of Black Americans as dangerous, deviant, and depraved creations that are debatably human means that the legal rights, duties, and protections afforded by the law do not attach to those who bear the Mark of Cain—a conclusion the Supreme Court reaches in *Dred Scott.*

apologist, but from a love of 'the truth of history.'"[71] This ambitious project contains several quotations and excerpts from the writings of slave traders and anti-abolitionists. One set of quotations from the work of William Winwood Reade is particularly illustrative of the concepts of the 3Ds:

> It will be understood that the typical negroes, with whom the slavers are supplied, represent the dangerous, the destitute, and the diseased classes of African society... The typical negro is the true savage of Africa, and I must paint the deformed anatomy of his mind, as I have already done that of his body. . . .
>
> The typical negro, unrestrained by moral laws, spends his days in sloth, his nights in debauchery. He smokes hashish till he stupefies his senses or falls into convulsions; he drinks palm wine till he brings on a loathsome disease; he abuses children; stabs the poor brute of a woman whose hands keep him from starvation, and makes a trade of his own offspring.[72]

Although only "dangerous" appears explicitly in Reade's quotation, the substance of the 3Ds permeates his description. His claims about the "typical negro" being a "true savage" and possessing a "deformed mind" are consistent with the concept of deviance I described earlier. Similarly, the closing paragraph describing the behavior of the "typical negro"

---

71 George Williams, *History of the Negro Race in America from 1619 to 1880: Negroes as Slaves, as Soldiers, and as Citizens.* (New York: G. P. Putnam's Sons, 1883), x.

72 Williams, *History*, 47–48, quoting William Winwood Reade, *Savage Africa: Being the narrative of a tour in equatorial, southwestern, and northwestern Africa; with notes on the habits of the gorilla; on the existence of unicorns and tailed men; on the slave-trade; on the origin, character, and capabilities of the Negro, and on the future civilization of Western Africa* (New York: Harper, 1864), 430.

reflects the alleged perversity and debauchery encapsulated in my use of the term depravity. Whether specific descriptions of African Americans invoke Cain or the 3Ds explicitly, the preceding examples reflect the consistently pejorative portrayals of black personhood that were common in the seventeenth to nineteenth centuries.

After the abolition of chattel slavery, Cain's villainy and the cultural/theological typologies he represented continued to appear in a myriad of post Civil War contexts, including twentieth century literature and movies.[73] In the 1993 movie *Menace II Society*, one of the central characters in the story is named Caine—a violent, drug-dealing black man. Erin Runions notes the choice of the character's name "read straight off both racist identifications of the biblical Cain as black and the scriptural promise that Cain would be forever marked, always tragically flawed."[74] Runions's analysis suggests, however, the movie's appeal to the Cain/Caine tradition departs somewhat from the biblical record and the racialized traditions described earlier. According to Runions, the Cain/Caine naming is (in part) an attempt to nuance the associations between Cain and villainy by showing "excluded [persons are] indispensable to cultural innovation and organization."[75] Similarly, Carolyn Jones argues Toni Morrison uses the myth of Cain in innovative (if not subversive?) ways to describe aspects of the

---

73 The appearance of Cain and his attributes when describing African Americans (even without explicit references to the Bible) is part of Harvey's analysis about the cultural currency of certain images. See Harvey, "A Servant of Servants," 25.

74 Erin Runions, "Signifying Proverbs," in *Theorizing Scriptures: New Critical Orientations to a Cultural Phenomenon*, ed. Vincent Wimbush (New Brunswick: Rutgers University Press, 2008), 148.

75 Runions, "Signifying Proverbs," 150.

relationship between Sethe and Sula.[76] Specifically, Jones concludes "both Sula and Sethe must embrace and even, finally, celebrate the mark of Cain which sets each apart but which also makes each unique—and so must their communities."[77] This pattern among some African Americans to appropriate and subvert the traditional racialized villainy of Cain is discussed in a recent article by Nyasha Junior. In this article, Junior illustrates how various interpreters of Genesis 4 linked Cain's mark with "white skin and white violence."[78] Although the racialization of Cain is inverted, the fundamental characterization of him remains constant. Thus, whoever is categorized as a descendant of Cain cannot escape the linkage between their lineage and being interpreted as a source of evil, violence, and suffering.[79] In Junior's words, "all these stories, whether told by blacks about whites or whites about blacks, are etiologies accounting for the 'unusual' skin color of the Other.[80]

These examples, particularly from antebellum white traditions, highlight one of the most pernicious aspects of racializing Cain—namely, the demonization of black people. Within the Christian imagination, the devil is the embodiment of evil. This character functions as the quintessential enemy and polar opposite of God. God creates life; the devil kills and brings death. God gives freely; Satan steals. God is Truth; the devil is a liar. Put another way, the devil

---

76 See Carolyn M. Jones, "Sula and Beloved: Images of Cain in the Novels of Toni Morrison." *African American Review* 27.4 (1993): 615–26.

77 Jones, "Sula and Beloved," 625.

78 Junior, "White Violence," 661.

79 See Junior, "White Violence," 672.

80 Junior, "White Violence," 667, quoting David Goldenberg, *Black and Slave: The Origins and History of the Curse of Ham*, SBR 10 (Berlin: de Gruyter, 2017), 41–42.

is dangerousness, deviance, and depravity. The false racial syllogism building upon these theological claims about Cain, the devil, and his progeny permits blacks to be portrayed as not just dangerous, deviant, and depraved but also as literal "demons."[81] By connecting Cain and his mark to the devil and blackness, the theological groundwork is fully laid to erect the 3Ds. When such theological assertions about the nature of blackness are translated into law, centuries of statutes, judicial decisions, and legally sanctioned practices develop that identify Black Americans as threats to the civil order that must be excluded, exterminated, or regulated—rather than integral and valuable citizens contributing to the success of the American experiment who deserve protection. The remainder of this section investigates how the 3Ds and demonization of blackness appeared within aspects of American jurisprudence prior to the conclusion of the Civil War.[82]

AMERICAN LEGAL RECEPTION

Because the following section focuses on racialization of Cain as expressed in the legal definitions of and restrictions upon blackness, a brief comment on Critical Race Theory ("CRT") is

---

81 As I will discuss in the final section, the pattern of some law enforcement officials referring to black men as "demons," "devils," or "monsters" is connected to the cultural afterlife of the reception of Cain and how that contributed to the demonization of blackness and the construction of the 3Ds.

82 Although the survey of laws and court decisions stops with the mid-nineteenth century, the patterns, perspectives, and approaches identified during this era I contend are operative today. My choice to stop with the antebellum period relates to space constraints and my contention that the patterns of racialization, demonization, and legalizing discrimination are sufficiently established during that era in American history.

warranted.[83] Scholars of CRT recognize this movement began within legal studies during the last quarter of the twentieth century.[84] Situating CRT within its proper legal context, Delgado and Stefancic argue this approach arose "to embark on a race-based, systemic critique of legal reasoning and legal institutions themselves."[85] Foundational to this critique and my investigation of how the law reflects, receives, and reifies ideas of blackness derived from the Cain story is that the law is a tool in creating and maintaining "a regime of white supremacy and its subordination of people of color."[86] Consistent with CRT, my approach in this essay recognizes that categories of whiteness and blackness have political, economic, and cultural significance that the law advances.[87] Rather than asserting law is "objective" or "neutral," the racialization of Cain and demonization/criminalization of blackness in America evinces the ways laws and actors within the legal system (e.g., judges, legislators, police officers, etc.) are affected by wider cultural trends—including racist ideals and stereotypes.[88] As Higginbotham states, "rac-

---

83 Within the past year, CRT has become the subject of increased and heated debates in many aspects of American society, including school board meetings in which individuals are concerned about CRT's presence within K–12 education. As Crenshaw and others have often stated, CRT is a scholarly approach to legal analysis, history, and reasoning that is typically taught as an elective for law students in their final semesters of law school. For a recent article discussing the conflation of CRT with broader conversations about the prevalence and deleterious effects of racism within our society, see Muskaan Arshad, "The Conversation Around Critical Race Theory is a Manufactured Danger," *Harvard Political Review*, 6 October 2021, https://harvardpolitics.com/crt-manufactured-danger/.

84 See e.g., Delgado and Stefancic, *Critical Race Theory*, 6–7. In recent conversations about CRT where scholarly literature is invoked, this introduction by Delgado and Stefancic is quoted most often. If a "mother" and "father" of the movement can be claimed, Kimberlé Crenshaw and Derrick Bell would be strong candidates for those positions.

85 Delgado and Stefancic, *Critical Race Theory*, xv.

86 Kimberlé Crenshaw, Neil Gotanda, Gary Peller, and Kendall Thomas, eds., *Critical Race Theory: The Key Writings that Formed the Movement* (New York: New Press, 1995), xiii.

87 See Delgado and Stefancic, *Critical Race Theory*, 85–87.

88 For a similar perspective, see Delgado and Stefancic, *Critical Race Theory*, 140. See also Higginbotham, *Matter of Color*, 13.

ism in the courts is reflective of significant symptoms, signals, and symbols of racism in the broader society."[89]

The history of the effects of the 3Ds on America's legal systems is almost as old as the history of America's laws. A. Leon Higginbotham dedicated a significant portion of his scholarly energies to unearthing and summarizing this history. A major purpose of his scholarship is to illustrate "how the law has contributed to perpetuating villainy on millions of Americans, solely because of their darker color."[90] He correctly notes the impacts of "moral or religious rationales" upon the passing and enforcing of these laws in America against Black Americans.[91] Higginbotham joins other legal scholars and historians who recognize the legal support of slavery and its brutality in colonial times, the laws regulating Black Americans throughout American history, and the discriminatory legal practices of today are only sustainable because of the religious/divine sanction biblical interpretation provided.[92] Because his primary focus does not require a discussion of how moral and religious rationales shape legal treatments of African Americans, in this section, I will focus briefly upon a few laws that illustrate the perception of African Americans as

89 Higginbotham, *Shades of Freedom*, 128. This perspective on racism in the courts (and wider legal system) is consistent with a common tenet of CRT—namely, racism is "ordinary, not aberrational." (Delgado and Stefancic, 8). In addition, a helpful metaphor Lani Guinier and Gerald Torres offer is the experiences of people of color (BIPOC in current parlance) are a "miner's canary," indicating the toxicity of the environment, rather than reflecting the weakness, inferiority, etc. of the suffering communities. See Lani Guinier and Gerald Torres, *The Miner's Canary: Enlisting Race, Resisting Power, Transforming Democracy* (Cambridge: Harvard University Press, 2002).

90 Higginbotham, *Matter of Color*, 16. See also, Higginbotham, *Shades of Freedom*, xxiv.

91 Higginbotham, *Matter of Color*, 10. See also, Higginbotham, *Shades of Freedom*, 4.

92 See Higginbotham, *Shades of Freedom*, 26. The significant role religion and scripture played in American chattel slavery is well documented in the secondary literature. A classic text, which Higginbotham also references, is Albert Raboteau, *Slave Religion: The 'Invisible Institution' in the Antebellum South* (New York: Oxford University Press, 1978).

dangerous, deviant, and depraved and their connection to the racialization of Cain. To further narrow the scope of the discussion, I will discuss some legal precedents (statutory and judicial) that connect most directly to the recent violence against Black individuals in the late-twentieth and early-twenty-first century American contexts.[93] The ultimate legal effect of the 3Ds is to ensure enslaved Africans and their descendants are "not entitled to the privileges of the Christian freemen."[94] Legal personhood for African Americans (as recognized by guaranteed rights, protection of the state, and full participation in civil government) was never the intention of colonial legislative bodies, including the Congress of the newly formed United States.[95] This intentional denial of the legal indicia of personhood and citizenship received its clearest articulation in *Dred Scott v. Sanford*, 60 US 393 (1857).[96] The Supreme Court framed the central question of the case as follows: "Can a negro, whose ancestors were imported into this country, and sold as slaves . . . become entitled to all the rights, and privileges, and immunities, guaranteed by that instrument [the United States Constitution] to the citizen?"[97] The Court ultimately answers this question in the negative, concluding

---

93 Given the scope of this study, a thorough accounting of every law is impossible. Therefore, the examples selected are simply to illustrate the pervasiveness of the legal codification and enforcement of the "mythoracial" ideologies I contend are influenced by racialized interpretations of Cain.

94 Williams, *History*, 121–22 (discussing first prohibition against "Negroes" within Virginia's seventeenth century race laws).

95 See Higginbotham, *Matter of Color*, 59–60.

96 See Higginbotham, *Shades of Freedom*, 61–67. The Dred Scott decision has received significant attention among legal scholars around issues of race, law, citizenship, and the role of the Supreme Court. A resource that was often recommended for understanding this case and its significance is: Don E. Fehrenbacher, *The Dred Scott Case: Its Significance in American Law and Politics* (Oxford: Oxford University Press, 1978).

97 *Dred Scott*, 60 US 393, 403.

"[Negroes] are not included, and *were not intended to be included* under the word 'citizens' in the Constitution, and can therefore claim *none of the rights and privileges* which that instrument provides for and secures to citizens of the United States."[98] In reaching this decision, the Court reviewed over 200 years of legislative history in the former colonies, now charter members of the new republic, to illustrate how Black Americans were "marked" to live as inferior beings, regulated by white freemen, and excluded from citizenship in the new republic.[99] For the Court, the degraded nature of "Negroes" and their unfitness for participation in the affairs of the state was not only a legal understanding, but also a "moral axiom" supported by "the laws of nature and nature's God."[100] Thus, enslaved Africans and their descendants had no guaranteed rights. Rather, any and all "rights" were the possession of the "dominant race" which they "might not withhold or grant at their pleasure."[101]

From this apex of legal othering, the "mythoracial" constructs around the 3Ds and their legal expressions can be summarized briefly. Throughout the colonial period and formative centuries of America, legislatures passed and courts upheld increasingly restrictive and violent laws intended to control "the rebellious and vindicative impulses of blacks."[102] In states as disparate as Mississippi, Pennsylvania, and South

---

98 *Dred Scott*, 404–5 (emphasis added).

99 See *Dred Scott*, 406–17.

100 See *Dred Scott*, 407 and 410.

101 *Dred Scott*, 412.

102 See William W. Fisher III, *Ideology and Imagery in the Law of Slavery— Symposium on the Law of Slavery: Theories of Democracy*, 68 *Chi-Kent L. Rev.* 1051, 1061.

Carolina, laws were passed to restrict Black Americans' "liberties."[103] In each case, essentialist notions about the "inferior" or "barbarous, wild, savage natures" of the individuals being regulated are invoked.[104] Moreover, these laws were often cast as protective measures for the white citizens who were entitled to guard their lives and property from the ever present threat Black Americans posed.[105]

For the discussion that follows, one legal expression of the 3Ds requires attention—the policing power over Black bodies. Because of the presumptive danger, depravity, and uncontrollable impulses Black Americans were alleged to possess, increased power and authority over Black persons was given to white citizens. Higginbotham quotes a 1705 Virginia statute that made it lawful for any person or persons (meaning white citizens) to kill, dismember, or otherwise cause bodily harm to any "slave" as a way of "terrifying others from the like practices," without fear of criminal liability.[106] As Higginbotham notes, rather than the law protecting blacks, it gave "sanction (for) brutalizing blacks."[107] Throughout the seventeenth and eighteenth centuries, colonies from Massachusetts to South Carolina passed laws effectively empowering white citizens to detain, physically punish, and even kill slaves for offenses as minor as not showing a pass while traveling.[108]

---

103 See e.g., Higginbotham, *Matter of Color*, 292.

104 See Daragh Grant, "Civilizing the Colonial Subject: The Co-Evolution of State and Slavery in South Carolina, 1670–1739," *Comparative Studies in Society and History* 57.3 (2015): 606–36, 623.

105 See Fisher, *Ideology*, 1071 (discussing Vance v. Crawford, 4 Ga. 445, 447–48 [1858]).

106 See Higginbotham, *Matter of Color*, 56. An aspect of the "punishment as deterrent" ideology seems to be operative to prevent slaves from seeking their freedom, an impulse the VA statute labels "incorrigible."

107 Higginbotham, *Matter of Color*, 57.

108 See Higginbotham, *Matter of Color*, 171–76

For Higginbotham, both northern and southern states implemented these laws on the assumption that "nonwhites were the cause of all disorder and inconvenience."[109] In most, if not all, of the statutes and judicial rulings Higginbotham reviews, language drawn from the register of the 3Ds appears, including explicit appeals to Christian traditions.[110] Additionally,, the justification of slavery and the racial caste system it created increasingly relied upon notions that black phenotypical characteristics were the divine mark of the 3Ds, which sanctioned violent regulation for the good of all.

In essence, skin color alone became *prima facie* evidence of the 3Ds.[111] Ultimately, the legal codification of biblically based and theologically constructed blackness supports Oliver Wendell Holmes's famous conclusion that "the life of the law has not been logic . . . the prevalent moral and political theories . . . even the prejudices which judges share with their fellow-men have a good deal more to do than the syllogism in determining the rules by which men should be governed."[112]

The implications and applications of these legal precedents for American current events are hopefully as clear as they are chilling. A repeated theme in various antebellum laws and judicial pronouncements is that Black Americans are *not* persons in the eyes of the law. A consequence of the legal logic and theological worldview that informed these

---

109 Higginbotham, *Matter of Color*, 81. See also, Fisher, *Ideology*, 1071 discussing a Mississippi Supreme Court decision justifying enslavement, travel restrictions, and the violent enforcement of them as necessary for the order and self-preservation of the white citizens.

110 See Higginbotham, *Shades*, 26 and 41–47 (discussing the color of black skin made them "savage," while the color of white skin made them "civilized.").

111 See Higginbotham, *Shades*, 33 and 49.

112 Higginbotham, *Shades*, 129 (quoting Oliver Wendell Holmes Jr., *The Common Law* [Boston: Little, Brown, 1881], 1).

legal precedents is that no rights, liberties, or immunities are legally guaranteed to those who bear "the indelible marks" of separation from whites. This mark and its substance, which I contend are related to the racialized interpretations of Cain and his mark, subjected (and subjects) Black Americans to similar "strict police regulations" for the alleged safety of the real citizens of America. Moreover, legal protections guaranteed to citizens, as well as the moral assertions connected to them, are frequently absent to those who are "raced" black. Given the ubiquity of the 3Ds and the demonization of black people outlined earlier, the final section sketches how these 3Ds inform modern treatment of African Americans by briefly investigating two case studies—Rodney King and Michael Brown.

RACED CAIN, BLACK "DEMONS," AND LAW ENFORCEMENT: TWO MODERN CASE STUDIES

As a teenager during the late 1980s–1990s, Los Angeles was a focal point for many in my community—artistically (2Pac, NWA); athletically (LA Lakers); and racially (O. J. Simpson and Rodney King). When I first saw the video of Rodney King's beating, I was horrified, but not surprised, by the assault. Like many, I assumed the video was sufficient evidence of the officers' guilt, and their conviction was simply a matter of time. I remember conversations with friends, classmates, and family in which we were all certain, "they won't get away with this one." As history reminds us, they got away with it—at least initially. Stunned by the acquittal, I began looking for reasons to explain why and how this happened. One answer I found, which relates to this essay, was how the officers described Rodney King. Although the officers do not quote directly from Genesis 4 or the 3Ds, their language resonated precisely within the racial registers sketched in this essay. For example, Officer Stacey Koon testified that Rodney King was a *"monster-like figure akin to a Tasmanian devil."*[113] Moreover, King's assailants described him as possessing "hulk-like strength."[114] Later, when transcripts of the Internal Affairs investigation were released, Officer Powell added his perspective to the assault on King: "I know if he gets hold of me and grabs me in the neck . . . it's going to be like a death grip, and you can have all 8,300 members of this police department pull this guy off and it's not going to work."[115] Officer Powell also testified, despite being accompanied by approximately half-a-dozen armed officers trying to subdue one African American man, "I was in fear for my life, scared to death that [if] this guy got back up, he was going to take my gun away from me."[116]

Within these quotations, the constellation of pejorative attributes the 3Ds intend to capture are evident. As these excerpts demonstrate, Rodney King is never described as a human being. Instead, he is monstrous, devilish, and seems

---

113 Linda Deutsch, "Defense Tries to Put Rodney King on Trial, But Latest Witness Backfires," *AP News* 27 March 1993, https://apnews.com/article/6c823876d40222f6dd454a1cc4734370. Perhaps, not surprisingly, similar efforts to put the assaulted Black person on trial in the court of public opinion appeared in the Ahmaud Arbery incident I mentioned earlier in this essay. See Barnini Chakraborty, "Video surfaces of Ahmaud Arbery being arrested on suspicion of shoplifting in 2017," *Fox News*, 20 May 2020, https://www.foxnews.com/us/ahmaud-arbery-shoplifting-video.

114 See Deutsch, "Defense Tries."

115 See Professor Douglas O. Linder, "Famous Trials," https://famoustrials.com/lapd/580-kingownwords.

116 See Professor Douglas O. Linder, "Famous Trials," https://famoustrials.com/lapd/580-kingownwords.

out of control, if not uncontrollable. As a result, King is viewed as such a dangerous threat to one officer's life that (from this officer's perspective) the entire LAPD could not save the officer from King's alleged violent strength. At one point in the trial, Officer Koon further testified that he assumed King's physical build was the result of prison workouts. The entire incident with King is, in many ways, a direct result of the assumption that King was a danger to the officers and other citizens. Moreover, the abundance of mythic language (e.g., hulk-like, monster, devil, etc.) reflects the perception that Black Americans are deviant, i.e., non-human.[117] Finally, the repeated discussions of King's alleged drug use and the constant fears of his presumptively violent nature (i.e., depravity) became one of the justifications for the police's response.[118]

Over twenty years later, the memories of this moment from my teenage years returned when Michael Brown was killed. The policeman in this case, Officer Wilson, used similar language as Officer Koon to portray the incident in the same light. For example, Officer Wilson describes that when he grabbed Michael Brown he "felt like a five-year-old holding onto Hulk Hogan."[119] This quasi-superhuman description

---

117 A further example of this alleged deviance is the testimony of an officer who presented a rationale on the use of choke holds against Black people. The officer unexpectedly argued that such methods should not be used, with a destructive rationale for this position. Specifically, he argued that Black peoples' "veins or arteries do not open up as they do in *normal people.*" According to this officer, the determination of what type of force to use was based on an assumption that there is something abnormal (i.e., deviant) about Black people. See Lou Cannon, "Officer Testifies King Beating Was "Violent . . . Brutal' and Justified," Washington Post, 20 March 1992, https://www.washingtonpost.com/archive/politics/1992/03/20/officer-testifies-king-beating was-violent-brutal-and-justified/2a610d51-f1b6-4d69-88f5-424ec18c7531/.

118 A similar tactic using the 3Ds was used in the Ahmaud Arbery case. See Indivisible Ventura, "Standing Indivisible with Ahmaud Arbery: Two Actions," 7 May 2020, https://demcastusa.com/2020/05/07/standing-indivisible-with-ahmaud-arbery-two-actions/.

119 See Josh Sanburn, "All the Ways Darren Wilson Described Being Afraid of Michael Brown," *Time*, 25 November 2014, https://time.com/3605346/darren-wilson-michael brown-demon/.

of Brown continues when Officer Wilson says it looked like Brown was "bulking up to run through the shots, like it was making him mad that I'm shooting at him." While Wilson does not use the specific words "hulk-like," those familiar with the Marvel character will recognize the commonalities between this description and portrayals of the Hulk.[120] In concluding his description of Brown's approach, Wilson simply states: "The only way I can describe it, it looks like a demon, that's how angry he looked."[121] Once again, the perception of uncontrollable emotions (depravity), the sense of threat (dangerousness), and the coupling of super-human attributes with demonic appearance (deviance) appears in an officer's testimony about his encounter with an African American male. As one expert noted, a major reason for these descriptions was to create a greater sense of fear and danger, which could then justify the use of force.[122]

The fact that these two police officers, separated by more than twenty years, two time zones, and almost 2,000 miles, invoked similar language compelled me to ask—how did we get here? While it is impossible to know everything in the hearts and minds of Koon and Wilson, the living legacy of Cain's racialization sketched in this essay is one source for the cultural vocabulary describing black persons as "demons"

---

120 A relatively recent article (2014) discusses how attributing superhuman attributes to African Americans is a form of dehumanization. Moreover, an effect of this dehumanization is a willingness to accept greater violence being directed towards Black Americans, in part because it is assumed we feel less pain. See Adam Waytz, Kelly Marie Hoffman, and Sophie Trawalter, "A Superhumanization Bias in Whites' Perceptions of Black," *Social Psychological and Personality Science* (2014): 1–8.

121 See Sanburn, "All the Ways."

122 See Emily Wax-Thibodeaux, "Wilson said the unarmed teen looked like a 'demon.' Experts say his testimony was dehumanizing and 'super-humanizing,' *The Washington Post*, 25 November 2014, https://www.washingtonpost.com/news/post nation/wp/2014/11/25/wilson-said-the-unarmed-teen-looked-like-a-demon-experts-say-his testimony-was-dehumanizing-and-super-humanizing/

and "hulk-like." As Harvey notes, the biblical/theological underpinnings of this perception of blackness are obscured to many, but the "category of blackness lives on, supported now more by cultural prejudices and the simple weight of history."[123] Imbedding these cultural prejudices in legal decisions and procedures about the citizenship, rights, and immunities available to Black Americans gives these prejudices a crushing weight—one that so many of us witnessed resting upon the neck of George Floyd.

CONCLUSION

Written almost fifty years ago, Higginbotham's summary of the connections he saw between America's racist past and present still resonates in 2021: "For there is a nexus between the brutal centuries of colonial slavery and the racial polarization and anxieties of today. The poisonous legacy of legalized oppression based upon the matter of color can never be adequately purged from our society if we act as if slave laws had never existed."[124] In this essay, I sought to illustrate how a racialized set of interpretations about Cain contributed to this "poisonous legacy of legalized oppression." By focusing on the demonization of black people and the 3Ds of Blackness (dangerousness, deviance, and depravity), I tried to capture a constellation of associations that continues to place black lives at risk. It is a risk earned not through individual (or even collective) misconduct, but through the perpetuation

123 Harvey, "A Servant of Servants," 25.

124 Higginbotham, *Matter of Color*, 391.

of "mythoracial" constructs that remain integral to the moral, legal, and social fabric of this nation. As an African American attorney, biblical scholar, and minister, the question with which I began this essay—how did we get here?—has become another, equally pressing one: where do we go from here?

DEALING WITH THE DEVIL AND PARADIGMS OF LIFE IN AFRICAN AMERICAN MUSIC[1]

Anthony B. Pinn

Finally, be strong in the Lord, and in the strength of his might.
Put on the whole armor of God, that you may be able to stand
against the wiles of the devil.
For we wrestle not against flesh and but against principalities,
against powers, against the rulers of the darkness of this world,
against spiritual wickedness in high places.

—*EPHESIANS 6:10-12 (KJV)*

The imagery and assumed theo-existential truth of the above passage has both explicitly and implicitly haunted and guided the ethical sensibilities of the dominant modalities of African American religion in the United States – i.e., African American Christian churches – for centuries. African American Christianity has drawn its vocabulary and grammar, its imagery, symbolism, and posture toward the world from the rich stories that make-up the Hebrew Bible and the New Testament. Perspectives on the complex nature

---

1 This was first published as: "When Demons Come Calling: Dealing with the Devil and Paradigms of Life in African American Music," in Christopher Partridge and Eric Christianson, editors, *The Lure of the Dark Side: Satan and Western Demonology in Popular Culture* (London: Equinox, 2009), 60-73.

and framework of human relationships are given their weight and content in large part from the workings of situations outlined in scripture. In this regard, African American Christianity, as the above scripture would suggest, presents life struggles as tension between physical forces and non-physical forces, between transcendent realities and mundane presences intertwined within human history—angelic and demonic personalities.

Theological imagery and doctrinal assertions, in various regions of the United States, speak to this arrangement of synergy between celestial and mundane forces. This is certainly the case within African American evangelical circles, where this rhetoric and perception of the workings of the world are most vividly expressed. The Church of God in Christ, the fastest growing Christian denomination in African American communities, says the following concerning the reality of angels and demons:

> The Bible uses the term "angel" (a heavenly body) clearly and primarily to denote messengers or ambassadors of God with such scripture references as Revelations 4:5, which indicates their duty in heaven to praise God (Psalm 103:20), to do God's will (St. Matthew 18:10) and to behold his face. But since heaven must come down to earth, they also have a mission to earth. The Bible indicates that they accompanied God in the Creation, and also that they will accompany Christ in His return in Glory....Demons denote unclean or evil spirits; they are sometimes called devils or demonic beings. They are evil spirits, belonging to the unseen or spiritual realm, embodied in human beings. The Old Testament

refers to the prince of demons, sometimes called Satan (Adversary) or Devil, as having power and wisdom, taking the habitation of other forms such as the serpent (Genesis 3:1). The New Testament speaks of the Devil as Tempter (St. Matthew 4:3) and it goes on to tell the works of Satan, The Devil, and Demons as combating righteousness and good in any form, proving to be an adversary to the saints. Their chief power is exercised to destroy the mission of Jesus Christ. It can well be said that the Christian Church believes in Demons, Satan, and Devils. We believe in their power and purpose. We believe they can be subdued and conquered as in the commandment to the believer by Jesus. "In my name they shall cast out Satan and the work of the Devil and to resist him and then he will flee **(withdraw)** from you." (St. Mark 16:17).[2]

Not all historical African American denominations provide such strong statements concerning the reality of unseen forces influencing human existence. Yet, such commentary finds its way into African American Christianity in ways not confined to the formal doctrinal creeds and official theological postures of particular denominations. Paul Tillich's remark holds true in this case: Religion is the substance of culture; and culture is the language of religion. Regarding this, one is just as likely to find discussion of these invisible forces battling for influence in human history expressed in both oft-called "sacred" and "secular" songs as in formal theology.

---

2 http://www.cogic.org/dctrn.htm.

SPIRITUALS AND THE WORLDS AT WAR

Scholars such as John Lovell, Jr., have argued for the existence of spirituals long before the formation of independent African American churches in the 19th century, and it is through these haunting musical tunes that enslaved Africans articulated their rudimentary religious sensibilities and theological assumptions.[3] These songs speak of the slave's sense of a God present in the world, poised to bring about the redemption of the enslaved and the "righting" of the world. This God is understood to be loving, kind, just, and author of history understood as teleological in nature, both during the time of the biblical stories and the historical moment in which the slaves found themselves. In the words of one song: "Didn't my Lord deliver Daniel, deliver Daniel, deliver Daniel? And why not everyone?" Or,

> God is a God!
> God don't never change!
> God is a God
> An' He always will be God.[4]

God's plan for the fulfillment of human history, complete with its reframing of African American life, is accomplished through the perfect blend of divinity and humanity in the form of the Christ Event. Drawing from stories of the activities and attitudes of Christ, along with a deep sensitivity to Christ's

---

3 John Lovell, Jr., *Black Song: The Forge and the Flame: The Story of How the Afro-American Spiritual Was Hammered Out*, Reprinted Edition (New York: Paragon House Publishers, 1986).

4 James H. Cone, *The Spirituals and the Blues* (Maryknoll, NY: Orbis Books, 1972), 35.

humble family context, enslaved Africans embraced him and drew bold existential and ontological links between themselves and this representative of God on earth. They found in the material poverty surrounding his biblically rehearsed birth, and in the suffering that informed his *raison d'etre*, epistemological links and similarities to themselves: Enslaved Africans faced hardship and undeserved pain and, more to the point, their plight would be rectified through the workings of God in human history.

> Children, we shall be free
> When the Lord shall appear.
> Give ease to the sick, give sight to the blind,
> Enable the cripple to walk;
> He'll raise the dead from under the earth,
> And give them permission to talk.[5]

The uniqueness of Christ is the perfect balance between transcendent forces or realities and physical presence represented through the God/man, Christ.

The absurdity of the slave system, with its Christian tendencies, gave raise to a cartography of struggle bringing into play a host of forces, only some of them physical but all of them deeply important and felt. The Christ Event confronts the evil found in the world guided by the workings of Satan and Satan's dominion. In the spirituals, enslaved Christians spoke of the battle between good and evil, and noted their souls and their existential condition as the prize and the battlefield respectively. In the words of one song:

---

5 James H. Cone, *The Spirituals and the Blues* (Maryknoll, NY: Orbis Books, 1972), 34.

Kneel and pray, so the devil won't harm me
Try my best for to serve the lord
Kneel and pray, so the devil won't harm me
Hallelujah[6]

Juxtaposed to the work of demonic forces, spirituals speak of the company of angels as a life affirming and heaven-assuring event:

O, I'm going to march with the tallest angel
O, yes, march with the tallest angel
O, yes, march with the tallest angel
When my work is done[7]

Within the spirituals, proper human activity involves a push against demonic forces and an embrace of angelic forces—the assumption being the ultimate welfare of humanity is tied to the triumph of good over evil—the kingdom of God over Satan.

BLUES AND DEALS WITH THE DEVIL

In the blues such a distinction is not assumed. What is best for the individual (only limited attention is given to community) as outlined in the blues might entail a relationship with demonic forces over against the Christian God. Such a willingness to entertain demonic forces might suggest one rationale for calling the blues the "Devil's music" in that the music was conversant

---

6 "All I Do, the Church Keep A-Grumbling," http://www.negrospirituals.com/songs/all_i_ do_ the_chunrch_keep_a_grumbling.htm

7 "Members Don't Get Weary," http://www.negrospirituals.com/songs/members_don_t_ get_ weary.htm

with Christian principles, grammar and vocabulary, but showed a willingness to entertain forces Christians fear and fight.

Some strains of the blues, perhaps to signify Christian assumptions within African American communities or as a genuine acknowledgement of a spiritual realm, speak to the workings of spiritual forces often presented in physical form.

Devil's gonna git you,
Devil's gonna git you,
Oh, the devil's gonna git you,
The way you're carryin' on.[8]

In this way, blues artists acknowledged the manner in which we move through the world accompanied and influenced by unseen forces:

Black ghost, black ghost, please stay away from my door
Black ghost, black ghost, will you please stay away from my door
Yeah you know you worry po' Lightnin' so now, I just can't sleep no more.[9]

Whereas the boundaries between these forces and their effectiveness in human life are clear and based on the Christian faith for those singing the spirituals, for those motivated by the blues there is a more utilitarian approach—one that allows for flirtation with both angelic and demonic forces

---

8 Bessie Smith, "Devil's Gonna Git You," http://www.geocities.com/BourbonStreet/delta/2541/blbsmith.htm#devil

9 Lightin' Hopkins, "Black Ghost Blues," http://www.geocities.com/BourbonStreet/delta/2541/bllhopki.htm#black

depending on which might offer the most efficient assistance. The blues lack the certainty of a teleological arrangement of history that gives the Christian comfort; instead, the blues romance a comfort with paradox, or with a blending of opposites, manipulated and celebrated by the cleaver. Blues chronicler Robert Palmer captures this epistemological complexity when saying,

> Blues lyrics could be light, mocking, risqué, or could deal forthrightly with the most highly charged subject matter—intimate details of love, sex, and desire; a fascination with travel for its own sake that was rooted in the years of black captivity; the hypocrisies and foibles of preachers and other upstanding folks; the fantastic and often disturbing imagery of dreams; the practice and tools of magic and conjury; aggressive impulses that had to be severely repressed in everyday life; and in some blues, particularly the Delta Blues of Robert Johnson, an unabashed identification with the leader of the world's dark forces, the ultimate other.[10]

The blues speak casually of life circumstances, the play and interaction of contrary forces—both visible and invisible—in ways of great discomfort to those singing the spirituals. There is, in the blues, no great fear of "hell," nor great yearning for "heaven" in that the former can't be any worse than the oppression they currently encountered. The latter takes a back seat to the significance and "feel" of life's earthbound pleasures and desires. The sense of commonality found in the blues is premised on the desire for advancement, for goods,

---

10 Robert Palmer, *Deep Blues: A Musical and Cultural History, from the Mississippi Delta to Chicago's South Side to the World* (New York: Penguin Books, 1982), 18.

for good feelings, for the good stuff of life. "Powers and princi-palities" offering excess to the riches of life, regardless of their nature or disposition, are approached. In most cases loyalty is first to the individual, based on the interests and desires of the individual, and codified by any force capable of making those desires real. Perhaps flirting with this understanding suggests one of the reasons for Pettie Wheatstraw's labeling as the "Devil's Son-in-Law and the High Sheriff from Hell."[11]

I take no moral stance here, and I make no effort to judge the rhetoric and imagery of demonic forces in partnership or as foe. Rather, my concern is to suggest the rich and robust sense of operative forces pervading and influencing human existence found within the blues.[12] I am aware of musicolo-gist Jon Michael Spencer's critique of blues scholarship that uncritically assumes the blues to have evil intentions, a certain reading of blues as "devil music" in ways that simply re-en-force stereotypical depictions of African Americans, and sug-gest a rather flat and reified notion of the nature and meaning of evil. I would agree with Spencer that the blues are not "evil" per se. That is to say, there is nothing about the blues suggest-ing it is intrinsically flawed; rather, the tension regarding the non-"godly" dimension of the blues seems an imposed par-adoxical arrangement as opposed to being generated inter-nally. In other words, the dilemma of commitments regarding blues and evil stems from a dominant Christian worldview projected onto the blues. Yet, even in saying this, I would not go so far as to say there is no interaction (if not in actuality at least in rhetoric) with forces considered evil by blues artists.

---

11 Robert Palmer, *Deep Blues*, 115.

12 See Jon Michael Spencer, *Blues and Evil* (Knoxville: The University of Tennessee Press, 1993).

I want to suspend Spencer's assumptions concerning the normative state of Christianity as the religious orientation of African Americans, and thereby avoid his rather flat depiction of evil's function in American religion and life. Applying this to musical talent in African American communities, I argue while some gave thanks to God for their abilities—assuming God favored them with great talent as a gift—others spoke of a bargain with demonic forces as the source of their musical (and social) prowess. None represent this arrangement better than Robert Johnson.

Born in Mississippi, Robert Johnson is perhaps the blues artists most closely linked, as folktales would suggest, to demonic forces. The hardships of his early life—relocations, family disruptions—may have had something to do with his early interest in the blues, which was nurtured through the mentoring of Willie Brown, Charley Patton and Son House in Robinsonville, Mississippi. During these early years, legend has it Johnson's musical ability was of limited appeal, pale in comparison to the other musicians making their way through the Delta. However, this changed after Johnson left the area for an uncertain period of time and returned with staggering musical abilities. Accounts by scholars suggest he worked under the tutelage of another musician, practicing his craft, and only returned when his abilities were at a high level.

For others, the account more explicitly involves demonic forces in the service of humans—for a price. By accounts provided by family members and others, Johnson's new abilities resulted from him selling his soul to the Devil in exchange for unparalleled talent. Certain of his songs are pointed out as testimony to this exchange.[13] While some artists give visual depictions of the demonic—often portrayed consistent with negative color symbolism as a large black figure—Johnson gave no such attention to the appearance of the demonic. Rather, his concern revolved simply around the ability of such forces to impinge upon human existence. Johnson recognizes the presence of such forces impinging on his life:

> I got to keep moving, I got to keep moving
> Blues falling down like hail, blues falling down like hail
> Mmm, blues falling down like hail, blues falling down like hail
> And the day keeps on remindin' me, there's a hellhound
>   on my trail
> Hellhound on my trail,
> hellhound on my trail.[14]

Or, the connection between Johnson and the Devil as one of exchange is also present in shaded ways in the following lines:

> Early this mornin'
> when you knocked upon my door
> Early this mornin', ooh
> when you knocked upon my door
> And I said, "Hello, Satan,
> I believe it's time to go."[15]

---

13 Robert Palmer, *Deep Blues*, 111-131.

14 Robert Johnson, "Hell Hound On My Trail," http://www.geocities.com/BourbonStreet/delta/2541/blrjohns.htm#Hellhound481

15 Robert Johnson, "Me and the Devil Blues," http://xroads.virginia.edu/~MUSIC/blues/matdb.html

Johnson alludes to the consequences of securing musical abilities from the Devil: One must surrender one's soul, one's self to forces beyond one's control. Hence, even this deal with invisible forces is only a temporary correction to fulfilling desires and wants in that after a period of time comes damnation. And, much of the time prior to that is spent anticipating the inevitable, feeling the pursuit by "hell hounds." The alternative for Johnson appears to be movement, unpredictable and constant movement:

> I got ramblin', I got ramblin' on my mind.
> I got ramblin', I got ramblin' all on my mind.[16]

Had Johnson simply worked hard, under the guidance of formidable musicians, absorbing lessons without distraction, nor competition; or, had he made a deal with evil forces? Even if the answer to the latter is "no," Johnson recognized the significance of such imagery for projecting a reputation as a "bad man," a formidable figure whose activities and music produced a deep gut reaction that both repelled and attracted listeners. Death for blues performers familiar with the world of diverse forces did not necessarily entail an end to all events. Rather it marked a transition, a movement to a new venue for activity; but one arranged in exchange for a liminal period of prowess. There is a sense of the tragic in this move in that life often remained difficult – marked by recognition, but not without its downside. They lived "hard" and died "hard."

In certain ways, even a deal with the Devil involved a signifying of such demonic forces in that at times bad men "ruled" hell through the maintenance of their self-centered and destructive

---

16 Robert Johnson, "Ramblin' On My Mind," http://www.theonlineblues.com/robert-johnson-ramblin-on-my-mind-lyrics.html

ways. Or, in other cases, they joined the ranks of unseen forces and continued to move through human time and space—the "deal" with demonic forces and its aftermath both shrouded in mystery. Perhaps such awareness accounts for Robert Johnson's request for burial near the highway so that his evil spirit might continue to travel vis-à-vis the bus line. The need to hit the road, to traverse time and space, is not dampened by death:

You may bury my body, ooh
down by the highway side
So my old evil spirit can catch a Greyhound bus and ride.[17]

Such deals with feared forces could only enhance his reputation in that Johnson understood lyrics alone (many of which he borrowed from other artists) could not cement his success and musical legacy. Rather, the personae of the artists, the overall ethos of *being* surrounding him needed to entail the wiles of the trickster and the dealings of the "bad man." In short, association, real or imagined, with demonic forces served the purpose.

Even this affiliation, this connection to the demonic, served as a modality of resistance to staid and reified notions of morality and ethics tied to what these blues men considered the hypocrisy of the Christian faith. They, in dealing with the Devil, signified the claims of the Christian faith (its doctrine, theology—particularly its theodicies) to the sources of the good life in ways that centered on the validity of the desires and wants Christianity condemned roundly—erotic desires, material goods, and revenge. In this way, Johnson and other blues figures like him

17 Robert Johnson, "Me and the Devil Blues," http://www.deltahaze.com/johnson/lyrics.html

were involved in an inverted spiritual arrangement—whereby the needs and wants of the body were given priority over what Christians considered the proper welfare of the soul.

Despised black bodies sought assistance from despised "dark" forces. By so doing, it is possible artists sought to use metaphysical evil to battle the damage done by the socio-political and economic fall-out of racism as demonic force: Evil negates evil. Put another way, novelist James Baldwin in reflecting on his years as a young minister in a black evangelical church argued that, in his neighborhood, everyone belonged to someone: This was the nature of survival in a predator world. Belong provided a "space" and socio-cultural arrangements, the nurturing of talents and abilities. Early on, for Baldwin, belong meant the development of preaching ability that generated acceptance and appreciation. Musical artists seek commitment to a similar philosophy of relationship: They belong to something. For some, the proper modality of belonging was guided by the "rightness" of the Christian faith and it's commitment to Christ. Yet, for others, the proper space for development of self and talent involved a relationship with demonic forces.

THE DEMONIC AND RAP MUSIC

The bad man, the rebellious figure, continues his flirtation with demonic realities within the form of certain rappers. Such rap artists share many of the existential commitments and the moral sensibilities of blues performers like Johnson, and this includes a similar stance on synergy between demonic forces and rebellious humans.

While rap tends to avoid a direct appeal to demonic forces for the development of musical abilities and other markers of success in a troubled world, rap is not devoid of references to sensitivity to the presence and workings of demonic forces. Yet, rather than joining league with them actively, some rappers simply work in ways that seem influenced by the negative tendencies and character of the demonic, while others step through the world seeing the demonic lodged firmly around them. At the very least, some rap artists note an awareness of a delicate balance between life influenced by the divine and by the demonic, and press it into a macabre worldview. Such a tortured existence, one hanging between an absurd world and the workings of invisible forces impinging upon human existence, marks, for example, lyrics by Scarface.

Born November 9, 1970, Jordan Bradley, in Houston, Texas, Scarface made his early fame (or position as infamous) through the rap group "The Ghetto Boys," whose lyrics spoke without remorse of the "dark" side of ghetto existence. This group presented itself as predatory and determined to exercise its wants and desires without attention to moral and ethical consequences.

Since the early 1990's, Scarface has produced solo projects that continue along the same path of existential angst but with a glimpse here and there into the world of "powers and principalities" that influences but is not synonymous with the arrangements of human history.[18] As blues artists note the manner in which evil can follow "bad men," from birth,

---

18 Whether or not Scarface converted to Islam does not negatively affect this analysis in that the lyrics to the referenced tracks do not clearly indicated an Islamic orientation vs. a Christianity orientation. To the contrary, the imagery and theological language embedded tends to shadow the Christian faith, and the awareness of demons and divine forces appears drawn from the Christian faith.

Scarface presents himself as dogged by the demonic even before he is able to consciously choose sides. He notes,

> I don't remember much about being born
> But I do remember this: I was conceived on February 10th
> Complications detected in my early months of ballin'
> Around my sonogram you could see the evil was swarmin'[19]

Furthermore, death is ever present and in some instances Scarface dissects the details of life's surrender to death: "you start your journey into outer space. You see yourself in the light but you're still feeling outta place."[20] Scarface, like so many other rappers, makes an appeal to relationship with the Divine as the best last out reach of humanity; but, he also recognizes the tensions between the forces of "good" pushing for this sort of relationship and the demonic that influences humans to behave in less than ethically robust ways. From his perspective, the existence of these two competing forces is real, oozing from every aspect of human existence in the 'hood. Death lurks around the corner, and the life of a "G" requires recognition of this and a willingness to accept the negatively serendipitous nature of such a life. Think in terms of the lyrics to "Make Your Peace" in which Scarface frames the demonic in terms of an alternate world invisible to human eyes, but nonetheless real:

> I had a dream and seen a double sun,
> a different world was in the makin'
> The rule of this new world was Satan.[21]

19 Scarface, "Last of a Dying Breed," *Last of a Dying Breed* (2000).

20 Scarface, "I Seen a Man Die," *The Diary* (2004).

21 Scarface, "Make Your Peace," *Balls and My Word* (2003).

Deals with demonic forces do not appear as commonplace in rap, although 2Pac's verse to "Smile," on Scarface's *Untouchable*, directly addresses this arrangement through which goods and prowess are secured:

No fairy tales for this young black male
Some see me stranded in this land of hell, jail, and crack sales
Hustlin' and heart be a nigga culture
Or the repercussions while bustin' on backstabbin' vultures
Sellin' my soul for material riches, fast cars and bitches
Wishin' I live my life a legend, immortalized in pictures.[22]

In spite of the above, on the whole, rap artists do not generally suggest that one try to bargain with and out maneuver these demonic forces. On the other hand, one should simply recognize their presence and their impact on life in that such forces are everywhere, identifiable in the activities of neighbors and friends by the observant. In Scarface's words, "who the fuck is you gonna trust when your road dog is scheming? And every other corner, you're passin' a different demon...."[23] The world involves an absurd arrangement of forces that one cannot completely control, but that one can embrace or signify. It is this perspective that artists such as Scarface accept and articulate in their music, absorbing the paradox of life with a rather knowing way and with a somewhat defiant posture.

The difficulty of moving through a world haunted by such forces is not limited to Scarface and his existential angst and metaphysical uncertainties, artists such as Snoop Dogg also

22 2Pac on Scarface, "Smile," *Untouchable* (1997).

23 Scarface, "Heaven," *The Fix* (2002).

wrestle with the various forces present in the world. Born October 20, 1971 in Long Beach, California, to Beverly Broadus and Vernall Varnado, Snoop Dogg's (aka Calvin Broadus) life was marked by the deep concern and religious orientation of his mother and the absence of his father. One of the few things given to him by his father, Snoop Dogg remarks, was a love for music. This love, combined with talent and skills given by God, mark the emergence of a rap career. In short, he notes, "In every rap I ever recorded, in the mad flow of every street-corner freestyle I ever represented, there was only one thing I wanted to get across: the way it is. Not the way I might want it to be. Not the way I think *you* might want it to be. But the way it *really* is, on the streets of the 'hoods of America, where life is lived out one day at a time, up against it, with no guarantees... My raps describe what it's like to be a young black man in America today."[24]

Snoop Dogg's rap shares with the blues a deep sensitivity to the nature and "flow" of life, the manner in which human relationships of all sorts shift and change in a variety of ways. He, like blues artists before him, recognizes the "dark" corners of life, noting both the promise and struggle associated with human existence. His is an existentially driven reality, but one that is also sensitive to the presence of realities uncontrolled by human intension. And, the bad man is best equipped to maneuver through this troubled terrain. That is to say, "there was a whole new class of hero coming up—the pimp and the outlaw, the thug and the gangster—and if you wanted to stay alive on the streets of Long Beach or Watts or Compton or anywhere else where the American Dream was falling apart

---

24 Snoop Dogg, with Davin Seay, *The Dogg Father: The Times, Trials, and Hardcore Truths of Snoop Dogg* (New York: William Morrow and Company, Inc., 1999), 2-3.

and fading away, you better get with their program. It was the only game in town."[25] Like the bad men of the century before him, Snopp Dogg is not troubled by this philosophy of connection; rather, he sees it as being a matter of fact and he embraces the paradox that is life: Stagger Lee reincarnated as a late twentieth century gangbanger.

While the often ethically questionable nature of some of his lyrics might suggest a paradox, Snoop Dogg views his musical history as teleological in nature, a purpose driven development framed and orchestrated by a God who has provided him with talent and opportunity. That is to say, "Just when you think you've got Him figured out, some blindside twist of fate makes you understand that you *can't* figure Him out. That's why He's God and you're whoever the hell you are. He calls the shots, makes the moves, and keeps it all in check."[26] He views his rap lyrics and music, as described above, as a matter of ministry, a way of transforming life and regenerating relationships. From his perspective all of life (and death) are controlled by forces unseen but felt: "...most of the time, most of us don't sit around thinking on how God can snap our string any time He gets mad or bored or needs another angel in heaven or another demon in hell. Most of the time, if we're honest, we don't give a thought o any of that metaphysical shit."[27]

Increased sensitivity to the fragile nature, the complex arrangements, of life came to Snoop Dogg, he recounts, when faced with the possibility of life behind bars without

---

25 Snoop Dogg, with Davin Seay, *The Dogg Father: The Times, Trials, and Hardcore Truths of Snoop Dogg* (New York: William Morrow and Company, Inc., 1999), 41.

26 Snoop Dogg, with Davin Seay, *The Dogg Father: The Times, Trials, and Hardcore Truths of Snoop Dogg* (New York: William Morrow and Company, Inc., 1999), 149.

27 Snoop Dogg, with Davin Seay, *The Dogg Father: The Times, Trials, and Hardcore Truths of Snoop Dogg* (New York: William Morrow and Company, Inc., 1999), 25-26.

the possibility of parole. It was with the threat of freedom removed, of space reified and time controlled by others, that Snoop Dogg's interest in metaphysical questions and concerns was sharpened. He writes, "My guess is, we all wonder about the time we've got set out for us on the planet and what we're going to do with it before the clock stops ticking and they put us in the ground...And that might be because, for those few, the reality of their life coming to a stone-cold stop is more than just some what-if trick their minds play on them. Every once in a while, a human being, no different from you or me, really does face down those odds, and when that happens, nothing is ever the same again."[28]

Unlike Robert Johnson and numerous other blues performers, there is no hint of conjuration, of folk practices, at work in Snoop Dogg's tale; but the existence of "powers and principalities" seems just as felt, just as compelling. There's a rhetoric of responsibility and accountability in the autobiographical voice of Snoop Dogg that one does not find in blues artists like Robert Johnson; yet, there is a paradox to life that resembles the depiction of life offered within so many blues tunes. Perhaps this paradox is even heightened in Snoop Dogg's story in that the battle between the demonic and the divine is made much more vivid.

On August 23, 1993 a man lay dead on the street, and Snoop Dogg and two others would be implicated in his murder. It is this tragic event, from which he was found innocent, that sparked his theological and existential reflection on and wrestling over deals with unseen forces as a framework for navigating the uncertainties of human (non) existence. As

---

28 Snoop Dogg, with Davin Seay, *The Dogg Father: The Times, Trials, and Hardcore Truths of Snoop Dogg* (New York: William Morrow and Company, Inc., 1999), 188.

Robert Johnson hauntingly portrayed such a deal for talent in several blues tunes, Snoop graphically suggests a deal in exchange for continued life and prowess in "Murder Was the Case," a project spearheaded by Dr. Dre (with Snoop Dogg as one of several receiving writer's credit for the title track). According to some, the title track was loosely "tied" to the murder charge Snoop Dogg faced at the time of its release. In his autobiography, however, Snoop Dogg is less than enthusiastic about that project, seeing it as potentially distracting from his solo project, *Doggystyle* ("Murder Was the Case" is also a track on *Doggystyle*).

While arguing the murder charge brought him closer to prayer and God, thereby recognizing the inability of humans to ultimately shape history and control visible and invisible forces, the lyrics suggest a world of forces at work. More important than an autobiographical authenticity to the lyrics—or the validity of seeing the piece as commentary on the trial—is the reflection on demonic vs. divine influence open to human use. Shot, one assumes, due to jealousy over his success, Snoop encounters the various forces marking the geography of human existence – all attempting to gain control of his soul:

> My body temperature falls
> I'm shakin and they breakin tryin to save the Dogg
> Pumpin on my chest and I'm screamin
> I stop breathin, damn I see demons
> Dear God, I wonder can ya save me...[29]

---

29 Snoop Dogg, "Murder Was the Case," *Doggystyle* (1996).

Based on Snoop Dogg's personal narrative of relationship to God, one would assume the deal struck in the track is with the Divine. However, the storyline is not so clear and the ethical system in large part leaves room to wonder. Is the voice he hears after praying that of God, or one of the demons he sees?

> I think it's too late for prayin, hold up
> A voice spoke to me and it slowly started sayin
> 'Bring your lifestyle to me I'll make it better"
> How long will I live?
> "Eternal life and forever"
> And will I be the G that I was?
> "I'll make your life better than you can imagine or even
> dreamed of."[30]

The life Snoop secures as a result of the deal with the unnamed force entails the material goods and control that might make Robert Johnson proud. Yet, it is one that does not mirror the more narrow and rigid moral and ethical outlooks generally associated with surrender to Christ, at least as typically presented by African American churches. The theological and ethical message is muddied in that the character's behavior results in a prison sentence. Is this punishment for not practicing more conservative Christian values, or is it simply the uncertain, perhaps double-crossing, arrangements of a deal with the Devil? Is it divine punishment, or the end of one's "run" through life—similar to Robert Johnson's deal with the Devil not preventing what legends call a painful death? Only Snoop knows; we are left to wonder with only a

---

30 Snoop Dogg, "Murder Was the Case," *Doggystyle* (1996).

few certainties—one being the presence of both "good" and "evil" forces shaping and shifting the nature and substance of human existence.

A NOT SO FINAL WORD...

A sensitivity to a world packed with both visible and invisible forces mark the lyrical content of African American forms of music such as the blues and rap. In both cases, the more ethically and morally aggressive artists flirt with such forces, signifying them and/or partnering with them based on a deep sense of individualized need and desire. The lyrical content offered by these artists, whether blues figures such as Robert Johnson or rappers such as Scarface and Snoop Dogg suggest a theological articulation of life premised on the reality of the biblical notion of powers and principalities. While they might not approach such forces as did New Testament writers or as contemporary Christians might hope, they nonetheless move through the world sensitive to the host of forces and realities impinging on life, shaping and transforming it—all the while, in an ironic way, also enriching it. This is certainly one way to read Johnson's deal with the devil, or Snoop Dogg's dream of an arrangement that provides wealth and power, while delaying death. In either case, there's a haunting and eerie narrative of the battle for the human soul, one firmly lodged in the lyrics of African American music.

"A HOME IN DAT ROCK": AFRO-AMERICAN FOLK SOURCES AND SLAVE VISIONS OF HEAVEN AND HELL[1]

Lewis V. Baldwin

I got a home in dat rock,
Don't you see?
I got a home in dat rock,
Don't you see?

Scholars such as John W. Blassingame, James H. Cone, Eugene D. Genovese, Lawrence W. Levine, Albert J. Raboteau, David Roediger, Sterling Stuckey, and Thomas L. Webber have made use of orally transmitted slave sources as an index to slave thought on the afterlife.[2] This essay is designed to contribute

---

1 First published in *The Journal of Religious Thought* 41, no. 1 (Spring-Summer 1984): 38-57.

2 John W. Blassingame, *The Slave Community: Plantation Life in the Antebellum South* (New York: Oxford Univeristy Press, 1972), chap. 2; James H. Cone, *The Spirituals and the Blues: An Interpretation* (New York: The Seabury Press, 1972), chap. 5; Eugene D. Genovese, *Roll, Jordan, Roll: The World the Slaves Made* (New York: Panteon Books, 1974), 248ff.; Lawrence W. Levine, *Black Culture and Black Consciousness: Afro-American Folk Thought from Slavery to Freedom* (New York: Oxford University Press, 1977), 34-46; Albert J. Raboteau, *Slave Religion: "The Invisible Institution" in the Antebellum South* (New York: Oxford Univeristy Press, 1978), 291-293; David Roediger, "And Die in Dixie: Funerals, Death, and Heaven in the Slave Community, 1700–1865," *The Massachusetts Review* vol. 22, no. 1 (Spring, 1981), 163-183; Sterling Stuckey, "Through the Prism of Folklore: The Black Ethos in Slavery," in Eric Foner, *America's Black Past: A Reader in Afro-American History* (New York: Harper & Row, Publishers, 1970), 99-102; and Thomas L. Webber, *Deep Like the Rivers: Education in the Slave Quarter Community, 1831-1865* (New York: W. W. Norton & Company, Inc., 1978), 48-49, 86-89, 143.

further to that effort. It is an examination of the concepts of heaven and hell.

My thesis is that African slaves in America shaped a more humane and realistic set of values than their white oppressors where heaven and hell were concerned. Narratives, tales, songs, sermons, aphorisms, prayers, and other slave sources—representative of the attitudes of a very large number of slaves toward the afterlife—make it amazingly clear that slaves did not subscribe to the slave-masters' vision of a heaven where racism and slavery would persist, and of a hell where disobedient slaves would meet their eternal fate. This picture of the afterlife was inconsistent with their belief in the biblical God who valued all human beings as equals. Thus, the slaves critically redefined and reshaped Christian dogma concerning heaven and hell in accordance with their own experiences, values, and traditions. In short, they fashioned an autonomous body of thought on this subject, thereby demonstrating that under the dynamics of the human spirit no system is airtight. This is one example of how slaves created *a Neo-Chrisitanity*.[3]

Many Africans who were brought to America as slaves had their own religious consciousness regarding the afterlife, but not specifically heaven or hell in the Euro-American Christian sense. Most came as adults steeped in African traditional religions which embraced notions of reincarnation and life beyond death. These notions were blended with Christian conceptions, as the number of American-born slaves began to outnumber African-born slaves, and as more and more slaves were exposed to white Christian teachings concerning heaven and hell. This contention is supported by W. E. B.

---

3 I am indebted to Professor Sterling Stuckey of Northwestern University for much of this idea.

Du Bois brilliant discussion in *The Souls of Black Folk*, where he referred to the breakdown of African religious systems and values among the slaves.[4]

Some African traditional views concerning the afterlife were strikingly similar to certain beliefs characteristic of Euro-American Christianity, thus making it easier for slaves to draw from and add to Christian notions of heaven and hell. First, both African traditional religions and white Christianity affirmed the reality of life beyond death. It was held in both that after death the departed ones live forever in a world beyond, in which they have a joyful, lasting reunion with other departed souls. Second, both emphasized the remembrance of the deceased by those who continued to live on earth, particularly surviving relatives. Finally, the ancient African belief that witches, thieves, and other evil people are excluded from the paradise of the departed closely resembled the Euro-American Christian notion that evil and immoral persons will not be accepted into heaven. Parallels of this nature undoubtedly helped prepare Africans in America for an acceptance of Christianity.[5]

As early as the seventeenth century white Christians used the language of heaven as a tool to indoctrinate African slaves with those teachings designed to make them docile. They constantly reminded slaves that faithfulness, honesty, and obedience were necessary preconditions for their salvation. This has been corroborated by the testimonies of ex-slaves like Anderson Williams of Mississippi,

---

4 John Hope Franklin, ed., "Souls of Black Folk," in *Three Negro Classics* (New York: Avon Books, 1965), 344.

5 See John S. Mbiti, *Death and the Hearafter in the Light of Christianity and African Religion* (Kampala, Uganda: Department of Religious Studies and Philosophy, Makerere University, 1973), 11-19.

who recounted for his interview how "De preacher would say to us, 'Be good to de massa an' missus, don't steal dey chickens and eggs, an' when you die dey will carry you to Heaven.'"[6] Slaves were often told of the immense beauty and the lavish material goods which awaited deserving persons in heaven—the "golden streets," the "pearly gates," and the "land flowing with milk and honey." But when describing the beauty and joy of heaven, whites were careful to avoid giving the impression that freedom and equality would abound between the races. Ex-slave Frank Roberson related how the white preacher told his black hearers that

> you slaves will go to heaven if you are good, but don't ever think that you will be close to your mistress and master. No! No! there will be a wall between you; but there will be holes in it that will permit you to look out and see your mistress as she passes by.[7]

Former slave Jack Jones laughingly shared with one WPA interviewer how the white preacher on his plantation taught the slaves that "they would go to the Negro Heaven, or Kitchen Heaven."[8]

The whites did not restrict themselves to describing the eternal paradise which was in store for faithful and obedient slaves. They also painted frightening pictures of the fire and brimstone of everlasting hell which would engulf slaves who

---

6 George P. Rawick, ed., *The American Slave, A Composite Autobiography, Mississippi Narratives*, 31 vols., Supplement, no. 1, vol. 10, pt. 5 (Westport, Conn.: Greenwood Press, 1977), 2300.

7 Quoted in John Cade, "Out of the Mouths of Ex-Slaves," The Journal of Negro History, vol. 20, no. 3 (1935), 329.

8 Rawick, ed. *Mississippi Narratives*, Supplement, no. 1, vol. 8, pt. 3, 1212.

cheated, lied, stole, ran away, plotted rebellion, or engaged in other acts of sabotage. The Mississippi ex-slave Polly Cancer remembered that her mistress frequently used such imagery to discourage bad behavior on the part of slaves:

> She wud read de Bible to us to tell us what de ole Bad Man was goin' to do to us; she wud sho' us de pictsher ov him; he had a pitch fork in hiz han' an' a long forked tail an' a club foot an' horns on hiz head; he wud be dancin' roun' pinchin' folks an' stickin' de pitch fork in dem.[9]

Henry Box Brown, born a slave in Virginia in 1816, said, after escaping from the South to Philadelphia, that "the great end to which religion is there made to minister is to keep the slaves in a docile and submissive frame of mind, by instilling into them the idea that if they do not obey their masters, they will infallibly go to hell."[10]

The visions of the afterlife presented to the slaves by their white oppressors were permeated with inconsistencies. This was inevitable, considering that the major concern was to convince black men and women of God's love for them without calling racism and slavery into question. The dilemma confronted by whites who attempted this task was illustrated in the case of the Rev. William Meade of Virginia. In one sermon he told a group of slaves that their masters and mistresses were God's overseers, and that faults against them constituted faults against God, while in another message he used the story of the rich man who went to hell and

---

9 Rawick, ed. *Mississippi Narratives*, Supplement, no. 1, vol. 7, pt. 2, 344-45.

10 Henry Box Brown, *Narrative of Henry Box Brown* (Boston: Brown & Stearns, 1849), 45.

the beggar at his gate who went to heaven to show that "God is no respecter of persons."[11] Even the most illiterate slaves were prone to see the contradictions inherent in such teachings. Consequently, they could not but be suspicious of a gospel which enjoined them to be honest and obedient, when they daily observed white people beating, killing, selling, and exploiting their people. Many of the slaves shared the view of fugitive slave Charles Brown, who claimed that, "I told my master one day, said I, 'You white folks set the bad example of stealing—you stole us from Africa, and not content with that, if any got free here, you sold them afterward, and so we are made slaves.'"[12]

Slaves generally, imbued with a strong sense of how Christianity was being used to oppress them, did not see themselves as sinners as readily as whites if they lied, stole, ran away, or killed for freedom. It was rather uncharacteristic of slaves to dwell on their own sinning, or to believe that they would go to hell for what whites regarded as slave crimes or sins. To the contrary, slaves tended to view themselves as God's chosen people even when their behavior patterns seemed to suggest otherwise. Even a devout slave woman could believe that "it's all right for us poor colored people to appropriate whatever of the white folks' blessings the Lord puts in our way."[13] Charles Ball, the author of an important slave autobiography, said that he was "never acquainted with a slave who believed that he violated any rule of morality by appropriating to himself anything that belonged to

---

11 Levine, *Black Culture and Black Consciousness*, 46.

12 Quoted in Raboteau, *Slave Religion*, 295.

13 Quoted in Julius Lester, *To Be A Slave* (New York: Dell Publishing Company, Inc., 1968), 101.

his master if it was necessary to his comfort."[14] These sentiments, coupled with former slave Rachel Fairley's wry remark that "you didn't eat if you didn't steal," bear witness to Lawrence Levine's thesis that the slaves shaped a new system of ethics which permitted them to justify their need to lie, cheat, and steal, without holding such actions up as models to live by in all instances—"without creating, that is, a counter-morality."[15]

Even in slave tales, which had to speak to the deeply felt needs of a large number of slaves in order to survive, one senses the conviction that it was all right for slaves to take what they needed from white people. Ex-slave Simon Brown of Society Hill, South Carolina, shared with young William John Faulkner a trickster tale, called "Brer Tiger and the Big Wind," which the slaves commonly told to express in a subtle way this conviction. In this tale Brer Rabbit and other little creatures symbolizing the slaves, caught in a time of drought and famine, were confronted by Brer Tiger who, representing the master, sought to deny them water and their share of a big pear tree, "just a-hanging down with juicy pears, enough for everybody."[16] The small creatures are compelled to trick Brer Tiger into allowing them to tie him up so they could take their share of the water and the pears. After Brer Tiger was carefully tied to a pine tree, Brer Rabbit encouraged all the little animals to "get all the pears and drinking water you want, because the Good Lord doesn't love a stingy man. He put the

---

14 Charles Ball, *Slavery in the United States: A Narrative of the Life and Adventures of Charles Ball, a Black Man* (New York: John S. Taylor, 1837), 299.

15 Rawick, ed., *Arkansas Narratives*, vol. 8, pt. 2, p. 259; and Levine, *Black Culture and Black Consciousness*, 123.

16 William J. Faulkner, *The Days When the Animals Talked: Black American Folktales and How They Came to Be* (Chicago: Follett Publishing Company, 1977), 89–94.

food and water here for all His creatures to enjoy."[17] A similar outlook is revealed in these words from a slave secular song:

> Our Father, who is in heaven,
> White man owe me eleven and pay me seven,
> They Kingdom come, thy will be done,
> And if I hadn't took that,
> I wouldn't had none.[18]

The attitude conveyed here contained elements of protest, and it developed naturally out of the slaves' perception of their own humanity and of the degree to which they were being exploited.

The existential situation of the slaves made it possible, and indeed necessary, for them to use a tremendous amount of critical judgement in evaluating the teachings of whites concerning the afterlife. Knowing that white Christian teachings on this subject could have no application to their world, the slaves redefined Christian dogma on heaven and hell to make it apply to their own peculiar experiences as an abused and exploited people. Thus, to them heaven necessarily represented something entirely different from the slavemasters' image of a Promised Land where the races would be separated, or where black people would be confined to the kitchen of heaven. The slaves envisioned a heaven where "Dere's no whips a-cracking"...."No more partin'"—a transcendent reality where "Dere's no hard trials"...."No evil-doers"...."No more

---

17 Ibid.

18 Sterling Brown, "Negro Folk Expression: Spirituals, Seculars, Ballads and Work Songs," in August Meier and Elliot Rudwick, eds., *The Making of Black America*, 2 vols., vol. 2 (New York: Atheneum, 1974), 216.

sunshine for burn you."[19] Slave thought was literally saturated with visions of freedom in heaven, implying a strong dislike for the limitations imposed by racism and slavery. One detects this in one of the favorite sermons of John Jasper, who was a slave preacher for twenty-five years. "What will I do ef I gets thar?" cried Jasper in his reference to heaven:

> I 'spec I'll make er fool of myself....I sometimes thinks if I's 'lowed to go free–and I 'specs to be free dar–I tell you, b'leve I'll jest do de town–walkin' an' runnin' all roun' to see de home which Jesus dun built for His people.[20]

Slave tales and songs also reverberate with this sense of freedom. In a tale gathered after the Civil War, "The Hopkins Nigger" goes to heaven "a-throwin' them foots an' shoutin'." After being given wings by the Lord, "he riz up an' he fly an' he flewed and there never been seen such flyin' since heben been heben...."[21] Another fascinating tale told by ex-slave Simon Brown focuses on the death of Sister Dicey, a strong spiritual force in the slave community. The slaves were not really sad when Sister Dicey died because they felt that she "was freed from all the trials and tribulations of slavery and was safe in Heaven, at rest and in peace forevermore. She wouldn't be a bare-foot slave dressed in rags anymore...." Her suffering had finally been transcended as her soul took flight for heaven.

---

19 Quoted in William F. Allen, et al., eds., Slave Songs of the United States (New York: Peter Smith, 1951), originally published in 1867, 45-46, 93.

20 Quoted in William E. Hatcher, *John Jasper: The Unmatched Negro Philosopher and Preacher* (New York: Fleming H. Revell Company, 1908), 177.

21 Quoted in Edward C. L. Adams, *Congaree Sketches: Scenes From Negro Life in the Swamps of the Congaree and Tales by Tad and Scip of Heaven and Hell With Other Miscellany* (Chapel Hill: University of North Carolina Press, 1927), 2-4.

The slaves knew, Brown continued, that Sister Dicey "was better off with a Loving Heavenly Father than she had even been in this wicked world of slavery." At Sister Dicey's funeral the slaves sang one of their favorite spirituals:

> I got shoes, you got shoes—
> All God's children got shoes.
> I'm going to put on my shoes
> And walk all over God's Heaven.[22]

Here the slaves were actually singing of a shared experience of suffering in bondage, of being "shoeless," while rejoicing in the firm conviction that the new order which is to come will afford both bodily freedom and the security of shoes. The "walking all over God's Heaven" points to a kind of freedom indeed, a freedom that transcends freedom. This freedom is to be realized not in the slavemasters' heaven, but in God's heaven.[23] The slaves were not simply dealing in escapism or telescopic idealism here. They were singing about a world that *ought to exist,* that *would exist.* Simon Brown remembered that some of the slaves got so happy thinking about heaven at Sister Dicey's grave "that they burst out crying and shouting for joy." The "crying and shouting for joy" as Walter E. Fluker puts it, was a foretaste of the glorious freedom which the concept of heaven embodied. In theological terms, it was "realized eschatology." The future event of liberation had broken into the present for these slaves. They were happy, not in some blitheful, ephemeral sense, but happy in conviction

---

22 Faulkner, *The Days When the Animals Talked*, 34-39.

23 See Gayraud S. Wilmore, *Last Things First* (Philadelphia: The Westminster Press, 1982), 84-85.

that they were indeed free regardless of what white people thought. Heaven and earth are one liberating frenzy. Whites cannot define their humanity—they live vicariously through Sister Dicey's death. Paradoxical notions of suffering and celebration are present here. Joy triumphs over sorrow, as sustained by Brown's recollection that "the singing was mostly sad songs with happy endings."[24] This is a clear indication of how pain and affirmation exist side by side in slave art, just as tragedy is so often the catalyst for great art.

In the minds of the slaves, the freedom which the concept of heaven entailed would allow them, in a manner similar to their West African forebears, to relate on familiar terms with God. The ex-slave preacher John Jasper often preched about greeting not only the patriarchs, prophets, apostles, and martyrs but also of visiting the throne of God: "I'll take er trip to de throne an' see de King in 'is roy'l garmints. . . . Oh, what mus' it be to be thar!"[25] In some spirituals, the slaves even talked about engaging in a dialogue with God:

> I'm gwine ter tell the Lawd all about it,
> When I reach de Promus land.

and

> When I get to heaven, gwine be at ease,
> Me and my God gonna do as we please.
> Gonna chatter with the Father, argue with the son,
> Tell um 'bout the world i just come from.

---

24 Walter E. Fluker, "Suffering and Community: Defining Motifs of Black Slave Existence," (unpublished paper, Fall, 1978), 9-11; and Faulkner, *The Days When the Animals Talked*, 36.

25 Stuckey, "Through the Prism of Folklore," 102; and Hatcher, *John Jasper*, 180.

Such lyrics show that some slaves, in the words of Sterling Stuckey, "would keep alive painful memories of their oppression even when released from the burdens of the world."[26]

Aside from being a place of unfettered freedom, heaven for some slaves represented that dimension in which white people would suffer the same abuses and exploitation they had visited upon black people on earth. Emily Burke, a white woman who studied slave life in Georgia, reported that the slaves ". . . believe, and I have heard them assert the same, that in life to come there will also be white people and black people; but then the white people with be slaves, and they shall have the dominion over them."[27] The fugitive slave Charles Ball wrote:

> It is impossible to reconcile the mind of the native slave to the idea of living in a state of perfect equality, and boundless affection, with the white people. Heaven will be no heaven to him, if he is not to be avenged of his enemies. I know, from experience, that those are the fundamental rules of his religious creed; because I learned them in the religious meetings of the slaves themselves.[28]

The slave notion of a revolution in the conditions of blacks and whites in heaven afforded a sharp contrast to the slave masters' view that blacks would continue to be servants in heaven. This slave attitude raises serious questions about

26 Rawick, ed., Georgia Narratives, Supplement, no. 1, vol. 3, pt. 1, p. 134; and Stuckey, "Through the Prism of Folklore," 100-102.

27 Quoted in Raboteau, *Slave Religion*, 291.

28 Ball, *Slavery in the United States*, 220-21.

Genovese's notion that there was an absense of personal vin-
dictiveness on the part of most slaves.[29]

There were persons in the slave community who were not
obsessed with a future paradise which insured the security
of shoes, intimacy with God, and retribution for their masters.
For those slaves, there may have been an existence beyond
the grave which was neither heaven nor hell. "I'll lie in de grave
and stretch out my arms" could imply a desire for eternal rest,
for relief from even the memory of the experience of slavery.
The Virginia slave Austin Steward wrote about such a slave:
"He toils on, in his unrequited labor, looking only to the grave
to find a quiet resting place, where he will be free from the
oppressor."[30] Solomon Northup, a talented slave musician,
described one slave woman who "entertained but confused
notions of a future life, not comprehending the distinction
between the corporeal and spiritual existence." "Happiness, in
her mind," continued Northup, "was exemption from stripes,
from labor, from the cruelty of masters and overseers. Her idea
of the joy of heaven was simply rest, and is fully expressed in
these lines of a melancholy bard":

I ask no paradise on high,
With cares on earth oppressed
The only heaven for which I sigh,
Is rest, eternal rest.[31]

---

29 See Genovese, *Roll, Jordan, Roll*, 251ff.

30 Thomas W. Higginson, *Army Life in a Black Regiment* (1869; reprint, New York: Collier, 1962), 199; and Austin Steward, *Twenty-Two Years a Slave, and Forty Years a Free Man* (1856; reprint; New York: Negro Universities Press, 1968), 19.

31 Solomon Northup, Twelve Years a Slave (1853; reprint; Baton Rouge: Louisiana State University Press, 1968), 200.

A significant number of slaves, again like their West African ancestors, looked to heaven as a place where they would have a happy, unending reunion with their friends and relatives. The slave's preacher who eulogized Sister Dicey proclaimed, as her body rested over the grave, that "On that Great Getting Up Morning, when the trumpet of God shall sound to wake up all of the dead, we will meet you in the skies and join the hosts of saints who will go marching in." Although Sister Dicey was dead, she did not cease to exist. The thought of meeting her in heaven, Simon Brown recalled, was greeted with an outpouring of joy: "Before the preacher could finish his benediction, some of the women got so happy that they drowned him out with their singing and handclapping and shouting."[32] Slave songs reflect this same sense of joy and community in heaven:

Meet my father
When I git home.
Meet my father
When I git home.

And there was this song which acknowledged a familial tie which went beyond kinship:

Oh, shine, de brudders shine,
Dey sisters shine ever mo',
When we all gits to heaven,
An' dey meets us at de do.[33]

---

32 Faulkner, *The Days When The Animals Talked*, 39.

33 Howard W. Odum and Guy B. Johnson, *Negro Workaday Songs* (Chapel Hill: University of North Carolina Press, 1926), 204.

The importance of heavenly reunions is further illustrated by the fact that slaves were most apt to think of heaven while standing at the foot of the auction block, where they were always faced with the painful reality that friends or relatives would be sold and taken away never to be seen by them again in their earthly life. A South Carolina-born slave gave a touching account of his mother's reaction when she learned he was being sold:

> On the morning I was sold and went to tell my mother goodbye, she fainted. She was in the bed, and I went to the door and said, "Goodbye, Mama, goodbye." It nearly broke her heart. She just cried out, "Goodbye, son! Meet me in glory." Then she turned her face from me. I never expected to see her again in this life.[34]

Jacob Stroyer, also a South Carolina slave, remembered that one of the spirituals slaves were accustomed to singing for the consolation of those who were being sold was:

> When we all meet in heaven,
> There is no parting there;
> When we all meet in heaven,
> There is no parting there.[35]

The slaves obviously experienced intense, perhaps the sharpest form of suffering, in the breaking up of their families and in being separated from loved ones. This explains

---

34 Clifton H. Johnson, ed., *God Struck Me Dead: Religious Conversion Experiences and Autobiographies of Ex-Slaves* (Philadelphia: United Church Press, 1969), 71.

35 Jacob Stroyer, *My Life in the South* (Salem, Mass: Newcomb & Gauss, 1898), 41.

why family reunions in heaven were such a persistent theme in slave sources. But the sorrow which accompanied the breakup of families and friends, as proven by the discussion above, was always superseded by the faith that in God's heaven there would be no auction blocks, slave catchers, drivers, and traders to destroy family ties and relationships with friends. Although broken and dispersed on earth, the slaves would be restored in heaven with all their friends and relatives as a community.

Aside from the auction block, gravesites were the scenes where slaves were most inclined to think of heaven. On such occasions, the sense of the ultimate unity of the slave community and family was always strong, and many wept at the thought of reuniting families in heaven, and sang together:

> My mother prayed in de wilderness,
> In de wilderness,
> In de wilderness
> My mother prayed in de wilderness,
> And den I'm a-going home.[36]

Bondsmen were also most likely to think of heaven on Sundays when friends and relatives met for worship in slave cabins, in "hush harbors," or in other places unattended by whites. The consciousness of being a suffering community had to be most compelling at such meetings. This is why some slave spirituals portray heaven as "a bright land of never-ending Sabbath":

---

36   Gold R. Wilson, "The Religion of the American Negro Slave: His Attitude Toward Life and Death," The *Journal of Negro History* 8 (January 1923): 65-68; and Rawick, ed., *Mississippi Narratives*, Supplement, no. 1, vol. 7, pt. 2, 139.

Help me, Lord, to live so
That when I'm through down here,
I'll have a place over there,
Where every day will be Sunday
And Sabbath will have no end.

And there were these lines:

Bye an' bye, bye an' bye,
Good Lord!
Bye an' bye
Ev'ry day'll be Sunday
Bye an' bye.[37]

The impact of this vision of heaven cannot be diminished by the contention that whites also tended to think of heaven on Sundays. Indeed, such thinking was common among whites, but it was more intense among slaves, due to the pain of earthly existence. It is conceivable that slaves generally endured the greatest physical and mental exertion and pain during the first six days of the week, which means that Sunday was most often the day which afforded the most rest and peace. Some slaves saw in this day an opportunity to visit each other, to talk with each other, and to share their pain with each other. Others saw it as a time to feel like somebody in their own worship services—a chance to have their spirits lifted by the consolatory words that fell from the lips of their own preachers.[38] These realities have to be considered if

---

37 Wilson, "The Religion of the American Negro Slave," 65.

38 Howard Thurman, *Deep River* and *The Negro Spiritual Speaks of Life and Death* (Richmond, Ind.: Friends United Press, 1975), 17-18.

we are to grasp the deeper significance of what slaves meant when they sang of a heaven where "Ev'ry day'll be Sunday."

A pervading sense of community with the dead, heightened by the vivid, imaginative conception or anticipation of reunions in the afterlife, was quite evident in slave rituals and "art for the dead." Slave rituals demanded that deceased slaves be "put away properly," or given a decent burial. Great care was usually exercised in the washing, drying, and shrouding of the dead. Wakes—euphemistically known as periods of "settin' up wid de dead"—were commonly held in the cabins of the deceased. At such times the slaves would kiss, touch, embrace, or say goodbye to the departed friend or relative. Other slave funeral rites were also expressions of a desire to bid a proper farewell to the dead. They included the large and slowly paced funeral processions, attracting as many as 700 slaves; the passing of the smallest child over or under the coffin; the powerful funeral sermons which evoked feelings of hope and solidarity; the sprinkling of handfuls of dirt over they coffin by slave mourners; the artistic decoration of graves with the belongings of the deceased; and the intimacy of communal sorrow reflected in the dancing, singing, chanting, praying, clapping, and weeping which normally occurred at gravesites and in post-funeral celebrations.[39] Examples of such rituals and practices are provided in Arna Bontemps' account of the funeral of Old Bundy, and in former slave Simon Brown's tale concerning Sister Dicey. At Bundy's grave the slaves, in a gesture of farewell, exclaimed: "We going to miss you just the same, though we going to miss you bad, but we'll meet you on

---

39 Roediger, "And Die in Dixie," 174-177; and Robert F. Thompson, "African Influence on the Art of the United States," in Armstead L. Robinson, et al., eds., *Black Studies in the University* (New Haven: Yale University Press, 1969), 122-170.

the other side. We'll meet you just as sure as you're born." The chant at Old Bundy's gravesite was:

> Put a jug of rum at his feet.
> Roast a hog and put on the grave.
> How them victuals suit you Bundy.

In the case of Bundy's death, the idea of freedom was communicated in these words:

> The smoke goes free....Can't nobody hurt smoke....A smoke man, that's you now, brother. A real smoke man.[40]

When Sister Dicey died, the slave women bathed her body, put on her best dress they could find, pinned a flower on her bosom, and laid her out in a homemade casket resting on two chairs. Slaves from plantations "all about came to the cabin and sat around while they sang and prayed." At the gravesite, the slave preacher gave a message of hope and unity, and the womenfolk "laid some flowers and ribbon grass on top and put colored bottles, broken glass, and seashells all around the grave of Sister Dicey." "In that way," Simon Brown reminisced, "they showed their love for her. It was the best that slaves could do in those days when everybody was poor and owned by their masters. But no one could own their souls or keep them from loving one another. These gifts come only from God."[41] Such attitudes and practices put the lie to Stanley M. Elkins' thesis regarding the total

---

40 Arna Bontemps, *Black Thunder: Gabriel's Revolt in Virginia, 1800* (Boston: Beacon Press, 1968), 52-53.

41 Faulkner, *The Days When the Animals Talked*, 34-39.

infantilization of many slaves; Eugene Genovese's stress on the dependency complex which slavery produced in blacks; and Kenneth M. Stampp's and C. Vann Woodward's views on the common culture of blacks and whites.[42]

The slave burial customs represented both a bridge into the afterlife and a continuity with the African past. The slaves, reflecting the influence of their African religious background, believed that the spirit of the dead had to be comforted, protected, and sustained in its journey to the afterlife. This meant that the proper "goodbyes" had to be said and the appropriate objects had to be placed on the grave.[43] Some relationship between slave customs and West African traditions is also suggested in the notion of surviving spirits. "Ghosts" or "hants," which maintained interest in the affairs of the living and punished or frightened them for misdeeds, played a significant role in traditional African religions and cosmology, and they reflected traditions connected with the process of ancestor reverence, and it was symbolic of what slaves and their African forebears thought about death and the afterlife. Like the artistic grave decorations, this belief in surviving spirits was indicative of the supreme value that people of African descent attached to the family and the community.[44]

What slaves thought about hell is equally important as support for the general argument that they created a distinctive

42 Stanley M. Elkins, *Slavery: A Problem in American Institutional and Intellectual Life* (Chicago: The University of Chicago Press, 1968), chap. 3; Genovese, *Roll, Jordan, Roll*, 3ff.; and Kenneth M. Stampp, *The Peculiar Institution: Slavery in the Antebellum South* (New York: Vintage Books, 1956), chap. 1.

43 Fluker, "Suffering and Community," 5-13: Roediger, "And Die in Dixie," 176; and Thompson, "African Influence on the Art of the United States," 122-170.

44 Mbiti, *Death and the Hereafter*, 12-13; and Mary F. Berry and John W. Blassingame, "Africa, Slavery, and the Roots of Contemporary Black Culture," *The Massachusetts Review*, vol. 18, no. 3 (Autumn, 1977), 507-08.

and autonomous body of thought concerning the afterlife. The slaves placed absolutely no value on the slavemakers' images of the everlasting hell, fire, and damnation which supposedly awaited disobedient and rebellious slaves. To the contrary, slave sources substantiate Thomas L. Webber's thesis that "slaves had little interest in hell except as an eternal depository for slaveholders."[45] Henry Box Brown spoke for most slaves when he admitted that he believed in a "hell, where the wicked will dwell, and knowing the character of slaveholders and slavery, it is my settled belief, as it was while I was a slave, even though I was treated kindly, that every slaveholder will infallibly go to hell, unless he repents." A correspondent of *The Southern Workman* reported in 1897 that some ex-slaves were even convinced that "No white people went to heaven."[46] Slaves pondered the issue of the slavemasters' role in the afterlife in spirituals like:

> Jorden stream is wide and deep...
> Jesus stand on't oder side...
> I wonder if my massa deh.

and this spiritual, which, in black theologian Howard Thurman's terms, was sung by the slaves while "looking up to the big house where the master lived":

> Oh, heaven, heaven.
> Everybody talkin' bout heaven.
> Ain't goin' there.[47]

---

45 Webber, *Deep Like the Rivers*, 89.

46 Brown, *Narrative of Henry Box Brown*, 18-19; and quoted in Levine, *Black Culture and Black Consciousness*, 34.

47 Allen, et al., eds., *Slave Songs*, 23; and Thurman, *Deep River* and *The Negro Spiritual*, 48.

Ex-slave Levi J. Coppin of Maryland recounted a slave aphorism repeated many times over when whites were seen riding in fine carriages: "That is all the heaven you will ever get."[48] In a popular tale, Mac, a slave, explained his master's doom to a group of fellow slaves while "old Boss" stood outside the window listening: "Sisters and brothers," he said, "there's only two places to go after you die, and that is Heaven or Hell. And since Boss can't go to Heaven, there's no other place for him to go but to Hell."[49] The slave preacher evidently had a similar notion in mind when he declared to his slave hearers in a sermon on the Judgement Day: "Breddern and sisters, in dat day, de Lord shall divide de sheep from de goats, and bress de Lord, we know who wears de wool." The sheer power of this statement comes through when one considers that goats symbolize white people in slave folklore. As to why white oppressors would not be allowed in heaven, former slave J. Maddox explained: "Lord God, they'd turn heaven wrong side out and have angels working to make something they could take away from them."[50] This conviction was not only reflective of the acute degree to which slaves realized that they were being exploited, but also suggestive that they were far more perceptive and realistic than most whites in their understanding of what constituted *right* and *wrong*.

Only in rare cases did slaves think of hell as a place where fellow slaves would be infinitely tortured. Charles Ball mentioned that the slaves on his plantation generally agreed that wicked

---

48 Levi J. Coppin, *Unwritten History* (Philadelphia: A.M.E. Book Concern, 1919), 54.

49 Richard M. Dorson, *American Negro Folktales* (Greenwich, Conn.: Fawcett Publications, Inc., 1967), 160.

50 Genovese, *Roll, Jordan, Roll*, 265-266; and John G. Williams, *De Ole Plantation* (Charleston, S.C.: published by the author, 1895), 2ff.

slaves would be the companions of the masters and mistresses after death.[51] Wicked slaves included those who were notoriously irreligious, those who abused and betrayed the confidence of fellow slaves, and those who collaborated with whites in keeping their own people enslaved. Levi J. Coppin commented on what was generally believed about the slave who persisted in his (or her) indifference to the religion of the slave community:

A man thus characterized by our people who was one who would swear, drink whisky and perhaps gamble; one who never went to church. They were called hard-hearted sinners. Some of them were supposed to have "dealings" with the Devil. When such a person died, you could not get a neighborhood child to go any distance alone at night. The impression was, the devil had come for the wicked person, and was probably still sneaking about there in the darkness. This doctrine was quite generally believed by the older ones, and the children had no inclination to go out into the darkness and investigate it, in order to be convinced whether it was true or false. There was always a superstition that the death of such a person was accompanied by a storm, a terrible storm, preferably a snow storm. By some kind of coincidence, the biggest snow storm of the season came at the time of the death of such persons.[52]

The conviction that slaves who cheated, killed, or mistreated fellow slaves in other ways would be subjected to everlasting hell was symbolic of the tremendous importance

---

51 Ball, *Slavery in the United States*, 219-20.

52 Coppin, *Unwritten History*, 27-28.

which the slaves attached to the need for community among the oppressed. Thus, it is clear why a slave from Georgia could say that, as a rule, any one of the slaves he knew "would have thought nothing of stealing a hog, or a sack of corn, from our master," but "would have allowed himself to be cut to pieces rather than betray the confidence of his fellow slave....[53]

Slaves who kept whites informed about the plans and activities of blacks, or who collaborates with the oppressors in other ways to insure the enslavement of their people, were characterized as "the same as white folks," and were known to be the targets of slave folklore concerning hell. One folktale from the collection of Edward C. L. Adams, called "the King Buzzard," told of an African slave who became well-known because of the ways in which he assisted whites in capturing and enslaving his own people. When this slave died, his spirit wandered eternally because "dere were no place in heaven for him an' he was not desired in hell." The lesson communicated here is that a slave committed a virtually unforgivable sin by plotting with whites against blacks. In short, the slave who had a reputation for such behavior was considered by "de Great Master" to be "lower dan all other mens or beasts....[54]

Lawrence Levine contends that "for the slave, Heaven and Hell were not concepts but places which could well be experienced during one's lifetime; God and Christ and Satan were not symbols but personages with whom meetings or confrontations were quite possible."[55] This contention is borne out by slave narratives, sermons, and accounts of conversion

---

53 John Brown, *Slave Life in Georgia: A Narrative of the Life, Sufferings, and Escape of John Brown, a Fugitive Slave, Now in England* (London: W. M. Watts, 1855), 83.

54 Edward C. L. Adams, *Nigger to Nigger* (New York: Charles Scribner's Sons, 1928), 12-15.

55 Levine, *Black Culture and Black Consciousness*, 37.

experiences. WPA interviewee Joana T. Isom of Mississippi related that "One time I wuz sick an' I went rite up to heaven an' saw de angels playin' on golden strings stretched over all heaven. They wuz singin' 'Happy Home, Sweet Home; Where Never Comes de Night,'"[56] William E. Hatcher wrote a tenderly moving account of how John Jasper's sermons often "took him into the neighbourhood of heaven," and how on such occasions the famous slave preacher "took fire at once and the glory of the celestial city lit his face and cheered his soul." A South Carolina ex-slave claimed that while praying one day, "I died and found myself at the greedy jaws of hell":

> I saw the devil, a terrible, club-footed man, with red eyes like fire. I called upon God to deliver me from that place, for the weeping and gnashing of teeth was awful. I saw a big wheel that seemed full of souls, and as it turned the cry of "Woe! Woe! Woe!" was pitiful.[57]

The fact that slaves labeled certain earthly locations as heaven and hell is equally significant, in light of Levine's argument that heaven and hell from the slaves' viewpoint could be experienced in this life. Places like Africa, Canada, and the northern Unied States were usually seen as lands of freedom and called heaven, whereas the slave South was known as hell. Many of the African slaves tended to believe that upon death their triumphant spirit would return to Africa. As one slave trader remarked, "Many of the blacks believe, that if they are put to death and not dismembered...they shall return again

---

56 Rawick, ed., *Mississippi Narratives*, Supplement, no. 1, vol. 8, pt. 3, 1099.

57 Hatcher, *John Jasper*, 174; and Johnson, ed., *God Struck Me Dead*, 121.

to their own country." This belief was manifested in a powerful manner at the grave of Old Bundy, "Where the Negros...,
throwing themselves on the ground and wailing savagley...,
remembered Africa."[58] This same conviction is obvious from
the testimony of Charles Ball, who once took part in the burial
of the small son of two African-born slaves. The child's body
was interred along

> ...with...a small bow and several arrows; a little bag of
> parched meal; a miniature canoe and a little paddle (with
> which it was said he would cross the ocean to his own
> country)...and a piece of white muslin with several curious
> figures painted on it...by which...his countrymen would
> know the infant to be his son.

Ball went on to stress that African-born slaves "were uni-
versally of the opinion, founded in their religion, that after
death they shall return to their own country and rejoin their
former companions."[59] Apparently, the image of Africa was
quite significant in the shaping of distinctive slave attitudes
toward the afterlife. In some slave songs, which were composed when African influences were still considerably strong,
"the crossing of the River Jordan" after death may well have
meant a crossing back to the African homeland:

My army cross ober,
My army cross ober,
O Pharoah's army drownded,

---

58 Elizabeth Donnan, *Documents Illustrative of the Slave Trade to America*, 4 vols., vol. 2 (New
York: Octagon Books, 1965), 266 and 359; and Bontemps, *Black Thunder*, 52.

59 Ball, *Slavery in the United States*, 265.

My army cross ober.

We'll cross de Riber Jordan.

We'll cross de danger water.

We'll cross de mighty myo.[60]

Among some Christianized slaves, visions of freedom in heaven brought vivid memories of the freedom they had known in Africa. For example, the slave Thomas Johnson recalled that his mother taught him "all about heaven where all would be free. Then she would talk of Africa; how they were all once free there."[61] The feelings vibrating from the recollections of slaves like Charles Ball and Thomas Johnson suggest that the slaves who were brought from Africa were literally obsessed with a desire to return there. However, this does not mean that Miles Mark Fisher was right in saying that most references to "home" and "heaven" in early slave spirituals reflect an intense desire to return to Africa, specifically Liberia. Fisher's thesis is questionable as a generalization about most slaves because during the 1820s and 1830s, when many spirituals were being assembled, African-born slaves made up a small minority of the general slave population in the United States.[62]

Frederick Douglass and Harriet Tubman reported that heaven was identified in the minds of many slaves with the North and Canada. This idea, coupled with the early tendency to equate Africa with heaven, shows that there was indeed a complex interrelationship between worldly and otherworldly

---

60 Allen, et al., eds., *Slave Songs*, 38.

61 Thomas J. Johnson, *Twenty-Eight Years a Slave* (London: Christian Workers, 1909), 4.

62 Miles Mark Fisher, *Negro Slave Songs in the United States* (Itaca, N.Y.: Cornell University Press, 1953), 129, 146, 156, 178; and Roediger, "And Die in Dixie," 177.

concerns in slave visions of heaven. Douglass skillfully illustrated the point when he wrote:

> A keen observer might have detected in our repeated
> singing of
> O Canaan, sweet Canaan
> I am bound for the land of Canaan,
> something more than a hope of reaching heaven.
> We meant to reach the North, and the North was
> our Canaan.[63]

After making it to the North, Harriet Tubman declared, "I
looked at my hands to see if I was de same person now I was
free. Dere was such a glory ober everything, de sun came like
gold trou de trees, and ober de fields, and I felt like I was in
heaven." This inclination to associate the North with heaven
must have been seriously discouraged when Congress passed
the Fugitive Slave Act as part of the Compromise of 1850, and
when the Dred Scott decision was made known in 1857. These
developments undoubtedly convinced many slaves that the
North was not much better than the South as far as the situation of black people was concerned.[64]

In the thinking of most slaves, hell was the best way to
characterize the South. In the South, the slaves saw the devil
when they confronted white people, and they experienced
hell when their fellow slaves were whipped, maimed, burned,
lynched, or sold on the auction block. This explains why one

---

63 Frederick Douglass, *Life and Times of Frederick Douglass*, rev. ed. (1892; reprint, New York:
The Crowell-Collier Publishing Company, 1962), 159-160.

64 Sarah Bradford, *Harriet Tubman: The Moses of Her People*, 2d ed. (1886, reprint, New York:
Corinth Books, 1961), 27-28.

ex-slave, in a reference to the slave South, could say that "in them days it was hell without fires." This view of the South as a kind of hell on earth is reinforced by the slave poem:

My body is weak and sickly
But it done served marse well
I'se gonna land in heaven
Already been through hell.[65]

Indeed, slaves underwent a sort of spiritual death and hell as they were cut off from their ancestral homeland, enslaved on these hostile shores, and not allowed to define their own destiny. All the talk about heaven in slave sources has often been interpreted as a fixation which diverted the slaves' attention from earthly woes and directed their hopes upon a peaceful eternity beyond time and space. This interpretation fails to do justice to the complex interrelationship between worldly and otherworldly concerns implicit in the spirituals, narratives, tales, and other slave sources. The compensatory hope for otherworldly freedom, justice, and pleasure was clearly a major theme in slave eschatology, but this does not mean that slaves were totally pessimistic about the possibility of freedom and triumph in their earthly existence. As W. E. B. Du Bois wisely put it, "The coming of the Lord, for the slaves, swept this side of death, and came to be a thing hoped for in this day."[66] The slaves knew from their reading of the Bible that God had indeed acted in history by freeing the Hebrew children from Egyptian captivity and

---

65 Quoted in Raboteau, *Slave Religion*, 291; and quoted in Elma Stuckey, *The Big Gate* (Chicago: Precedent Publishing Company, Inc., 1976), 21.

66 Franklin, ed., *The Souls of Black Folk*, 345.

Daniel from the lion's den. Thus, they could sing with every fiber of their being:

> My Lord delivered Daniel.
> My Lord delivered Daniel.
> My Lord delivered Daniel.
> Why can't He deliver me?[67]

Another point is essential in light of the general contention that there was a complex interrelationship between worldly and otherworldly concerns in slave thought concerning the afterlife. Since heaven was defined as the very antithesis of slavery, visions of the otherworld were marked by a subtle but powerful strain of social protest. Many of the slave songs which focused so heavily on the resurrection of the faithful to a renewed life in heaven also resounded with discontent and a condemnation of slavery. Examples are:

> Massa sleeps in the feather bed,
> Nigger sleeps on the floor,
> When we get to heaven,
> There'll be no slaves no more.

and

> Got hard trials in my way,
> Heaven am my home.[68]

---

67 Brown, "Negro Folk Expression," 213.

68 Lester, *To Be A Slave*, 106; and Allen, et al., eds., *Slave Songs*, 7.

190

The activities of some slaves to usher in the Kingdom of God on earth leave the impression that there was a side to slave eschatology which encouraged open rebellion against white society. Gabriel Prosser, Denmark Vesey, Nat Turner, and countless other slaves who planned rebellions, ran away, poisoned whites, and engaged in other acts of sabotage, not only believed in the possibility of God's deliverance in the here and now, but in their very actions sought to make that possibility a reality. Therefore, it is understandable why Nat Turner, a black preacher who led a slave revolt which resulted in the death of some sixty whites in Virginia in 1831, would prophesy that "the time was fast approaching when the first should be last and the last should be first."[69] For such slaves who attempted to fulfill their millenial vision here on earth, the picture of heaven as a place of eternal freedom and triumph contributed to a willingness to accept death rather than slavery:

Before I'll be a slave,
I'll be buried in my grave
And go home to my Lord
And be free.[70]

One last comment is in order, in view of the argument that slaves were not preoccupied with the afterlife to the point of anxiously awaiting and seeking death. The slaves had a strong survival ethic, as evidenced by the Br'er Rabbit tales and by the fact that their suicide rate was far lower than that of whites. The slaves' love of life was made abundantly

---

69 Nat Turner, *The Confessions of Nat Turner, Leader of the Late Insurrection in Southampton, Va.* (Miami, Fla.: Mnemosyne Publishing Company, Inc., 1969), 1-12.

70 Thurman, *Deep River* and *The Negro Spiritual*, 113.

evident in their tales concerning heaven and hell. According to one tale from "The Slave Who Prayed To Go To Heaven" series, a pious slave named Ephraim developed a habit of praying to God: "Oh, God, my master's so mean to me, please take old Ephraim home out of the miseries of dis life." A group of white boys passing by Ephraim's cabin one day overheard the slave's prayer, and, sensing this as a chance to have some fun, knocked on his door. "Who's thar?" asked the slave. "It's the Lord come to take Ephraim home," the boys said. "He's not here, Lord. He's gone. He's been gone from home for months," replied old Uncle Ephraim. In another tale inspired by slavery, the "sinner man" Sam Finklea had to be tied to his deathbed because of a deep fear of dying and going to hell. He met death "a-screaming and kicking and swearing."[71] In tales and in other slave sources, a desire for peace and freedom in the afterlife coexisted with a passionate love of life that was grounded in the slaves' sense of their own worth as human beings.

---

71 Rawick, ed., Indiana Narratives, Supplement, no. 1, vol. 5, p. 129; and excerpts from a tale told to me by my grandmother, Fannie B. Baldwin, when I was a boy in Camden, Alabama. Tales like that involving the "sinner man" Sam Ficklea were often told to children as a warning that they should live a life pleasing in the sight of God.

MODERN SLAVERY BY ANOTHER NAME:

A BLACK CHURCH RESPONSE TO GENDER-BASED VIOLENCE AND THE HUMAN TRAFFICKING OF BLACK WOMEN, GIRLS, AND QUEER FOLX FOR THE PURPOSE OF SEXUAL EXPLOITATION

Brandon Thomas Crowley, PhD

Abstract: *Modern Slavery By Another Name: A Black Church Response to Gender-Based Violence and the Human Trafficking of Black Women, Girls, and Queer Folx for the Purpose of Sexual Exploitation* is a theological reflection on the effects of Black faith/spirituality/religion/churches and the American #MeToo Movement. This chapter explores how gender-based violence and human trafficking are modern forms of slavery by another name.

The work argues that Black churches, whose silence about such matters, make them complicit in upholding and reinforcing the contemporary chains and intersectional fetters of American racism, transphobia, sexism, biphobia and homophobia. For this reason, Black churches need to recognize, and confront the reality of gender-based violence and human trafficking with strategic and tangible responses, because African American Christianity and Black churches bear the stains of such violence.

This chapter also acknowledges the importance of Black churches and Black spirituality as sources of healing for those who have experienced sexual and gender-based trauma and it also constructs a strategy called congregational queering for Black churches who wish to become allies for survivors and advocates for anti-sexual violence. The themes within this chapter describe "spiritual justice and queering" as a guiding principle for advocates and Black churches who want to incorporate human services and pastoral care for Black Queer and Black female survivors of gender-based violence and human trafficking.

VOCABULARY

Heteronormative - denoting or relating to a world view that promotes heterosexuality as the normal or preferred sexual orientation.

Hegemony - leadership or dominance, especially by one country or social group over others.

Psychoanalytic - method of treating mental disorders, shaped by psychoanalytic theory, which emphasizes unconscious mental processes and is sometimes described as depth psychology.

Queering - a theoretical and theological technique that came out of queer theory in the late 1980s through the 1990s and is used as a way to challenge heteronormativity by analyzing places in a text that utilize heterosexuality or identity binaries.

Ecclesial - relating to or constituting a Church or denomination.

Mysticism- is defined as the response of the individual to a personal encounter with God within his own spirit.

INTRODUCTION

On April 26, 2010, Eddie S. Glaude Jr., the William S. Todd Professor of Religion and Chair of the Center for African American Studies at Princeton University, wrote a provocative opinion editorial in the *Huffington Post* titled "The Black Church is Dead!" In the article, Glaude argued that "the idea of this venerable institution as central to Black life and as a repository for the social and moral conscience of the nation had all but disappeared."[1]

Glaude posited that the concept of socially conscious, morally prophetic, and culturally relevant Black churches is a phenomenon of the past, because the Black church has grown silent concerning matters of Black human suffering.[2] Glaude sees Black churches as dying or a dead ecclesial breed that only exists in the nostalgic memories of Black religious historians and middle-class mainline African American protestants.[3] Glaude assesses that 21st-century Black churches are complicated spaces that are often viewed as progressively prophetic institutions when in reality, they are mostly quite conservative, apolitical, and silent about important matters for the

---

1 Glaude, "Black Church Is Dead." https://www.huffpost.com/entry/
the-Black-church-is-dead_b_473815

2 Glaude, "Black Church is Dead."

3 Glaude, "Black Church is Dead."

sake of cultural, political, and evangelical correctness rooted in biblical literalism.

While most of Glaude's argument is rooted in social criticism and analytical provocation, the latter half of his ecclesial assessment is deliberately prescriptive. He essentially tells Black churches how to resurrect and re-enliven themselves with breaths of new life. According to Glaude, these breaths will enable Black churches to reimagine and rethink what it means to be simultaneously Black and Christian.[4]

He argues that Black churches, however dead they may be, can be resurrected and brought back to life by breathing something new into their ecclesial structures. Glaude interprets this refreshing breath of new ecclesial life as a rekindling of the prophetic voices and social progressiveness of pre-reconstruction Black churches.[5] Through such rekindling, Black churches can regain life and reclaim their original mission to work on behalf of those who suffer most.[6]

One of the areas of perpetual silence and ecclesial ignorance within the social and moral conscience of Black churches is the matter of gender-based/sexual violence and human trafficking. Black churches need a new breath and breadth of ecclesial mission and structure that reimagines gender while acknowledging and queering the sexist, heteronormative, and biblically literalist worldviews that prohibit survivors of gender-based violence and human trafficking from feeling safe in Black congregations.

I believe that such a discussion should begin with a reimagining of gender because most issues pertaining to

---

4 Glaude, "Black Church is Dead."

5 Glaude, "Black Church is Dead."

6 Glaude, "Black Church is Dead."

sexual violence in Black churches, or the silence thereof, are rooted in gender inequality and ignorance about the non-biological nature of gender construction. For instance, when considering the level of silence and revictimization of survivors of gender-based violence in Black churches, one must consider the historic Christian understanding of Black women's bodies as inferior to males, especially white American Christian males.

Such an ingrained indoctrination about cisgender heterosexual male superiority makes it easy for Black clergy persons and parishioners to perpetuate negative stereotypes about Black female and Black trans survivors of gender-based violence as casualties of their own sins because of the "clothes that they were wearing" or because of their abominable identity as an LGBTQIA+ person.

What is most frightening is not that Black churches have the capacity to practice violence, but that the sexually violated, which includes LGBTQIA+ persons and Black female should often go unattended, and their traumatic pain is often not recognized! Black churches and clergy persons must acknowledge the silent roles that they have taken in ignoring the cries of survivors of gender-based violence and human trafficking within their own congregations and Christian families.

For this reason, Black churches must begin to acknowledge and queer their sexist, heteronormative, and biblically literalist claims that have historically scourged the St. John 3:16 "whosoever" Christian understanding of human dignity. Black churches must also learn to courageously speak up about the truths of sexual violence and gender-based violence within our communities with the same fervor with which we stand up for racial (*Black Lives Matter*), political

(*Blacks' unwavering support of the democratic party*), and economic (*prosperity gospel*) rights.

As a Black queer practical theologian, I see the need for a critical, theory-laden, and psychoanalytic naming and queering of the theologically oppressive and sexually secretive injustices out of which Black sexism, Black homophobia, and Black sexual violence oppressively thrive.

This chapter explores how American white supremacy and Black ecclesial sexism are used as tools of oppression and re-traumatization for survivors of gender-based violence. I begin by arguing that the #MeToo Movement, the American justice system, and Black churches have failed Black women and Black LGBTQIA+ survivors of gender-based violence by ignoring them. Gender-based violence and the human trafficking of Black women, girls, and Queer Folx for the purpose of sexual exploitation is modern slavery by another name. Black churches, whose silence about such matters, are complicit in upholding and reinforcing the contemporary chains and intersectional fetters of American racism, transphobia, sexism, biphobia and homophobia.

However, I also believe that this problem presents Black churches with an opportunity to resurrect their moral consciouses by queering their traditionally male-centered concepts of justice to become centers and sources of safety, healing, resistance, and resilience for those who have experienced sexual trauma. As I will discuss in the forthcoming sections, I believe that Black churches have a responsibility to respond to the cries of and stand with Black women and Black LGBTQIA+ survivors of gender-based violence, because the current American culture continues to ignore the cries of Black victims of sexual assault and human trafficking for the purpose of sexual exploitation.

THE IGNORING OF BLACK WOMEN AND BLACK QUEER FOLX IN THE AMERICAN SOCIETY

In 2006, African-American sexual harassment survivor and activist Tarana Burke created the phrase *#MeToo* to help female survivors of gender-based violence stand up for themselves while simultaneously bringing awareness to the pervasive and endemic nature of sexual abuse and assault in America.[7] Nearly a decade later, on October 15, 2017, the phrase *#MeToo* resurfaced on Twitter when Caucasian American actress Alyssa Milano used the hashtag in response to Harvey Weinstein's sexual abuse and molestation allegations. After which, many high-profile white actresses like Ashley Judd, Gwyneth Paltrow, Jennifer Lawrence, Uma Thurman, and many others shared their *#MeToo* stories on Twitter, causing the hashtag to be used and retweeted more than 200,000 times by the end of the day.[8]

From that moment forward, *#MeToo* became a nationwide empowerment campaign for thousands of survivors to share their experiences and stand in solidarity with each other. By October 2018, nearly two hundred male executives were implicated and indicted for committing sexual crimes against women.[9] The pursuit to end sexual violence against women has undoubtedly grown into a national topic of discussion that

---

7 Garcia, Sandra E. (20 October 2017). "The Woman Who Created #MeToo Long Before Hashtags" – via www.nytimes.com.; Burke, Tarana (February 10, 2018). *Founder of #MeToo Movement Talk* (Speech). AUSG Women's Initiative Award for Excellence in Activism, American University.

8 Sini, Rozina (October 16, 2017). "'MeToo' and the scale of sexual abuse". *BBC News*. Archived from the original on November 7, 2017.

9 Carlsen, Audrey; Salam, Maya; Miller, Claire Cain; Lu, Denise; Ngu, Ash; Patel, Jugal K.; Wichter, Zach (October 23, 2018). https://www.nytimes.com/interactive/2018/10/23/us/metoo-replacements.html "#MeToo Brought Down 201 Powerful Men. Nearly Half of Their Replacements Are Women" Check /url= value (help). *The New York Times*. ISSN 0362-4331.

created substantial and quantifiable shifts in the social and cultural landscape of American patriarchy and sexism.

Despite the campaign's viral success, the *#MeToo* movement, like most ideas created by Black persons and Black women in America, was co-opted by the structural power of white American ethno-nationalist politics and culture. After Alyssa Milano used the hashtag to share her story, the privileged caricature of a presumed innocent white heterosexual cisgender woman became the face and primary focus of the *#MeToo* movement, thereby decentralizing the victimhood of Black women and Black queer folx.

It must never be ignored that the *#MeToo* movement created by a Black woman did not become a national topic of discussion until privileged white women began using the hashtag. After nearly 400 years of legalized and culturally induced gender-based sexual violence against Black and LGBTQ+ bodies in America, it took the cry of an "innocent white woman" to push the sexist structures of American oppression to listen, address, and subvert the systemic nature of sexual assault in American history and culture. The racialized, homophobic, and transphobic aspects of this inhumane reality compel me to examine the political whiteness of the *#MeToo* movement as a symptom of white feminist ignorance in American culture.

White feminism, which intentionally upholds the politics of American whiteness, ignores the surge of violence against transgender persons and Black women in the United States. As a result of its white feminist adaptation, the original Black female aims of the *#MeToo* movement were transfixed into a white heterosexual movement that solely preserves the lives and assumed purity of white cisgender American women. If the American *#MeToo* movement wishes to achieve the justice-oriented goals of its visionary and progenitor, it must advance beyond the American preoccupation with whiteness and center its focus on the oppressive aspects of power and privilege in the narratives of gender-based violence survivors notwithstanding race, gender, or sexual identity.

According to American moral and political philosopher John Bordley Rawls, most political theorists see justice as a guarantee of the state.[10] However, the lack of cultural empathy for Black queer and Black female survivors of gender-based violence reveals that while American ideals of justice and equality may be a state guarantee for white heterosexual men and women. Said ideals were not historically created for non-white or non-heteronormative bodies. In light of the overly sexualized perceptions and cultural stereotypes of Black women and transgender persons as sites of white pleasure and eroticism, Black or queer survivors of gender-based violence are viewed as politically insignificant and undeserving of civil and human rights protection under the law.[11] In order to right this wrong, there must be a queering of both justice and criminology to subvert the oppressive aspects of American culture and laws that prohibit Black women and queer folx from being valued as inviolable dignities. The American legal and health systems must conspire to assist in exploring the experiences of these uniquely traumatized populations that face insurmountable discrimination within the justice system and who are often ignored by local police departments and federal agents. The presumption of guilt that America places over the heads of Black female and queer survivors of gender-based violence is unethical, unjust, and evil. Therefore,

---

10 Rawls, J.A., *Theory of Justice: Revised Edition*. Oxford: Oxford University Press, 1999.

11 Case proof ....

if Rawls's theories of justice as fairness equaling basic rights, equality of opportunity, and the promotion of the interests of the least advantaged members of society are to become realities in America, then the American concepts of justice and equality must be queered to include all persons.

THE GREAT AMERICAN INJUSTICE

The concept of justice in America can be understood both idealistically and pragmatically. Idealistic justice is best understood as the moral ideal of equality afforded to all people equally. It is the belief that fair and impartial treatment of human "others" is both morally good and legally required in a just and democratic society. The best example of an idealistic concept of justice is found in the preamble of the Constitution of the United States. The Constitution is essentially a body of fundamental principles that frame justice and freedom as the ideals of American democracy. The preamble unequivocally describes all American citizens as equal and divinely endowed with unalienable rights. However, when the Constitution was created, Blacks in America were only considered 3/5ths of a person. The problem with solely defining justice idealistically is that it permits empowered persons to subscribe to just beliefs without acting upon said principles. For example, over the last four hundred years, America has legally inscribed laws and nationally professed belief in the concepts of fairness, justice, and liberty for all. However, due to the economically immoral and radicalized societal pathologies of white supremacists, the concept of American justice has never been fully legally or socially enacted for persons of color, especially Black women and Black queer folx. One could argue that it would be utterly impossible for America to ever live up to its romantic concepts of justice and freedom because of the evil and immoral means of conquest and slavery that paved the way for the establishment and economic stability of the American empire.

For this reason, many African-Americans, particularly Black women and Black Queer folx, who have long felt the denial of justice, have begun rejecting the notion that American justice is salvageable. Instead, they nihilistically argue that the entire American empire must be demolished, reimagined, and rebuilt with more than just a promise of justice at the helm of the enterprise.

For a new and more just America to emerge, justice must be embraced pragmatically and intentionally to make justice a living reality for all persons. I see pragmatic justice as an active and inclusive form of idealistic justice that faces the harsh intersectional realities of systemic injustices with cultural competence and social sensibility instead of just theoretically and idealistically.

THE IGNORING OF THE SUFFERING OF BLACK WOMEN AND BLACK TRANSGENDER PERSONS BY BLACK CHURCHES

In America, Black women, Black trans, Black intersex, Black queer, and Black gender nonconforming (LGBTQ+) survivors of gender-based violence face unprecedented levels of discrimination, harassment, health disparities, poverty, and exclusion in virtually every institution and setting, including Black churches. Gender-based violence is a sin that the Black church needs to recognize, confront, and subvert because African American Christianity and Black churches bear its stain. Additionally, for far too long, many of our inclusive Black churches and African-American queer theologians have centered their entire theological arguments for the full inclusion of LGBTQIA persons into the life of the church solely on the identities of gay men, lesbian women, and bisexual persons thereby thwarting all ethical, empathetic and intersectional demands to courageously and prophetically address the issue of transphobia within Black churches that also supports gender-based violence. For instance, in 2021, Tyianna Alexander, a 28-year-old Black trans woman, Bianca "Muffin" Bankz, a Black transgender woman, Dominique Jackson, a 30-year-old Black transgender woman, Fifty Bandz, a 21-year-old Black transgender woman, Diamond Kyree Sanders, a 23-year-old Black transgender woman, and so many others were killed at larger and more alarming rates than the number of Black men killed at the hands of the police. But not once did Black churches, in a sort of collective mass, come to the defense of Transgender persons as they did our sacred Black male. It is as if Black Christian America has chosen, like Pope Pius XII's knowledge of the Holocaust, to ignore the intersectional nature of American racism and Black American transphobia that continuously leads to the tragic and senseless murders of countless Black transgender persons.

Historically, Black churches have placed more authority and valued upon cisgender male bodies than other bodies. In fact, it could be argued that the preservation of the

Black male body is subconsciously one of the primary aims of Black churches. The Black ecclesial fear of and lack of African-American female senior pastors is a telltale sign of black ecclesial patriarchy and internalized masculinity. Black churches have historically taught a very heteronormative theology despite the fact that the congregational population of many Black churches is predominantly female and even queer. At the time of this publication, none of the Black conventions or denominational has elected a non-cisgender male senior Bishop or president. While this section of my work is intended to solely speak to the issue of transphobia in black churches, the theoretical and fundamental characteristics of queering, which was birthed out of feminism, mandates all queerers to acknowledge the intersectionality between oppressive measures like sexism and transphobia. According to Annamarie Forestiere's article *America's War on Black Trans Women* in the *Harvard Civil Rights—Civil Liberties Law Review*, "Violence against Black trans women has been accurately described as "a pandemic within a pandemic. In particular, Black trans women are killed at disproportionate rates because of 'the intersections of racism, transphobia, sexism, biphobia and homophobia.'"[12] The pandemic has created the deadliest era for violence against Transgender persons on record. But sadly, like the American culture in which they exist, Black churches have also traditionally ignored the experiences, criminalization, and inherent human worth of Black female and Black LGBTQ+ survivors of gender-based violence. Despite the vast amount of unjust incarceration, gender-based violence, and murder of Black trans women and gender-nonconforming

---

12 Forestiere, Annamarie. "America's war on Black trans women." *Harvard Civil Rights—Civil Liberties Law Review. Available at: https://harvardcrcl. org/americas-war-on-Black-trans-women* (2020).

persons, the inextricable links between Black homophobia, transphobia, and the Constantinian remnants of empire in Black Christianity prevent most Black churches from offering pastoral care and comfort to Black trans and Black queer or Black female cisgender survivors of gender-based violence.

After the murder of Trayvon Martin at the hand of George Zimmerman, black churches protested in overwhelming numbers by wearing hoodies and placing bottles of iced tea and bags of skittles on their communion tables as Eucharistic reminders of the tragic deaths of young black men like Emmett Till and Trayvon Martin. But during the deaths of Black Transgender persons and Black women, the Black church's prophetic enthusiasm seems to fade into a poor caricature of its Black prophetic tradition. The needless and senseless murders of black men like George Floyd incites a type of outrage in black churches that the murders of Black women and Black Transgender persons do not. The question that must be interrogated is why? What is it about Black churches that causes them to place great and needed emphasis on the murders of Black cisgender male bodies while intentionally and unintentionally devaluing the bodies of Black women and Black transgender persons by ignoring their narratives of trauma and senseless murders?

Like the white American stereotype that Black victims of race-based violence like George Floyd deserved their trauma by nature of their Black identities, many Black churches also ignore the high levels of killings, violence, and poverty amongst Black queer sex workers and transgender persons because of the theological assumption that they got what they deserved because: *the wages of their sin deserved death.*[13] The majority of Black churches still refuse to create atmospheres of self-actualization for Black heterosexual female and queer survivors of gender-based violence in the same ways that it has for Black heterosexual male survivors of race-based violence.[14] This forces me to wonder why are Black churches, the original spaces where all sexually traumatized bodies of enslaved Blacks could find peace and acceptance, so silent when it comes to matters of gender-based violence towards Black women and Black LGBTQ+ folx. My first response to such is simply: sexism, transphobia, and homophobia. Black churches are historically sexist institutions where hypermasculinity and heteronormativity breed sickening amounts of theological ignorance. The theologically undergirded systems of sexism and heterosexuality in Black churches are incapable of empathizing with survivors of gender-based violence first and foremost because their understandings of gender are flawed and innately unjust. The concept of gender must be queered in Black churches if they wish to become true allies of survivors of gender-based violence.

My second response as to why many Black churches are silent about gender-based violence is related to a matter of cultural assumption as a form of racialized resistance. Historically, and especially during American chattel slavery, Black men were frequently labeled as sexual predators and rapists of white women and Black women were regarded as sensual sites of erotic pleasure for white men. Consequently, to gain acceptance into the larger white homophobic society, many enslaved

---

13 Romans 6:23 (NRSV).

14 Riggins, "Loving Our Black Bodies," 249–69.

African males sexually repressed themselves to avoid extreme hardship and death and the raping of enslaved Black women was ignored. Much like the publicly uncivil civilian conviction and execution of Emmett Till and other nameless innocent Black men in the American South, many African-Americans, especially Black men, continue to find themselves extremely untrusting of the American legal concept of gender-based violence in which Black males are the victimizers. Many African-Americans males interpret the words gender-based violence as code language for the prosecution of African-American males on trumped-up and salaciously false accusations of sexual immorality and penetrative fallacies like that of the Black-buck-beast stereotype of the antebellum period. This false sentiment is often reflected in Black pulpits, which are predominantly male-led and phallically used by their occupants as positions of hypermasculine dominance and Black male preservation. As an African-American queer pastor who is keenly aware of the racialized and intersectional nature of gender-based violence, it has saddened me that the Black church has largely remained silent and lowered its prophetic voice that once spoke so courageously in response to the murders of Trayvon Martin, Michael Brown, and Philando Castile. This forces us to consider, what does the overarching silence of the Black church mean for Black women and Black Transgender survivors of gender-based violence? This sad but true reality begs the socially awakened consciousness of Black churches to ask where can Black women and Black LGBTQ+ folx go to receive support and safety? My coupling of the attack on Black trans women and Black women as one in the same will also require Black women to eradicate the assumption that Black trans women are not "real" Black women. Since Black women constitute the majority of Black church goers, Black women in the Black church and in America at-large should work to fight the issue of American heteronormativity in an inter-sectional manner. This type of womanist courage, especially amongst Black church women, is synonymous with the found-ing of Black churches. I say this because the founding of Black churches during the 18th and early 19th centuries was an act of Black ecclesial courage. Black churches were founded amidst the racist realities of slavery, Jim Crow laws, and segregation. However, this did not stop enslaved Africans from forging their way into the brush harbors and empty barns to make theologi-cal meaning out of their racially divided world. A recurring char-acteristic of Black churches is their prophetic courage, but as I mentioned in my introduction, Glaude argued that such courage has all but died.[15] For this reason, I offer that 21st Century Black churches must become resurrected sectors of Black ecclesial courage queering the traditional notions of justice to be inclu-sive of the concerns of survivors of gender-based violence.

QUEERING: TOWARDS A BLACK CONGREGATIONAL RESPONSE TO GENDER-BASED VIOLENCE

If twenty-first-century Black churches wish to resurrect their moral conscience, they should begin by queering gender-based injustices and homophobic practices within their own ranks. Queering is an academic and theoretical tool used to recon-sider or reinterpret a thing or concept from a perspective that

---

15 Wilcox, M. Melissa, *Coming Out in Christianity: Religion, Identity, and Community* (Bloomington: Indiana University Press, 2003); Glaude, "Black Church Is Dead." https://www.huffpost.com/entry/the-Black-church-is-dead_b_473815

intentionally rejects the traditionally oppressive categories of sexuality and gender. The queering of gender-based oppression and homophobic practices in Black churches is important because it will problematize and unearth the theological and cultural layers of homophobic oppression and gender-based violence by 1) redefining what it means to be a whole person beyond one's victimization, 2) reflecting on the cultural and theological oppression of gay Christians and Black women, and (3) calling into question the hegemonic institutional structures of Christian institutions and their unjust methodologies. As the long-term pastor of a one-hundred-and-fifty-year-old historically Black church, I believe that all Black churches have a critical role to play in the prevention, intervention, and healing from gender-based violence. This healing cannot and should not happen without Black church leaders and parishioners taking time to contemplatively and theoretically equip themselves with the proper tools to respond with prudence, wisdom, and care when they become aware of gender-based violence in our churches, within our immediate surroundings, or even on a national level. I believe that queering is the best tool to combat the structures of sexism and homophobia that prevent Black churches from successfully incorporating holistic trauma-informed human services and innovative pastoral care for LGBTQ+ and Black female survivors of gender-based violence.

Queering is the process whereby new dialogues on sexual violence, ideas, and frames of resilience are constructed and made acceptable to survivors of sexual violence with passion and prudence. The act of queering in Black congregations also obliges the "queerer" to thoroughly understand the histories, cultures, and theological ideologies that re-traumatize survivors with institutionalized patriarchy and gendered inequalities. This type of historical understanding is important because it aids the queerer to disrupt and challenge the status quo in a way that will force churches to communally re-examine sacred texts, stories, and institutional notions of sexual normalcy and appropriate sexual functionality that have traditionally terrorized LGBTQ+ persons most effectively. Queering also creates brave spaces for persons to freely see things in a different light and listen to marginalized voices and sources that have been ignored, silenced, and discarded because of Christian notions of decency and the politics of respectability.

Queering is also a theoretical procedure that encourages Black churches to think about their allyship with survivors of gender-based violence as an act of spiritual justice. Unlike the American notion of justice, spiritual justice is founded upon the principles of equity as opposed to equality. The American justice system claims to ensure equality by promoting fairness so that everyone gets the same things. On the other hand, spiritual justice is an act of empathic equity that goes beyond American fairness. Spiritual justice is a collective responsibility rooted in the Black prophetic tradition that calls upon Black churches to courageously work to preserve a free and just world while theologically promoting and ensuring the civil and human rights of all survivors of gender-based violence regardless of their ethnicity, nation of origin, sexual orientation, class, physical or mental ability, or age. Spiritual justice is essentially a queered version of American justice that aims not just to get Black women and Black queer folx the same things as straight white men, but spiritual justice also works to understand why survivors of gender-based violence were victimized in the first place and how the systems of Black churches and white society kept their narratives silent. Additionally, it is the spiritual aspect of spiritual justice that makes it queer. In this context, to queer something is to subvert it or to turn it on its head. It means to reveal and expose the intricacies and complexities of an unjust system of evil with the intent to demolish and reimagine its reconstruction with a preferential option for survivors of gender-based violence. Spiritual justice is social justice actualized and brought forth by spiritually subversive (queer) means.

Throughout Christian history, the Spirit has been a subversive force that worked with equity. For instance, in Joel 2:28-31, the Spirit is not restricted to a male heir but falls upon all flesh across the spectrums of gender and age: *"And it shall come to pass afterward, that I will pour out my spirit upon all flesh: and your sons and your daughters shall prophesy, your old men shall dream dreams, your young men shall see visions...The sun shall be turned into darkness, and the moon into blood, before the great and terrible day of the Lord come" (NRSV)*. Here we see the Spirit resisting heteronormative hegemony. And even in the book of Acts, when the Holy Spirit is given to the chosen persons in the upper room, she upends heteronormativity by giving authority to Lydia and Dorcas instead of men. The Spirit is even sexually ambiguous. The Spirit is described in male tenses in certain biblical passages and female tenses in other passages while being described as neither male nor female because it is a spirit. Except for God, the Holy Spirit appears throughout scripture as the only other entity within the trinity that does her earthly work without the strict personification of gender. All of this is very queer and very justice oriented. In response to gender-based violence, spiritual justice is the sacred Spirit work of resisting heteronormative hegemony and upending all theological normativity that prohibits the human flourishing of survivors of gender-based violence.

A more concrete example of how Spiritual justice could queer Black churches into being better allies and safe spaces for survivors of gender-based trauma would be for them first to acknowledge the ways in which they perpetuate gender-based violence through their denial of its existence. Many Black churches struggle with having conversations about gender-based violence because they believe that the stakes are too high. What they fail to realize is that since the Catholic church sexual harassment lawsuits, silence equals complicity. Black churches, like Catholic churches, have been guilty of ignoring the voices of survivors of gender-based violence within our own churches. Countless Black women, Black girls, Black boys, and Black queer folx have experienced gender-based violence in the Black church at the hands of empowered male clergy. And for centuries, the Black church has covered it up with silence or by disrespectfully dismissing offenders without providing faith-specific intervention or training for leaders about sexual violence.

The silence of Black churches not only denotes complicity but also protects the perpetrators of sexual violence. This harsh reality stands in stark contrast to the reputation of Black churches as places of spiritual healing and safety. Therefore, Black churches can be both sources of healing and traumatic roadblocks for those who experience gender-based violence. Some of these obstructions include a cultural unwillingness to have sexual conversations and the belief that "it doesn't happen here" or "it's not a problem in our church." All of these assumptions are drenched in the notion that denial is a valid solution. Even certain theologies of the cross prioritize beliefs about long suffering and forgiveness as Christian mandates that inadvertently force women to remain in abusive marriages or survivors to forgive their abusers. Pastors and pastoral counselors should never use scripture to encourage an abused person to remain with their abuser. Black churches must learn that silence and denial about sexual violence are antithetical to the mission of Christ, and abusive to gender-based violence survivors.

Black churches must also learn how to do no harm! By this, I mean that Black churches must begin to profile leaders by checking for criminal histories and training their leaders about sexual aggression and gender-based and transgender violence. Leaders should be informed that sexual harassment is not restricted to abuses such as the invasion of the body by force, rape, or unwanted forms of physical behavior.[16] Additionally, all leaders should be careful when making physical contact with members. For instance, hugging should be reconsidered in churches. Sexual harassment also includes verbally suggestive, demanding, and/or coercive advances that are unwanted and hostile. Churches should also have well-written and well-known policies about matters of gender-based violence and sexual harassment.[17] These policies should include clear messaging about leaders and misters not engaging in romantic or sexual relationships with other staff members or members of congregations. Even when an individual's intentions are pure, a congregational leader should never touch parishioners without their permission.[18]

---

16 Francois, Willie Dwayne, Simmons, Martha. *Christian Minister's Manual: For the Pulpit and Public Square for All Denominations.* (Atlanta, GA: The African American Pulpit Press, 2017), 29-31.

17 Francois and Simmons.

18 Francois and Simmons.

Leaders must be careful to never be act in a way that would cause a person to become squeamish or uncomfortable. Pastors and church leaders have a responsibility to make sure that parishioners have the right not to be violated. For too long female congregants have endured inappropriate touching out of their desire to not jump to conclusions, but this is unfair to the recipient of the aggression. The rules around hugging can be quite simple: (1) You should never initiate physical contact without permission.[19] (2) If you want to hug someone, ask first, and be prepared to normalize and graciously accept their no if they decline your offer.[20] (3) If they accept your offer, do not hug the person too long.[21] (4) Consider giving the person a side hug. Even with side hugs, pastors must be sensitive and keenly aware of a person's indication of discomfort. This is important because many people do not want hugs or to be touched at all. Persons should never be forced to fellowship in the form of giving or receiving physical touch if such is interpreted as a violation of their personal space.[22]

In addition to the issue of touch, there is also the matter of language. Pastors and church leaders should avoid giving parishioners unwanted comments on their appearances, style, clothes, hair, shoes, perfume, or body parts. Although giving a person a nice compliment may seem innocent, excessive commentary that is unwanted can become violent to the recipient when it appears excessive and over the top. And, lastly, it is also inappropriate for parishioners to harass their pastors and

19 Francois and Simmons.

20 Francois and Simmons.

21 Francois and Simmons.

22 Francois and Simmons.

clergy persons. As a young Black queer pastor, I have also been the recipient of countless acts of sexual harassment, unwanted advances, and sexually suggestive commentary from older women and men in churches. In my younger years of pastoring in my twenties, I often avoided naming their behavior as violent because I did not want to cause problems. But as I have matured, I have now begun establishing bolder boundaries with men and women. Often, we only think about the safety of parishioners while branding all church leaders as offenders without acknowledging that pastors and church leaders can also be victims of gender-based violence. Countless female clergy and musicians have been harassed in churches.

Lastly, Black churches should also develop social partnerships with their local health departments, women's clinics, mental health resources, and methadone clinics to offer gender-based violence survivors with wrap-around services and full support for children, women, or men who need drug rehab, healthcare, jobs, housing, academic support, and trauma therapy.[23]

QUEERING: TOWARDS A BLACK CONGREGATIONAL RESPONSE TO HUMAN TRAFFICKING AND ADOLESCENT ABUSE

Up until this point I have intentionally focused on the concept of gender-based violence because I see human trafficking as a vicious symptom of GBV, it's progenitor. Human trafficking

---

23 When churches have pre-existing relationships with social health providers, they are better equipped to provide support for survivors.

is a form of Gender-based violence. It is important to understand that Gender-based violence categorizes any form of physical, sexual, psychological, emotional or other personal harm inflicted on a person for gender-based reasons. Gender-based violence may include or be characterized as the following: Sexual and other physical assault, including murder; rape; sexual harassment (sometimes called bullying); sexual, physical and verbal abuse, including coercion; stalking; intimate relationship violence that includes employment, housing or educational intimidation and obstruction; elder abuse or child abuse; sex-specific torture; reproductive coercion; female genital mutilation; early and forced marriage; honor crimes; "mail-order" brides; dowry violence; practices used to decrease the number of girl babies, such as prenatal sex selection, infanticide or child neglect; sex tourism; forced prostitution; human trafficking for sex; pornography; and violence during armed conflict, including rape, enslavement, torture and murder.

So, the question becomes: how should a pastor or a church respond to human trafficking and adolescent abuse within their congregations?

As the senior pastor of the historic Myrtle Baptist Church, I am a mandated reporter in the state of Massachusetts. Over the last twelve years of pastoring, I have had numerous reports of gender-based violence and human trafficking reported to me. In every instance, I began by alerting the local chief of police, who I have a preexisting relationship with, about the matters in question. In moments when it was reported or suspected that there was evidence of adolescent abuse in the home, the first thing I did was to properly investigate what was happening in the home of my parishioner. If I sensed that the home was a non-child friendly environment, saw bruises, or discovered questionable behaviors from the parents and children after doing a random home check to see what the home environment was actually like, I would then alert the local housing authority, which I also have a relationship with, the local police department, and the child (or children's) school officials. It is important to note that in the Black community hitting is a cultural norm. Many people hit their children because they were hit by their parents as children, but this is a dangerous and slippery slope because it doesn't work. However, as a pastor I am quick to say that such is wrong. It is wrong to physically abuse your child. Some even think that the hitting of Black children by Black adults is an echo of a slave labor mentality of punishment and behavioral correction that do not work, much like the incarceration of addicts and adolescents does not work rehabilitatively.

Another response is for Black pastors to begin preaching on issues of gender-based violence and human trafficking. For instance, Black pastors must begin to sermonically acknowledge that gender-based violence is an ancient biblical sin that has gone unrecognized and even looked over in scripture for thousands of years. The truth is that the Bible is a book full of egotistical and small-minded men who chauvinistically use women as pieces of property in the name of God. Even in the Bible itself, we are able to find narratives about gender-based violence that reflect and exemplify the traumas that many domestic and gender-based violence survivors experience on a daily basis. For instance, in 2 Samuel chapter 13 we are introduced to a survivor of gender-based violence by the name of Tamar. Tamar was King David's daughter. Her half-brother Amnon, King David's firstborn son, raped her after tricking her into his home and bed chambers and subsequently threw her out into the streets. Before the violation, Tamar courageously begged her brother Amnon not to rape her and to follow Israel's laws that forbade sexual attacks. She tried to protect herself, but she could not do so because of the heteronormative structures of her time. Sadly, no one listened to Tamar, not even her family members. Her brother Amnon violated her intrinsic human dignity and ignored her pleas not to have her body sexually accosted. And even after the violation, she wanted her family to understand her pain and not cast her out but Absalom, Tamar's brother, told her to be silent about Amnon raping her.

Even her father, King David, did nothing. The one person that should have protected and fought for Tamar, her father, ignored her and left her to defend herself in the face of a male-centered sexist and oppressive patriarchal society. Instead of standing with his daughter in response to his anger when he found out what Amnon had done, David patriarchally protected Amnon by covering for him because he wanted him to be unblemished as the next king.

This narrative is extremely reflective of the realities of many survivors of gender-based violence. Especially considering the fact that most children are brought into the horrific trade of human trafficking and sexual violence by their own family members. Much like David, many Black churches have swept the issue of gender-based violence and human trafficking "under the rug" as a means of preserving the dignity of their ecclesial spaces. In other words, the preservation of the black church has often superseded the Black church's care for survivors and victims of gender-based violence. We have cared more about maintaining institutions than we have victims of gender-based violence, especially when those victims are girls, women, and members of the LGBTQIA community.

The behaviors of King David and his sons are also reflective of the toxic nature of too many Christian spaces as it pertains to sexual violence. For instance, Amnon was wrong, and he should be regarded as the quintessential epitome of evil in the Hebrew Bible. Like Amnon, the Black church and the Christian church at large has members of its fellowship who commit acts of gender-based violence. David was also wrong because his silence equals complicity. Like King David, Black churches have, as of the last sixty years, had the means to intervene, but have remained silent. And lastly, Absalom and the culture were wrong for forcing Tamar into silence. The culture is what allowed all of Tamar's troubles to happen. We need to be honest that the Black church contains Davids, Amnons, Absaloms, and Tamars. As Black Christians, we are quick to point fingers at the Catholic church and its awful behaviors, but we are often slow to sweep around our own victimizing front doors.

FOUR CONCRETE STEPS FOR QUEERING INJUSTICE:

First, like Black churches before Reconstruction, 21st Century Black churches must become spaces where Black victims of gender-based violence can find spiritual care and safety. 21st Century Black churches must rekindle and broaden the Black church's historical notion of African American ecclesial courage by resurrecting pre-reconstruction ideals. **Second**, 21st Century Black churches must begin to provide Black women, Black trans, Black intersex, Black queer, and Black gender nonconforming (LGBTQ+) victims of gender-based violence with the spiritual tools to believe in a God after trauma. Black churches must promote their belief in an "as-if" world of Black ecclesial mysticism and expressive modes of worship with proactive training and education on gender-based violence to effectively minister to survivors. **Third**, by "arguing from experience as well as Scripture," 21st Century Black churches must develop hermeneutics of suspicion about homophobia and sexist scriptures. 21st Century Black churches must learn to question and rethink their traditional, fundamentalist, and deep-seated homophobic and sexist Christian belief systems, doctrines, and theologies that oppress survivors.

The Fourth and most important thing that 21st Century Black churches must do to queer the concept and notion of Justice is to develop a theological and psychoanalytic response to Black female and LGBTQ+ victims of gender-based violence. In *Self, Culture, and Others in Womanist Practical Theology*, Phillis Sheppard reports that the field of American psychology ignores the sexual narratives, pains, and struggles of Black queer folx. She also reproves Black psychologists for portraying Black psychology as an explicitly heterosexual enterprise, thereby ignoring homophobia as an intrapsychic cultural symptom of heteronormativity.[24] Sheppard proposes the need for a psychoanalytic examination of Black sexuality, culture, race, gender, and religious experiences.[25] When we consider that most African-American queer bodies exist within and between multiple homophobic contexts, one cannot help but agree with Sheppard's assertion that a Black psychoanalytic discussion

---

24 Sheppard, Phillis Isabella. *Self, Culture and Others in Womanist Practical Theology*. (New York: Palgrave Macmillian, 2011) 121-123.

25 Sheppard, 121-123.

on sexuality and homosexuality is imperative. While it would be impossible for me to construct an entire psychoanalysis of Black sexuality within this brief writing, I will, with the aid of Sheppard, suggest what a Black psychoanalysis of Black homophobia would resemble.

In her chapter on psychoanalytic literary criticism, Sheppard argues what a womanist psycho-religious perspective would look like.[26] She describes womanist theology as a cultural work that brings to light the experiences of African-American women. Since womanist theology and Black queer theology are similar in their pursuit to subvert the destructive powers of white heteronormativity, I find it fitting to continue Sheppard's argument using an explicitly Black queer lens.[27] Hence, a Black practical theological and psychoanalytic analysis of Black homophobia and Black sexuality should bring to its theo-psychological discussion the unexamined cultural experiences of sexually traumatized African-American bodies, specifically the bodies of Black LGBTQ+ persons. Likewise, it should bring culture and society into dialogue with race and power as starting points for analysis. It should also seek to explicate, acknowledge, and queer the social, political, and religious structures that impact

---

26 Sheppard.

27 In her book *Our Lives Matter: A Womanist Queer Theology*, Pamela Lightsey presents womanist methodology as an excellent platform for doing queer theology. In the first chapter of her book titled "Black Woman's Experience and Queer Black Women's Lives," Lightsey surveys the work of several womanist scholars related to Black sexuality and the nature of Black homophobia. As a response to the lack of womanist scholarship on the theological conception of Black LGBTQ+ persons, Lightsey constructs a womanist queer theology that addresses what it means to be Black and LGBTQ+ in America. She states that there are "several layers of meaning that are womanist ways of loving 'the folk' and the one who is 'committed to survival and wholeness of entire people.' This being so, one can make the case that womanist methodology that allows for the examination of categories such as race, gender, sexuality, and class is an excellent platform for doing queer theology. Particularly as these are womanist methodology primary points of departure from western theology, which is critiqued are too often the perspectives of living and dead white men. The strength of this book is its utilization of womanist methodology to contextualize this work as useful for a broad range of persons."(xix)

Black female and Black queer victims of gender-based violence. This, like Sheppard's argument about womanism, should
be the guiding principles upon which Black churches, Black
pastoral/practical theologians, and Black clergy ground their
moral imperatives to subvert the heteronormative worldviews
that prohibit victims of gender-based violence from feeling safe
in Black churches. The acknowledgment and queering of gender-based violence as normal must include an interrogation
of the various Black Christian practices of violence disguised
in theological and cultural language. According to Sheppard,
Black psychological perspectives are needed to amplify the
silent narratives, uncover the wounds, and re-enliven the
embedded hope of Black people in America.[28]

CONCLUSION

Eddie Glaude is correct; the Black church is indeed dead.
However, the Christian faith is more than just a tradition of
sacrifice and death; it is also a conduit for individual and collective resurrection. Spiritual justice is the means by which
Black faith/spirituality/religion/churches can be re-enlivened
and resurrected with prophetic hope. The Black church must
awaken from her death with a calling to do spiritual justice
in the face of white supremacist and heterosexist American
culture and Black Christian sexism and homophobia.

Spiritual justice is the only means by which the tools
of oppression and the re-traumatization for survivors of
gender-based violence can be dismantled for good. Black

---

28 Sheppard, *Self, Culture and Others in Womanist Practical Theology*, 125.

churches must learn to harvest crops of spiritual justice to reinvigorate and rekindle the historical notion of Black churches and Black spirituality as sources of healing for those who have experienced sexual and gender-based trauma. Spiritual justice is a queer congregational strategy and guiding principle for advocates and Black churches who wish to incorporate trauma-informed human services and innovative pastoral care for LGBTQ+ and Black female survivors of gender-based violence and human trafficking.

THE BIRTH – AND REBIRTH – OF BLACK ACTIVIST ATHLETES: THEY REFUSED TO LAY THEIR BURDENS DOWN

Ron Thomas, *Director, Morehouse College Journalism in Sports, Culture and Social Justice*

When black athletes have laced up their spikes, cleats or sneakers, dressed in their uniforms, shorts or jerseys, and put on their caps or helmets, their original primary goal has been to beat their opponent. Often, they also have been burdened with another goal that superseded winning. That second, though not necessarily secondary, goal has been crushing racism in their respective sport.

My contribution[1] that follows will spotlight black activist athletes over the last 200 years. I contend that sometimes the athletes' mere presence was activism because it caused white society to react – and often lash out. Other black athletes earned the term activist by blatantly defying societal norms, what author Howard Bryant calls "The Heritage" in his book titled the same.

My contribution will be comprised of brief narratives about many of those athletes, and the photos were chosen by Devin Emory, the project coordinator of the Morehouse College journalism program.

---

1 *Based on a presentation I made on Aug. 13, 2020, for the virtual mini-course "The Black Body in the Public Eye" that was offered by Morehouse College Psychology Professor Sinead Younge and filmmaker Deborah Riley Draper, author and director of "Olympic Pride, American Prejudice."*

Sometimes the Black Athlete's Body takes him or her to freedom. Tom Molineaux was born enslaved in 1784 on a plantation in the Washington, D.C., area. He used his bare knuckles to defeat a fellow captive in 1809 to win a huge wager for the plantation owner. Molineaux's reward was his freedom, plus $500.[2] He took a ship to London, won several bouts there, and on December 18, 1810, battled British champion Tom Cribb in the ring. Thus, Molineaux became the first American to compete for a world championship.

Molineaux should have been declared the winner in the 28th round when Cribb was knocked down and could not return to the middle of the ring in the required 30 seconds. But Cribb's aide claimed Molineaux had "pistol balls" that were illegal weights in his hands, which gave Cribb time to recover and eventually win the match.[3] Molineaux also lost a rematch and died in 1818, but at least he died a free man.

Sometimes the Black Athlete's Body is assaulted on the playing field so it must invent ways to protect itself. In 1872, second basemen Bud Fowler, became the first black player in organized baseball. He and Frank Grant, a great minor-league baseball player in the 1880s, were both noted to shield themselves from white players sliding toward them with spikes high. Consequently, both Fowler and Grant have been credited with inventing baseball's first shin guards.

Here's how Fowler's travails in the International League were described by an unnamed white player in *Sporting News*

---

2 Virginia Museum of History & Culture: https://virginiahistory.org/learn/tom-molineaux

3 Robert Ecksel, Boxing History: Cribb vs. Molineaux (Sept. 27, 2016): https://www.wbaboxing.com/boxing-news/boxing-history-cribb-vs-molineaux#.Yc-kNSxOnUo

Tom Molineaux, credit: National Portrait Gallery, London

SECOND BASEMAN GRANT

Ulysses "Frank" Grant, courtesy Baseball Hall of Fame & Museum

on March 23, 1889. "Fowler used to play second base with the lower part of his legs encased in wooden guards. He knew that about every player that came down to second base on a steal had it in for him and would, if possible, throw spikes into him."[4]

Grant was targeted in the same way and resorted to Fowler's method of defending himself. On October 24, 1891, Sporting Life quoted major league infielder Ned Williamson talking about the dangers the Buffalo Bisons' Grant faced on the ballfield. Williamson said that white players in the Eastern League "were willing to permit darkies to carry water to them or guard the bat bag," but became upset if they had to play against a black player. Hence, Grant paid the price.

"The players of the opposing team make it a point to spike this brunett Buffalo," Williamson said. "They would tarry at second when they might easily make third just to toy with the sensitive shins of this second baseman. The poor man played only two games out of five, the rest of the time he was on crutches. To give the frequent spiking an appearance [sic] he put wooden armor on his legs for protection, but the opposition proceeded to file their spike to a sharper point and split the cylinder. The colored man seldom lasted."[5]

Grant led my hometown Buffalo Bisons in batting from 1886-1888, but in 1887 teams in organized baseball had been banned from signing black players to new contracts. So in 1889, Grant joined the Cuban Giants in the Negro Leagues and played there until 1903.

He was posthumously inducted into Baseball's Hall of Fame in 2006; Fowler will be inducted in 2022.

---

4 Sol White, *History of Colored Base Ball* (Lincoln, Nebraska: University of Nebraska Press, 1995), 137

5 White, 140

Sometimes the Black Athlete's Body dominates more than one sport. That's what Ora Washington achieved. She was undefeated for 12 straight years in the all-black American Tennis Association in the 1920s and '30s, winning 23 singles, doubles and mixed doubles titles. However, she highly resented the fact that racial discrimination prevented her from proving she was the world's best player.

"Ora was really angry about never getting a chance to play against the best white women," Bob Ryland, a former American Tennis Association champion, said in *Charging the Net* by Cecil Harris and Larryette Kyle-DeBose. "She'd hear about the white women winning at Wimbledon and the U.S. Nationals, and those other [Grand Slam] tournaments, and she'd be saying, 'I could best them.' She had to work as a domestic, and she was really angry that she couldn't play in the big leagues."[6]

In 1976, her name was inducted into the Black Athletes Hall of Fame, but she couldn't be found to receive a silver bowl, gold ring and medallion set aside in her honor.[7] That's because no one in the Hall of Fame knew that she had died in 1971 as just another deceased housekeeper.[8]

While being damned near infallible in tennis, Washington dominated women's basketball from 1930-1943. She made the Philadelphia Tribune Newsgirls a powerhouse as their captain and leading scorer for 11 consecutive years. Fortunately, when she was named to the Basketball Hall of Fame's Class of

---

6 Cecil Harris and Larryette Kyle-DeBose, *Charging the Net* (Chicago: Ivan R. Dee, 2007), 109.

7 Lena Williams, New York Times, *Black Net Star Who Hoped To Play Miss Wills Honored* (New York Times, April 11, 1976), 164.

8 Charles Pierce, SI.com: Dual-Sport Trailblazer Ora Mae Washington Get Her Due in Basketball Hall of Fame (March 31, 2018): https://www.si.com/college/2018/03/31/ora-mae-washington-tennis-hall-of-fame

2018, the WNBA's fellow inductee Tina Thompson made sure Washington was appreciated.

"She was a hard-worker," Thompson was quoted by SI.com. "The amount of time we get to put into our games and to practice, I couldn't imagine being able to do it at the level she had the privilege to do it with all those responsibilities. It just makes it all that more amazing that she was able to be not just a basketball champion, but a tennis champion, and then live a full life in the fashion she did.

"It's an honor to be in this class with her. I would think that she would be so proud of the number of young women now able to play the game. Both games, actually."[9]

Sometimes the Black Athlete's Body exhibits courage in the shadows. Two months after Brooklyn's Jackie Robinson famously integrated Major League Baseball's National League in 1947, Cleveland Indians owner Bill Veeck acquired Larry Doby from the Negro League's Newark Eagles on July 4th while Doby was batting a league-leading .458. The next day, Doby played his first game in the American League.

The movie "42" and numerous books chronicled Robinson's many stresses; Doby had different struggles to endure. "Jackie and I talked often. Maybe we kept each other from giving up," he was quoted saying in a 1974 Los Angeles Times article.

"The only difference [was] that Jackie Robinson got all of the publicity. You didn't hear much about what I was going through because the media didn't want to repeat the same story. I couldn't react to (prejudicial) situations from

---

9 Pierce

Larry Doby, courtesy Baseball Hall of Fame & Museum

a physical standpoint. My reaction was to hit the ball as far as I could."[9]

When Robinson debuted, the public already knew him as a three-sport star at UCLA and Brooklyn's minor-league sensation. Doby had no such reputation, and the team owner believed that publicizing his signing would put pressure on him. So Veeck didn't tell Cleveland's players that they would have a black teammate until the day before Doby walked into their clubhouse on July 5[th.]

"Larry Doby remembers being introduced to the Cleveland Indians, walking past each locker and extending his hand. Some of his new teammates shook it, some pulled their hand back. Some just turned away,"[10] Don Amore wrote in a 1997 Hartford Courant article.

Doby was joining the Indians only three months after Robinson broke in with the Dodgers. No racial miracles had occurred in the meantime, and Doby hadn't expected any.

"I'd like to say that Jackie made it easy for me," Doby told Amore, "but I didn't see any difference in 11 weeks. People were not going to change all over the world in 11 weeks. . . . There were 25 guys on the team, and 23 of them had never played with a black player, so the way I looked at it, it was as tough for them as it was for me."[11]

The next day, one of his new teammates, Texas native Eddie Robinson, refused to lend Doby his first baseman's glove. According to Joseph Thomas Moore, the author of "Larry Doby: The Struggle of the American League's First Black Player," the

---

10 Dom Amore, Hartford Courant: *Larry Doby Remembers Being Introduced To* (Hartford Courant, April 15, 1997): https://www.courant.com/news/connecticut/hc-xpm-1997-04-15-9704150685-story.html

11 Amore

Larry Doby (R) & Steve Gromek after winning game 4 of the 1948 World Series Credit: Bettman via Getty Images

glove incident exhibits how delicate and potentially explosive integrating a team could be 75 years ago.

On July 6th, player-manager Lou Boudreau listed Doby as the starting first baseman in the second game of a double-header. Problem was, the right-handed Doby didn't have a first baseman's glove, and Robinson, the player Doby replaced in the lineup, had the only glove Doby could use. So traveling secretary Spud Goldstein, acting as a racial go between, tried to arrange the Robinson-to-Doby glove transfer. Moore pieced together the following dialogue after interviewing Goldstein and several people who witnessed the incident but asked to remain anonymous.

"Would you lend your glove to Larry Doby?," Goldstein asked. "No," Robinson allegedly replied, "I won't lend my glove to no nigger."

"Persisting, Goldstein is supposed to have asked, "Eddie, would you lend it to me?" With that, Robinson tossed his glove to Goldstein, saying, "Here, take the glove."[12]

From one viewpoint, the "no nigger" comment, which Robinson denied and Goldstein did not verify, leaves Robinson in a bad light. But from Moore's viewpoint, Robinson avoided torpedoing the entire Doby experiment caused by Boudreau's unwise lineup change.

"Had Eddie Robinson been steadfast in his refusal to lend his glove, other members of the Indians sympathetic to him might have rallied around him," Moore wrote. "If that had happened, surely the other owners of other teams who were watching Rickey [Brooklyn owner Branch Rickey] and Veeck would have feared a player rebellion. Veeck could not have fired 30 or

---

12 Joseph Thomas Moore, *Larry Doby: The Struggle of the American League's First Black Player* (Mineola, N.Y.: Dover Publications, Inc., 2011) 53.

40 percent of his team. A chain reaction of resistance to integration might have exploded in both leagues. Given that potential outcome, then, Eddie Robinson deserves a certain kind of credit. When he threw his glove to Spud Goldstein, he saved a whole lot more than the career of Larry Doby."[13]

That season, Doby got only five hits in 29 games, batted a horrible .156, and struggled as an infielder. But in 1948, he moved to center field, helped Cleveland win the World Series that year, and again in 1954 World Series, and was on the way to a stellar career.

There's an iconic photo of him and teammate Steve Gromek celebrating a World Series victory. "That was a feeling from within, the human side of two people, one black and one white," Doby said at his Hall of Fame induction in 1998. "That made up for everything I went through. I would always relate back to that whenever I was insulted or rejected from hotels."[14]

Sometimes the Black Athlete's Body overcomes disabilities that would overwhelm most people, but not Wilma Rudolph. She was born in 1940 and survived double pneumonia, scarlet fever and polio, which mainly damaged her left leg. At age 6, she could hop on one leg. At 11, her mother saw her playing basketball outside. At 20, she became the first woman to win three gold medals in the same Olympics, taking first in the 100 meters, 200 meters and 400-meter relay in the 1960 Olympics in Rome, Italy.

Wilma said, "My doctors told me I would never walk again.

---

13 Joseph Thomas Moore, 54.

14 Larry Doby's 1998 Baseball Hall of Fame induction speech: https://www.youtube.com/watch?v=SnictfRm-rl

Gold medal winner Wilma Rudolph, XVI Summer
Olympic Games in Rome, Italy on Sept. 2, 1960. (Credit: AP Images)

My mother told me I would. I believed my mother."[15] Wilma's hometown of Clarksville, Tennessee, offered to hold a parade in her honor. She refused to participate unless it was integrated, so Clarksville held its first desegregated public event.

Sometimes the Black Athlete's Body refuses demands to step into the field of combat. That's what Muhammad Ali did on April 28, 1967, when he refused induction into the U.S. Army during the Vietnam War. That decision cost him badly: he was stripped of his heavyweight title, was suspended from boxing, convicted of draft evasion, fined $10,000, and sentenced to five years in prison. Many people would have cowered at that prospect; Ali just put it in perspective and shrugged it off.

"I met two black soldiers a while back in an airport," he told Black Scholar in 1970. "They said: 'Champ, it takes a lot of guts to do what you're doing.' I told them: 'Brothers, you just don't know. If you knew where you were going now, if you knew your chances of coming out with no arm or no eye, fighting those people in their own land, fighting Asian brothers, you got to shoot them, they never lynched you, never called you nigger, never put dogs on you, never shot your leaders. You've got to shoot your 'enemies' (they call them) and as soon as you get home you won't be able to find a job. Going to jail for a few years is nothing compared to that.' "[16]

As it turned out, Ali's suspension from boxing lasted three years, ended by his victory over Jerry Quarry on October 26,

---

15 Arlisha Norwood, National Women's History Museum: *Wilma Rudolph, 1940-1994:* https://www.womenshistory.org/education-resources/biographies/wilma-rudolph

16 *The Black Scholar Interviews: Muhammad Ali*, Vol. 1, No. 8, BLACK CULTURE (June 1970), pages 32-39. (Taylor & Francis, Ltd.): https://www.jstor.org/stable/41206252

Tommie Smith, center, and John Carlos during the playing of national anthem after Smith received the gold and Carlos the bronze for the 200 meter run at the Summer Olympic Games in Mexico City. (Credit: AP Images/file)

1970, in Atlanta. Ali never was imprisoned because the U.S. Supreme Court overturned his conviction by an 8-0 vote on June 28, 1971. He was on his way to becoming an internationally revered figure who lit the Olympic torch in 1996.

Sometimes the Black Athlete's Body steps up to the podium to draw attention to racism and poverty in America, which Tommie Smith and John Carlos did with fists raised after winning gold and bronze in the 200 meters during the 1968 Olympics. In an interview with Howard Cosell on ABC after their protest, Smith thusly described what their apparel signified on October 16, 1968:

My raised right hand stood for the power in black America. Carlos's left hand stood for the unity of black America. Together, they formed an arch of unity and power. The black scarf around my neck stood for black pride. The black socks with no shoes stood for black poverty in racist America. The totality of our effort was the regaining of black dignity.[17]

Their raised fists became the logo for the Black Power salute. Ironically, that never was their intention.

In his autobiography "Silent Gesture" co-authored with David Steele, Smith explained that their demonstration stemmed from their involvement in the Olympic Project for Human Rights – with the emphasis on "Human." Their main concern was about a social system that guaranteed rights for all but mainly reserved them for white people in power. Which in the 1960s mainly meant white men. Women, regardless of color, were almost powerless.

---

17 Tommie Smith with David Steele, *Silent Gesture: The Autobiography of Tommie Smith* (Philadelphia: Temple University Press, 2007)

SLAVERY AND ITS CONSEQUENCES

"To this very day, the gesture made on the victory stand is described as a Black Power salute; it was not," Smith said in his book. Instead, their gesture supported human rights. "It's just that pressure was taken by the black athletes; we stepped out and did what should have been done by young groups much earlier."[18]

Smith also is proud that their actions were done with dignity. "People expected us to go up there and hoo-rah, get loud, slap hands, or something," he wrote. "We did it with pride, and we wanted it to represent everybody without making a statement for anybody, just a silent gesture for anyone to interpret their way."[19]

Unfortunately, most of the white media and the public interpreted it as a gesture of disrespect for America. Even before the Olympics, fearing Smith might do or say something brash, a Pontiac car dealership near his school fired him. That left him with a wife, a 6-month-old son, and a "full" scholarship that included $85 a month and $25 a semester for books.

He had completed his college track eligibility, and any possible endorsement money he could have attracted as a gold medal winner had evaporated as he stood on the victory podium. In his book, Smith writes that he was disappointed by the lack of support he received even from black people, particularly fellow '68 Olympics hero George Foreman, the NAACP and its members, and retired football star Jim Brown.

There also was the pain inflicted by the white media, which largely ignored the humanistic, anti-racism message he and Carlos attempted to convey and instead painted them

18 Smith with Steele, 22

19 Smith with Steele, 139

as defiant ingrates. To Carlos, the worst among them was the column written by later-to-be-famous sports journalist Brent Musburger in the Chicago American.

In a June 4, 2012, column in *The Nation*,[20] Dave Zirin called for Musburger to apologize for his column headlined "Bizarre Protest By Smith, Carlos Tarnishes Medals."[21] In it, Musburger calls them "unimaginative blokes," accuses them of "insuring maximum embarrassment for the country that is picking up the tab for their room and board here in Mexico City" and refers to the always highly politicized Olympics as a "fun and games tournament."

He calls Smith "a militant black" and posited about he and Carlos, "Perhaps it's time that 20-year-old athletes quit passing themselves off as social philosophers." It was Musburger's precursor to the infamous "shut up and dribble." But to Carlos, worst of all was when Musburger wrote that they "looked like a couple of black-skinned storm troopers."

"We are talking about someone who compared us to Nazis," Carlos told Zirin. "Think about that. Here we are standing up to apartheid and to a man in [International Olympic Committee President] Avery Brundage who delivered the Olympics to Hitler's Germany. And here's Musburger calling us Nazis. That got around. It followed us. It hurt us. It hurt my wife, my kids. I've never been able to confront him about why he did this. Every time I've been at a function or an event with Brent Musburger and I walk towards him, he heads the other way."

---

20 David Zirin, The Nation, *After 44 Years, It's Time Brent Musburger Apologized to John Carlos and Tommie Smith:* https://www.thenation.com/article/archive/after-forty-four-years-its-time-brent-musburger-apologized-john-carlos-and-tommie-smith/

21 David Zirin

Sometimes the Black Body refuses to move – literally. On October 7, 1969, the St. Louis Cardinals traded Curt Flood, a superb outfielder and near .300 hitter, to Philadelphia – or so the teams thought. Flood, who was a friend of mine, refused to move to his new team in a city known for its racist fans. After 12 years with the Cardinals, Flood wrote Baseball Commissioner Bowie Kuhn that he refused to be treated like a piece of property.

In a 1970 interview, sportscaster Howard Cosell pointed out to Flood that his $90,000 salary "isn't exactly slave wages." Flood replied, "A well-paid slave is nonetheless a slave."[22]

In court, he challenged baseball's reserve clause that tied a player to his team until the team released him or he died. Flood lost in the Supreme Court, but scared owners into opening the door to free agency that thousands of players from several sports have profited from in the last 46 years.

"He helped to change the way they do business. Every day you read the sports page, whether his name is in there or not, Curt's there," his wife, actress Judy Pace, said in a New York Times video named "Rebel Without a Clause."[23]

However, age and stress-induced alcoholism stole Flood's playing talent and baseball denied him jobs after he retired as a player in 1971.

"I am pleased that God made my skin Black – but I wish he had made it thicker," Flood wrote in his autobiography *The Way It Is*.[24]

He needed an elephant's hide to endure being black as a minor leaguer in the Cincinnati Reds' farm system. After being

---

22 Howard Cosell Interview With Curt Flood on Vimeo: https://vimeo.com/91118362

23 New York Times: Rebel Without a Clause video (RetroReport): https://www.nytimes.com/2014/10/06/us/curt-flood-the-athlete-who-made-lebron-james-possible.html

24 Curt Flood and Richard Carter, *The Way It Is* (New York: Trident Press, 1971)

Curt Flood (Credit: AP Images)

raised in progressive Oakland, California, the Carolina League was a mental meat grinder he wasn't prepared for. Spring trainings in Georgia and Florida, and his first minor-league season in High Point-Thomasville, North Carolina, subjected him to vicious abuse in 1956.

"One of my first and enduring memories is of a large, loud cracker who installed himself and his four little boys in a front-row box and started yelling 'black bastard' at me," Flood was quoted in *A Well-Paid Slave: Curt Food's Fight for Free Agency in Professional Sports*" by Brad Snyder.[25]

Eventually, he called his sister, Barbara, to tell her he wanted to come home and that he needed to talk to someone. "I wanted to be free of these animals whose 50-cent bleacher ticket was a license to curse my color and deny my humanity. I wanted to be free of the imbeciles on my ball team."

Barbara called Reds scout Bobby Mattick, who said Flood should not quit. He didn't, wrote Snyder, because he understood the larger meaning of his survival in High Point-Thomasville.

"What had started as a chance to test my baseball ability in a professional setting had become an obligation to measure myself as a man," Flood said. "As such, it was a matter of life and death. These brutes were trying to destroy me. If they could make me collapse and quit, it would verify their preconceptions. And it would wreck my life."[26]

---

25 Brad Snyder, *A Well-Paid Slave: Curt Food's Fight for Free Agency in Professional Sports* (Viking Adult, 2006) Chapter Four: https://books.google.com/books?id=Tpt845rGohkC&p-g=PT47&lpg=PT47&dq=%E2%80%9CI+am+pleased+that+God+made+my+skin+Black+%E2%80%93+but+I+wish+he+had+made+it+thicker.%E2%80%9D&source=bl&ots=fpRuL_WyJt&sig=ACfU3U3qf8Wbu16DoRlYhP8Ykyg-PSO54A&hl=en&sa=X&ved=2ahUKEwjhi7-G3JH1AhUMRjABHb1eB9wQ6AF6BAgOEAM#v=onepage&q=%E2%80%9CI%20am%20pleased%20that%20God%20made%20my%20skin%20Black%20%E2%80%93%20but%20I%20wish%20he%20had%20made%20it%20thicker.%E2%80%9D&f=false

26 Snyder

If Flood could summon that much fortitude at 18 years old, he certainly wasn't going to let the Cardinals, the reserve clause, or Commissioner Kuhn determine his future after he had established himself as a star and helped St. Louis win two World Series. He had done his time in racial purgatory. No one was going to volunteer him for more.

Sometimes Black Bodies are told to wait ... and wait ... and wait some more.

It was 44 years ago when I wrote about the lack of black head football coaches for the first of many times. The first article of a two-part series for the Chicago Daily News appeared on January 3, 1978, and the headline was "Lonely at the Top" because Oree Banks at West Virginia State was the only black head coach at a predominately white college. At the time, and for 11 more years, the National Football League had no black head coaches.

As I write this on January 23, 2022, I could switch the topic to the NFL, swap the picture of Pittsburgh's Mike Tomlin for Banks, and write the same "Lonely at the Top" headline. Because 101 years after Fritz Pollard became the NFL's first black head coach, Tomlin is the only one in the league.

Mike Brown, a retired Bay Area-based diversity trainer, called this dilemma "tragically timeless" for black people who aspire to be NFL head coaches.

The first ever, Pollard, was named a player-coach with the Akron Pros in 1921. But it took 68 years and maverick Oakland Raiders owner Al Davis to hire the second, Art Shell, in 1989. The struggle has continued even though roughly 60% of NFL players are black.

When the 2021 season began, there were only five non-white NFL coaches out of 32: Tomlin with the Steelers; David Culley (Houston) and Brian Flores (Miami) are black; Ron Rivera is Hispanic (Washington); Robert Saleh is Arab American (NY Jets). Only one out of seven openings had been filled by hiring a black coach (Culley). Most egregious, Kansas City's Eric Bieniemy was passed over again even though he was offensive coordinator for a Super Bowl team the previous two years.

After the regular season, two of the three black head coaches were fired. On January 10, 2022, Miami fired Flores even though the Dolphins had finished 10-6 and 9-8 in his last two seasons, the first consecutive winning records for Miami since 2002 and 2003. To achieve that, the Dolphins overcame a 1-7 start in 2021 by winning their last eight games. Yet, owner Stephen Ross said he fired Flores because of a lack of collaboration within the organization. The consensus among NFL writers was that meant Flores lost a power struggle with general manager Chris Grier, who also is black.

Culley toiled 27 years as an NFL assistant coach before becoming head coach of the Texans, then was fired on January 13 after only one season. True, his team finished 4-13, but he had inherited a feeble 4-12 team after previous coach/general manager Bill O'Brien traded away star receiver DeAndre Hopkins for virtually nothing, three-time Associated Press Defensive Player of the Year J.J. Watt signed with Arizona, and potential superstar quarterback DeShaun Watson sat out the season as he battled sexual assault allegations. General manager Nick Caserio said he fired Culley because they had philosophical differences about the team's future, but he wouldn't specify what those differences were.

Those inexplicable firings left Tomlin as the NFL's one and only black head coach. It will be fascinating to see if, or how much, that changes with eight teams needing new head coaches and six highly accomplished black offensive and defensive coordinators competing in the divisional rounds of the 2021 season playoffs: Leslie Frazier (Buffalo), Bieniemy (Kansas City), Raheem Morris (Los Angeles Rams), DeMeco Ryans (San Francisco) and Todd Bowles and Byron Leftwich (Tampa Bay).

The colleges were no better during the 2021 season, with 12 black head football coaches among 130 in FBS major colleges. Just 1 out of 15 hires before the season were African American despite 54% of the players being black. In FCS, 25 out of its 124 head coaches are black: 20% compared to the FBS' 9%. But that's because the FCS includes 21 HBCUs. By researching college football websites and the internet, I found four black head coaches – Mike Minter (Campbell U.), Demario Warren (Southern Utah), Autry Denson (Charleston Southern), Mike London (William & Mary) – out of 121 predominantly white institutions.

Black aspirants for NFL head-coaching jobs must overcome an imposing list of pitfalls to achieve their goal.

- Their leadership skills are questioned:

Indianapolis' Tony Dungy and Chicago's Lovie Smith were competing head coaches in Super Bowl XLI to win the 2006 championship, and Tampa Bay just won the 2020 championship with four black coordinators and 12 black assistant coaches altogether. That question should never arise again.

▪ The whispered rumor: He doesn't interview well.

That accusation sometimes pops up after a black coach with excellent credentials keeps getting passed over. It has begun to victimize the Chiefs' Bieniemy, who interviewed with six teams last offseason and didn't get a job.

Last year, Sports Illustrated reported that in a radio interview with "The A Team with Wexler & Clanton" Aaron Wilson of the Houston Chronicle, said, "I'm going to be honest, very transparent. Eric is not interviewing very well with other teams, and (the Texans) haven't been interested in Eric through the entire process."[27]

On the other hand, the Atlanta Falcons "absolutely refuted" that Bieniemy didn't interview well with them, praising his interview instead. However, they hired Art Smith, another white coach.

It's a Catch-22 for black coaches. How do you prove that you interviewed well when your opinion doesn't matter?

▪ No legacy points:

Routinely, white head coaches gain football knowledge and networks from a family tree of former NFL coaches and administrators. This season's NFL head coaches John Harbaugh, Bill Belichick, Sean McVay and Kyle Shanahan – along with the deposed Jon Gruden – were among them. But the list of former black college and pro coaches is so short that aspiring black coaches don't get that legacy boost.

---

27 Dan Lyons, The Spun by Sports Illustrated: *Falcons 'Furious' About Last Night's Eric Bieniemy News.* (Sports Illustrated, Jan. 9, 2021): https://thespun.com/nfl/nfc-south/atlanta-falcons/eric-bieniemy-head-coach-candidate-interviews-atlanta-falcons-texans-kansas-city-chiefs

Houston Antwine (L) & Larry Garron (R) of the Boston Patriots;
AFL All-Star Game cancelled 1965, courtesy Todd Tobias

Legacy-wise, young white coaches can lean on a sturdy oak tree; black coaches cling to a twig.

Baltimore's John Harbaugh: His dad, Jack Harbaugh, was a college head coach for 19 years and a college or pro assistant coach for 25. That's 44 years of football knowledge and contacts his son benefited from.

New England's Bill Belichick: His dad, Steve Belichick, had a 40-year coaching career at four colleges. Bill started analyzing film with his father when Bill was 10.

Jon Gruden, who was fired by the Raiders after it was revealed that he made racist, homophobic and misogynist comments about NFL colleagues: His dad, Jim Gruden, had at least 25 years as a pro or college assistant coach or scout.

Los Angeles Rams' Sean McVay: His grandfather, John McVay, was a pro football (NFL and WFL) head coach for five years, college head or assistant coach for 11 years, and San Francisco 49ers general manager for nine years.

49ers head coach Kyle Shanahan: His father, Mike Shanahan, spent 38 years as an NFL and college coach, including 20 as an NFL head coach.

GRAND TOTAL of football family background:
5 of 27 White Head Coaches – a minimum of 172 years
5 Non-white Head Coaches – 0

• Relatively little head-coaching experience:

The media's focus is on high-profile NFL and Division I jobs. But outside of HBCUs, black coaches get almost no Div. I-AA and Division II jobs where whites often start their head-coaching resumes. No pressure to diversify is applied to presidents and athletic directors of small PWIs.

• Head-coaching success at HBCUs gets ignored:

Excellent Example: Morehouse's Rich Freeman – In 2010, he led 8-3 Morehouse to its first appearance in the NCAA play-offs. In 2018, his 6-0 Tigers were the last undefeated HBCU in the nation. In 2021, after missing a full season and not being able to practice much before the season began, his team started at 0-5 but roared back for a 4-1 finish.

That included beating arch rival Tuskegee University 31-15 and destroying Fort Valley State 51-3 during Morehouse's Homecoming game. Oh, one more thing, the Tigers' field was being renovated so they played no home games. Yet, after 27 years as a coach, including 15 as a head coach, not one PWI has invited Freeman for a job interview. HBCUs? Yes. PWIs? Never.

Sometimes Black Bodies act as one, which occurred in 1965 when black players boycotted the American Football League All-Star Game because of the racism they encountered in New Orleans. Black players couldn't get a cab, couldn't enter some night clubs, and at one restaurant when a black player hung up his coat, a white patron trailed behind him, took down the coat and threw it on the floor. Many black players flew home in disgust and the game was moved to Houston, where it was played two days later.

Black players in general stifled their voices in the 1970s-early 2000s, feeling they had to protect their jobs, growing salaries

The Honor Guard presents John-Miles Lewis, John Lewis' son, with the flag that shrouded his casket during the burial service of late Representative and Civil Rights leader John Lewis, South-View Cemetery, Atlanta, Georgia on July 30, 2020
Credit: Alyssa Pointer via Getty Images

Colin Kaepernick, 2016.
Credit: Image © Shutterstock.

Maya Moore (in mask) exulted as Jonathan Irons released from Missouri prison in Missouri after burglary and assault charges were vacated; credit: Julia Hansen for *The New York Times* — July 2, 2020

and commercial endorsements. They also felt pressured to remain silent by team owners and the predominately white media. To me, that began to change when the Miami Heat stood as one wearing hoodies in sympathy with the slain Trayvon Martin in 2012.

Sometimes, the Black Athletic Body can't stand the pain. The killings didn't stop as Michael Brown, Eric Garner, Sandra Bland, Philando Castile, Tamir Rice, Freddie Gray and Walter Scott were all slain by police or under police custody within only two years. 49ers quarterback Colin Kaepernick couldn't stand for it anymore, so he sat through national anthems at two preseason games to protest police brutality.

On the advice of teammate Nate Boyer, a former Army Green Beret, Kaepernick decided to take a knee before the game on September 1, 2016. He did it quietly, respectfully, just like the soldier who knelt before Miles Lewis to give him a folded American flag at the burial of his dad, Congressman John Lewis.

Sometimes the Female Black Athletic Body has to make change happen. After Jacob Blake was shot seven times in the back by a policeman in Kenosha, Wisconsin, the NBA's Milwaukee Bucks famously canceled their August 26, 2020, game in protest of the unjustified brutal injuries and deaths inflicted on black people by law enforcement officers. But as Erica Ayala's Washington Post column pointed out three days afterward, the women of the WNBA—80% of them black—had lit a pattern of protest that the NBA could easily follow after the previous four years.[28]

Ayala noted that WNBA players began their public stands on July 9, 2016, when the Minnesota Lynx wore T-shirts that read: "Change Starts with Us: Justice and Accountability" to honor black victims of police shooting Philando Castile and Alton Sterling, along with five recently slain Dallas police officers.

• The Indiana Fever became the first team to take a knee during the national anthem in support of Colin Kaepernick and black victims of police violence. They kept it secret beforehand, not even telling their coach, Stephanie White. Afterward, she expressed pride in their united effort.

> "There's a respectful way to affect social change, and I think any time our players have a conversation about doing it in a respectful way, I appreciate that and I applaud them for that," she said after their playoff loss to Phoenix on Sept. 21, 2016.[29]

• On August 27, 2020, the Washington Mystics "appeared on national television with hand-designed white shirts, each one with a single letter on the front to spell out Jacob Blake, with the backs portraying seven bullet holes to symbolize the number of times Blake was shot by police."[30]

---

28 Erica Ayala, The Washington Post: *The NBA's walkout is historic. But the WNBA paved the way.* (The Washington Post, August 29, 2020): https://www.washingtonpost.com/outlook/2020/08/29/nba-wnba-racial-injustice/

29 Gregg Doyel, IndyStar.com: *Doyel: Entire Indiana Fever roster kneels for national anthem* (IndyStar.com, Sept. 21, 2016): https://www.indystar.com/story/sports/basketball/wnba/fever/2016/09/21/entire-fever-roster-kneels-national-anthem/90692648/

30 Ayala

Brittney Griner — courtesy of Phoenix Mercury

• Before the 2020 WNBA season, the players union and the league established a Social Justice Council to hold conversations about "voting, girls and women killed by police, and increasing support and awareness for Black-owned and female-owned businesses" and other topics.

The WNBA took concrete, consequential political action, too.

• The WNBA strived to make sure every player was registered to vote in the 2020 election and had completed the 2020 U.S. Census. They also demanded that the attorney generals in Kentucky and Wisconsin arrest the killers of Breonna Taylor and shooter of Jacob Blake, respectively.

• The WNBA and NBA players association learned more about their voting rights by video conferencing with First Lady Michelle Obama.

• After Sen. Kelly Loeffler (R-Ga.), a co-owner of the Atlanta Dream, criticized the WNBA for supporting Black Lives Matter, players campaigned for her opponent, Rev. Raphael Warnock, who won her seat in a runoff. On February 26, 2021, Loeffler and her co-owner sold the team. One of the new owners is Renee Montgomery, formerly a black Dream player.

"It is our hope that no one will ever again attempt to use the players for individual political gain or favor," Washington National Basketball Association Executive Director Terri Jackson said in a statement. "Those actions were unbelievably selfish, reckless and dangerous. And those who would conduct themselves in that manner have absolutely no place in our sport."[31]

Finally, sometimes one Black Athletic Figure's Body expresses the concerns of all black people as we traverse a world filled with gunfire, health disparities, and environmental hazards that shorten our lives.

Speaking before an NAACP march on the Georgia state Capitol on June 15, 2020, former Atlanta Hawks coach Lloyd Pierce said, "I want to finish by saying, I was born a black man, and I know one day I'll die a black man. ... But I don't want to die because I'm a black man."[32]

31 Candace Buckner, *The Washington Post: Kelly Loeffler sells stake in WNBA team after clashing with players over Black Lives Matter* (The Washington Post, February 26, 2021): https://www.washingtonpost.com/sports/2021/02/26/kelly-loeffler-senator-sells-wnba-atlanta-dream/

32 Sarah K. Spencer, The Atlanta Journal-Constitution: *Hawks' Lloyd Pierce speaks on racial injustice, voting rights before NAACP march* (The Atlanta Journal-Constitution, June 15, 2020): https://www.ajc.com/sports/basketball/hawks-lloyd-pierce-speaks-racial-injustice-voting-rights-before-naacp-march/VafId5u3zMYmCtwziTYzRJ/

Hawks' Coach Lloyd Pierce (with daughter) joined protestors for a march through downtown, June 15, 2020. Credit: Rebecca Wright for the AJC (The Atlanta Journal-Constitution)

OCCUPYING THE CENTER: BLACK PUBLISHING AS ACTIVISM

An interview with Paul Coates & Barry Beckham
Jodi L. Henderson, Editor in Chief, Journal of Modern Slavery

Jodi Henderson: We're here to have a conversation about Black publishing, but before we get into that, I'd really like to hear about why you chose books as your path.

Barry Beckham: Paul, since you've been doing this far longer than I, why don't you begin?

Paul Coates: Okay. My experience with books is one that, I think books kind of found me. I do this as part of a passion that came to me when I was much younger, as a child. I don't know what it is about books, but they have a calming, warming, and sometimes a fiery side to them that attracts me. And they always have. As a child, they attracted me, and as I became older, my relationship with books deepened, particularly when I went into the military. They began to help me expand my understanding of the world as I became more politically conscious.

They gave me not only the pleasure of experiencing things; they gave me an understanding of the world and how things were in the world, and also how things could be changed in the world. I came out of the military loving books, and in pursuit of Black books in particular. And I followed that love and pursuit into the Black Panther Party. In the Black Panther Party, I worked with books. I worked with people who needed books, and I carried that same need and network out of the Black Panther Party into an organization called the George Jackson Prison Movement that had books as its core.

It was a three-part program that I created to help people who were incarcerated, particularly people in the movement who were incarcerated, and other people. But the first part of that program was a bookstore.

The bookstore was created so that when people that we were working with in the jail came out of the jail, they'd have a place to work. They'd have a base to be able to give back to the community that they had been taken away from, a place to land so that they could stabilize themselves and deal and deepen their knowledge about themselves, and consequently, become more valuable assets to their community. That was called the George Jackson Prison Program.

The second part of that program was the building of a publishing house. The publishing house was intended to publish books by and about people of African descent that aided in developing their consciousness and aided in literally correcting the mindset and establishing a value in the Black community in books. Our intention was to supply books, and we would publish books that we would supply to that bookstore, the George Jackson Prison Movement bookstore, and supply to other bookstores around the country.

The third part of that program was to establish a printing company that would print the books that we were going to be publishing, and that would eventually be sold in the bookstore and bookstores around the country. Each level was designed so that it would offer employment in the Black community and so that it would be a self-sustaining type of venture. So, it wasn't intended as a commercial press at all. My engagement and my romance with books was intended as a community project. And it went that way probably for about 10 years, when I realized that most of the things I had wanted to do as a community organizer had gone by the wayside, and I actually was running a business.

So, probably about ten years in, Black Classic Press was established as Black Classic Press. Twenty years in, we put together the resources and acquired the equipment to do printing, and about five years in, we closed down the bookstore because that part was not going to work. So, I still maintained the printing part and the publishing part as Black Classic Press and BCP Digital. And that's how I got into books.

Barry Beckham: That's quite a story. Now Paul, where was this?

Paul Coates: Historic Pennsylvania Avenue in Baltimore—the center, really, of West Baltimore, right around the corner from where Thurgood Marshall actually grew up. At one time, the Black Panther Party had an office that was right off Pennsylvania Avenue. When I came back from the West Coast and the Panthers, we selected an office for the George Jackson Prison Movement which was right around the corner from where that other Panther office was. And so shortly after we did that, the Panthers closed the office, and everybody went to California. That's what happened.

Barry Beckham: I knew you were with the Panthers, but I wasn't sure where you were located.

Paul Coates: In Baltimore, yeah, I was defense captain for Maryland.

We ended up with so many people in jail, including myself, you know that? Yeah, I didn't serve the Long Time. We had some people that did serve Long Time, but there were so many people, and we had so much of an organization in jail, that obviously, educating people with books became the revolution. That was the revolution.

Barry Beckham: Right.

Paul Coates: To touch the minds. And the whole idea that you could touch somebody's mind and flip that person over and have that person then become an asset in your community. That became the revolution.

Barry Beckham: And it certainly was.

Paul Coates: Yeah, and then the notion that you could do that for a whole community became a powerful motive, influence.

Barry Beckham: Absolutely.

Paul Coates: But now about yourself, please.

Barry Beckham: I will start with being about seven or eight years old and watching my mother sit in a chair reading all the time, books and magazines, and I thought, "God, this is fascinating. What's going on?" And I started picking up some of the magazines, mostly women's magazines and popular culture magazines. And I thought, "This is so fascinating; maybe I should start writing, and I can keep her attention also." So, I started writing, and I was copying stories from the magazines.

I would show them to my mother, who said, "You're not writing. You're just copying stories. You have to write your own stories." That's when I thought, "That's a great idea. I want to be a writer." So that was the influence and the first direction of me thinking, "I can be a writer."

I think I thought I was writing poetry at one point. And I remember the detective stories I tried to write because it always ended with the hero being a detective whom I had heard about on the radio stations, but he always said something that was worthwhile remembering and writing down at the end of every story, which was "crime does not pay."

Paul Coates: [laughs]

Barry Beckham: I wrote as many of those stories as I could. Finally, I got into high school and wrote as much as I could there. When I got to Brown University, I took a fiction writing course with John Hawkes. At one point in class, we had to talk about what we're doing. I said, "I'm writing a novel." And people just looked at me as if I had said something that made no sense at all. Why would I be talking about writing a novel in John Hawkes's fiction writing class and no one else says anything about taking such a venture? So, I started my novel based on the fact that John Hawkes was a premier surrealist and wrote all kinds of novels that really stretched reality.

I thought, "I can write a book like that. I think I'll write a book about a boy who kills his mother; that should make things really strange. Put him in Maine where I've never been in my life." But I thought, "He needs to be in some wild, crazy atmosphere." And so that was the beginning of my first novel. I called it *My Main Mother*—with main being spelled "m-a-i-n"—and started that novel and graduated from Brown. I went to Columbia Law School, stayed there for two months, and crazily enough thought, "Ah, I'll get a job in New York City." And I did as a PR writer with the Chase Manhattan Bank. So, I was writing answers to David Rockefeller's correspondence and press releases and stories for the press in the *Chase Manhattan News*. And I found out that there was a fiction writing course at NYU in the evening taught by Sydney Offit, who is my great friend and is now 92.

Paul Coates: Yeah? I did not know that.

Barry Beckham: Yes. I asked my supervisor if the Chase Manhattan Tuition Reimbursement Program would pay for a fiction writing class at NYU. And he said, "Why not? That's what we're doing anyway." So, I took the course with Sydney, brought out my four chapters I had written at Brown, and at one point he said, "This is really good." He says, "If you got an outline and some sample chapters, I think we've got a good chance. I can take them to publishers." I said, "Okay, I'll have an outline next week." I gave him the outline and some chapters, and after one rejection, he said, "I found a publisher for you."

And so that's how I got my first novel published, writing two years after graduating from Brown. And from that it was

"It's gotta be books from here." First, I was a writer and published, and before I knew it, I received a letter from the new and first director of Afro-American Studies, which is what we called it back then in the sixties.

He said he had read my novel, and I still remember the phrase, "with some interest," and wanted to know if I'd come back to teach at Brown part time. I thought, "Oh boy, what a life. I've got two kids living in Manhattan, a fair salary just making it, but it's expensive. It's dangerous. It's not like trees and the verdant atmosphere of Providence, Rhode Island." So, I grabbed the job and stayed there for 18 years, working, of course, in the English Department, being fascinated with books and teaching, and, believe it or not, fiction writing. I came up with some courses like Personal Reflective Writing, and even designed a course that focused solely on the novel *Invisible Man* by Ralph Ellison.

The one point I would say about books is that I loved the John Hay Library then; they had this fantastic collection of works that you would see nowhere else. I found all of these books written in the early part of the century by African-American writers, and I thought, "God, it's amazing what they've done. I've got to do that too." And the library kept me fascinated with the books and writing. One part of the library had this great newspaper and magazine section, and I could read *The Pittsburgh Courier* at the library and find out what's going on with Black people around the country.

One thing that fascinated me about books in my history is that there were so many antique classics in the library, particularly at the John Hay Library, which is a reservoir of classic works. These old bound books had a fascinating aroma, a smell to them. I liked taking the books and running my nose along the spine. Gosh, it was wonderful to smell those old books.

To end all this, I think that I started out with books because my mother was so fascinated with writing and with reading, and she got me interested in writing.

And at one point, I thought, "I don't see enough works being published by and about Black people. I think I'll start my own publishing company. Our focus will be books by and about the Black experience." So that's how I got from sitting on the floor, fascinated by my mother reading all these books, to thinking I should publish books, too.

Paul Coates: How old were you when she transitioned? Did she get to see you at Brown?

Barry Beckham: Yeah, she saw me at Brown. I do remember one part when I had published my first piece with *Esquire* magazine. I told her that my piece in *Esquire* was coming out. I think it may have been one of the few telegrams that she sent to me: "All Atlantic City is proud of you. They've read *Esquire*."

Paul Coates: Wow, good.

Barry Beckham: So many people think that *My Main Mother* is about her. And of course, it's not. [laughter] It's about a boy who kills his mother.

Paul Coates: Did she read *My Main Mother*? Did she read your books?

Barry Beckham: Oh, I'm sure she did. Yes, she knew that Aunt Helen was a woman in the family whom I knew. I changed her name, of course, in the book, but she knew that character was really Aunt Helen. [laughter]

Jodi Henderson: Barry, social commentary seems central in many of your works. What spurred that, and why has this been important to you?

Barry Beckham: Yes, that's a good question. My first novel was published in '69, so I guess I was certainly writing in the late sixties before it was published. All that came about from the sixties. There was so much going on. Martin Luther King being assassinated. And being in New York City in the sixties, and meeting Nikki Giovanni[1] at a party and walking her to her car in the snow with a baby. Larry Neal[2] and Imamu Baraka[3] and everybody was excited and militant and demonstrative during that time. I just picked it up, and I thought, "Geez, these are things that are important."

Although the novel may be about a boy who is mentally disturbed, there are other things going on too. I take him to New York City in the novel, and he sees people looking out the window and wondering what's going on and people fighting on the streets. I remember one scene I came up with where two Black teenagers are walking down the street, they see the

---

1 American poet, writer, and activist

2 Scholar of African-American theatre, active in the Black Arts Movement of the 1960s and 1970s

3 Born Everett LeRoi Jones, author, playwright, teacher, and political activist who disavowed his former life in 1965 and took the name Amiri Baraka; when he converted to Islam in 1968, he added "Imamu" (as he is referenced here). In 1974, he dropped "Imamu" when he began identifying as a Marxist, August 2, 2022, biography.com/writer/amiri-baraka#political-activism last accessed 2 August 2022 10:24AM

main character and his uncle and ask them questions. The main character's uncle says, "You guys shouldn't be on the streets. You should be in school." Of course, the answer was well, that wasn't the answer for them.

Then, in the novel, I have the police drive up the street, and the two brothers say, "Uh-oh, it's the man! Let's get out of here!" and run away, because that's what I saw.

Paul Coates: Right. Right.

Barry Beckham: That's what I felt. And this is way before "defund the police." What I saw was a world where things were not going well for us as a people. And I've got to put this somewhere in the book.

Paul Coates: Mmmm.

Barry Beckham: So *Runner Mack*, I think that was my second novel. It was about a main character who comes up from the South to make it in baseball. Of course it's more than that, because he joins a group that's going to take over the White House, because things are so bad. So, it's a novel of protest. And the main character is really a baseball player, he hopes. I didn't realize until one professor invited me to talk to students, and she said that it's the first novel about baseball written by a Black author.

Paul Coates: Hmmm, hmmm.

Barry Beckham: I never knew that [laughing]. And of course, it's not about baseball, solely.

Paul Coates: Right.

Barry Beckham: But it is about a baseball player who doesn't make it because he's a Black baseball player. So back to your question, it has so much social content, comment. The scholar picked up on it and said, "He's writing about baseball, and he's the first Black writer to do it." I said, "Wow. Really?"

Paul Coates: Interesting.

Barry Beckham: I have a friend, he read the novel and said that he was amazed at how many Black baseball players I had mentioned, because his father was in the Negro Leagues.

Paul Coates: Right, right.

Barry Beckham: And okay, I had to throw that in for reality. It wasn't a major, main part of the novel, but he was amazed with the fact that, "Oh boy, he mentioned some Black baseball players in his novel."

Paul Coates: [laughter] You know, I don't think I've read *Runner Mack*. I certainly read *My Main Mother*.

Barry Beckham: Yeah.

Paul Coates: Cause that was before. . . Your books were later published by Howard, right? You had two books published by Howard?

Barry Beckham: They reprinted what I would call the baseball novel, *Runner Mack*. I think that's all they did.

Paul Coates: I sold that book in the bookstore that I was telling you about, right?

Barry Beckham: Really?

Paul Coates: We used to sell out there. So that bookstore was like 1971 until about 1978.

Barry Beckham: Wow.

Jodi Henderson: And you started your publishing house in the late seventies, right?

Paul Coates: '78. I was preparing to go away to graduate school in '78 and already had the plans for the publishing house. I wanted to make sure that it was done before I went away to graduate school, so the first publications were done in 1978. We'd done some pamphlets, but *Survey Graphic* was the first actual publication.

Barry Beckham: Oh, yeah.

Paul Coates: The logic was that if I could publish this book and go away to graduate school, then I certainly would publish when I came back from school, you know what I'm saying?

Barry Beckham: Perfect logic.

Paul Coates: Yeah, that was the logic. That was really it. If I could do it before I went, then it would work.

Jodi Henderson: What was the situation with Black publishing back then?

Paul Coates: There were some presses that would do like how Barry got his book done. But most Black publishing was done more as an alternative to white publishing. I don't even want to say as a response to white publishing because it wasn't that at all. Our publishing was a statement. Most of the publishing that was done about Black folks was a statement about who we were and the times, and the fact that we had to publish our own stuff. Not as a negative, as a good thing. Barry, during that time, Haki [Haki R. Madhubuti][4] did a book. I don't know if you remember this, but it was called *Plan to Planet*.

Barry Beckham: Mm-hmm.

Paul Coates: And it was a chapter in that book—I had already decided I was going to publish when he did that book—but when that book came out, there was a chapter in that book that said who's responsible for publishing Black books. I think that was the title, "Who's Responsible for...", but basically what he was saying in that chapter solidified and verified that I was gonna publish. The bookstore was already established. The publishing company wasn't, but when that book came out, it verified it, because the question was like he was saying,

---

4 Member of the Black Arts Movement, poet, author, publisher, and founder/operator of Third World press; August 2,2022, poetryfoundation.org/poets/haki-madhubuti

"Italians don't wait for Black people to publish books on Italians. Jews don't wait on anybody to publish books on Jews. Germans don't wait; if it's a book on Germans, then Germans are going to publish the book. It's that clear."

So, who is responsible for publishing Black books? It was looking at the absence, if you will, of Black literature, but also the responsibility. And of course, Third World Press was stepping into that vacuum and saying, "Yeah, hell yeah, this is us. And we're supposed to be doing it, and we're going to do it."

It's not a question for me, but him posing the question still resonates with me, and it still motivates me to publish. So, Jodi, when you ask, what was it like at the time? It was like our declaration—and all the areas coming out of the '60s—was a declaration of "We're here to do this for ourselves."

It's an interesting period if you go back and look. Most of the national organizations that we know today as Black organizations, most of them were founded in the sixties. Along this same period, the publishers, particularly the publishers, are a part of that same effort.

So, you look at organizations like the National Association of Black Social Workers, for example, which began as a branch of the National Association of Social Workers. The Black folks in it are heated by what's going on in the community, and they're demanding a voice of their own and for themselves. They come out of it.

The Association for the Studies of African Civilization comes out of the African Studies Association. Same time, same period. There's so many Black organizations, and many of them still exist today as professional organizations, that came out of the white organizations at that time. It was a reflection really of the Black Power movement. And that's what Black publishing was. Black publishing was the expression of that. So, you find presses like Third World Press in Chicago. You find presses like Broadside Press in Detroit. You have presses like Ahidiana, which was based in New Orleans. You have Jihad Press, which is Amiri Baraka; that's based in Newark, New Jersey. You have The East; that's based in Brooklyn. All of these independent presses came about at that same time.

I come after them. I'm following in their tradition and following on the examples that they've already set, and it's very clear to me, especially with the question of who's supposed to publish Black stuff. It became very clear to me that's what I wanted to do, and that's what I had to do.

Barry Beckham: Um-hmm.

Paul Coates: Even though it was already built into that George Jackson Program, it just crystallized it and said, "Yes, this is what we're gonna do."

Barry Beckham: Mm-hmm. Well, Paul, I'd like to jump in and say that your influence was greatly responsible for why, and how, I got into book publishing. I had thought about book publishing, and I had published one book when I started teaching at Brown called *The Black Student's Guide to Colleges*.

Paul Coates: Yeah. I remember that.

Barry Beckham: When Paul and I became associated, primarily because I was following after him, and he was pretty much a director, if you will, and a mentor. And a supporter of Third World Press.

Paul Coates: Mm-hmm. Mm-hmm.

Barry Beckham: At some point, Paul would bring together a group because he was the person that others would call to say, "Oh, we need to talk to some Black publishers." And Paul would gather us, invite us.

Paul Coates: Mm-hmm. Mm-hmm.

Barry Beckham: I remember being with him, Haki Madhubuti, and do you remember Wade Hudson?

Paul Coates: Oh, yeah. Sure. Just Us Books. Sure.

Barry Beckham: Just Us Books. He was starting a book publishing company just for Black books for children, and it was amazing. In many cases, I saw myself at Howard University, and I think at some point we were invited to City University, one school in New York, to talk about Black publishing. And there I was on the panel with Paul Coates and his associates thinking that well, I'm part of this group too.

I should say also that Paul has been very low-key about his participation and his leadership.

Paul, he's so revered that he has actually published, as a Black publisher in America, Walter Mosley. He and Walter became friendly, and Paul publishes Walter Mosley, which is what nobody in Black publishing can say in terms of noteworthy writers.

And so, I say that Paul was more than what he says he was and did more than what he says. He is still probably the oldest accomplished Black publisher in the country, as we speak.

Paul Coates: Actually, Third World is older.

Barry Beckham: Ah, okay.

Paul Coates: They're 11 years older.

Barry Beckham: Wow. Goodness.

Paul Coates: Yeah, so they were quite the inspiration for us, and that's the way it should be. It should be that we're bringing folks along.

The only other thing I would say with that is, there's another capacity that I have. I went away to graduate school to become a librarian. I did that because I was not going to be able to survive being this Black bookstore owner, this Black publisher. It's wonderful to have high ideals and things like that, but it helps to have a paycheck, and I'm sure Barry can agree with that.

So, I went away to become a librarian so that I could work, but by the time I went away, I had operated in the bookstore long enough so that I understood I always had this love of Black books, but I didn't understand and know the history of Black books. And I didn't know the books that made up that history. Opening the bookstore as I did, it was like on-the-job training for me because people would come in, and they would ask for books. I would do the research on the books, and Barry, oftentimes people would come in for people who were in jail. So, they would send their mothers, and their girlfriends, and their wives, and their children in, and they would say my brother, father, whoever wants this book and wants you to find the book. They would give me titles, and they would say things like, "It's going to be hard to find because the white man don't want us to have this knowledge." And I would do research on the books. Most often I would find the books, even if the title was different or something, but I would find the books.

That type of research and that type of searching led me to appreciate the books that have been published before our time. That appreciation is what led me to focus on publishing books that had previously been published. Hence you have a company called Black Classic Press.

Barry Beckham: Mm-hmm.

Paul Coates: So it was an appreciation of the books that had come before us, but it also was the tutelage by people who were in jail. Now you have to remember, we set up this book-store to serve them, but they educated me. They have. And they're the ones that were sending me, because I travelled, and I used to travel to wherever Black book repositories were to find certain books.

We didn't have the internet then, so I'd have to travel. I was either at the Schomburg, or I would be at the collection at Fisk; I would go to Atlanta University and use that col-lection. I would spend time at Howard's collection, where I ended up working after library school. But it was because they inspired me and sent me looking for these books that I was able to put together the strong appreciation of Black people who had used books for 200 years, and I'm going back to David Walker, 200 years to fight against oppression in this country, to fight against racism in this country, to fight against slavery in this country. And those were the people who I revered at Black Classic Press.

Let me just say one other thing on that. So, I'd already

had the name Black Classic Press when I went to library school in Atlanta. It was in Atlanta that I knew the name was going to be Black Classic Press. We were sitting around the table at a lunchroom. I had some friends there, and they were introducing me to people. I'd been introduced as a publisher. I only had *Survey Graphic*. I only had one book out. And so, I'd been introduced as a publisher, and one of the brothers said, "Okay, so what is the name of your press?" And I said, "It's Black Classic Press." And he broke out, he said, "Black Classic Press. I love that! Niggas got classics too." And in that moment, he had it.

And I knew that was going to be the name because that really is what Black Classic Press meant to me when we set it up. It meant that white folks have a canon of literature, and that Black folks are entitled to have a canon of literature also. And we get to say what that literature is. We get to say who we are; we get to express ourselves.

To do that, we've got to have our own presses. I cannot be expressing myself dependent upon whether white people are going to publish me or not. Or publish the books that I find value in. Those books have to have a life that's independent from somebody white saying that those books don't have value. When those brothers were telling me that the white people didn't want them to see these books, and they were hiding the books or they destroyed the books, it really wasn't that. It really was that the white people had made economic decisions about what gets published, and they should make those decisions. But then, Black people should make decisions about what's important to them. That's what I understood. And that's what that brother I'm telling you about understood. So, the name was fixed after that.

Jodi Henderson: What was the reception like in the Black community? You're talking about publishing stories and books.

Paul Coates: Tiny, tiny reception, and it still is. But for those who knew of it, it was enthusiastic. And it always has been. We're not Random House, so we don't have that kind of outreach, but it's just like that. People who see these books, they see a body of work; they understand what it is. And they understand that it's an independent press and an independent effort. Consequently, it's appreciated like I appreciate the books. It's that core. And that's all I need to be satisfied. I just need that core. I need to know that one generation beyond me, two if I'm lucky, will have access to the same books that I pulled together, that I curated, that gave voice to those people who came before me.

Given technology, it has become easier and easier to reproduce books, and those books get reproduced. So even if the people reproducing them don't have the value, if they simply understand that those books will sell in our community, it's cool. It's really cool, because those books have another life, and in our way, we've helped to give them that life by identifying them.

Jodi Henderson: Barry, you mentioned that your social commentary grew out of what was going on in the sixties.

Barry Beckham: Yes.

Jodi Henderson: And the social justice movements, civil rights movements then, and Paul, you mentioned the prison movement. Those were social justice engagements. What do you see as a place for publishers in that larger context of civil and racial justice?

Barry Beckham: Well, if I can take another perspective. I had become fascinated with what we had produced as writers way before the 20th century because at Brown with, I think, five or six Blacks in my class and three of us Black males graduating in my class in '66, I was absolutely flabbergasted by the resources that this Ivy League college had despite the fact that there were only six of us in the class. At John Jay Library, they just had so much original material by Black writers that I thought, "I can't believe it. We never heard about this." And they would have the original editions of books that you can't find and didn't even know about.

I thought, "Boy, we've done so much!" And I think that was one of the encouraging circumstances that led me to think about publishing books by and about the Black experience. But my approach was, I guess having been in the Ivy League and seen my colleagues running up to Vermont for a weekend, skiing, and at least one student had a Ferrari driving around, that the answer was to be as big as Random House. And therefore, I needed huge resources. In order to get those resources, I had to take a different approach. I learned how to write business plans and learned about putting together projects, but it didn't work out, really. But I do remember putting together a business plan and even getting one of those loan guarantees from some shyster who advertised in the *Wall Street Journal*. They'd give you $500,000. You'd borrow the money; they'd give it back to you, and so forth. And one of my associates, a major publisher who was helping me out, said, "Yeah, I called that bank to find out about the guy who's gonna give you the money. He's a teller. He can't give you any money."

Paul Coates: [laughter]

Barry Beckham: I thought, "Okay. I still need a business plan." I was actually going to buy a company based on the fact that one of my associates was a venture capitalist, and he said, "You want to do publishing, and we've got the money. So, we're going to give you the money to buy other companies. We'll hold on to them for about 10 years, and they'll be worth so much that we'll sell them." That's where I got the name Beckham Publications Group, because we were going to own so many other publishers we had bought.

Several problems there. First, we couldn't find any companies that were in the $20 million range because the venture capitalist needed small companies that were making $20 million. And then if he got five of those, he could sell them for millions. That never worked out.

But one of the telling responses I got as I'm running around, trying to find money to be larger than Random House, because I wanted to publish all of these books, not one at a time. I sent the business plan to a consultant. He sent the plan back in 24 hours and said, "You don't have a publishing company; you have a project." And that's when I realized, "Yeah. Okay. That's what people are thinking, is that I don't have a publishing company. I've got one book called *The Black Student's Guide to Colleges* that got lots of response from the educational and African-American world. But that's all I have, plus an idea that 'darn it,' as Paul has expressed, 'we needed it. We needed a company that expresses who we are without having to say can we?'"

I should add also that my first book published was *The Black Student's Guide to Colleges.* Took me seven years to run after large houses in New York, before it occurred to me that it's not going to happen. I became so frustrated before finally EP Dutton offered me a contract, and then that contract could not continue for a new edition because they didn't want to support me financially.

Believe it or not, some fraternity brothers said, "You know we need a publishing company. Why don't we invest in you, and we'll go ahead and make your company the house that's going to be as large as Random House." I got enough money from the fraternity to do another edition of *The Black Student's Guide to Colleges* and had some other ideas, which I incorporated in my business plan that was sent around to everybody in the world, including the person who said "You don't have a company. You've got a project." He says, "You're not going to get anywhere trying to be a book publisher by and about the Black experience when you've only got three books and a bunch of ideas. If I were you—you're close to tenure at Brown—I would get tenure at Brown and keep that salary." And so, to say that my approach to publishing came about, because I thought, "We need this book. We need a Black student's guide to colleges" and no publisher in New York, believe me, thought that. They would say, "We've got Lovejoy's and we've got Yale, and we got others. We don't need a guide for Black students."

That's when I thought, "They don't think so," but as Paul would say, we need to make our own decisions about what we need. And my approach was, "If we're going to make our own decisions, we need to have a lot of money to fight Random House, as opposed to let's just do one book here and one book there."

That is what was slapped in my face as reality, that it wasn't going to work that way. And we still have no major, as far as I know, Black publishing company that is controlled by Black people and can even say that they're competing with Simon and Schuster. I think now we're down to about three or four or five publishers, thanks to Penguin, who I think has bought two or three other major houses.

One aside, we were talking about book publishing, but at the same time in the sixties, as all this was going on in New York City, there was a fellow named Ed Lewis, and there was Earl Graves. They decided that they had an answer for what we were trying to do in terms of representing the community, but they were going to do magazines. Earl Graves became quite successful with *Black Enterprise.*

Ed Lewis just finished his memoir four or five years ago about starting *Essence.* I still remember his describing how that magazine started and how it was difficult to find the money, particularly by, I think, four or five Black men whose idea it was to publish *Essence.* At one point, the hilarity and absurdity even got more telling when I read that the first idea for Black men who decided that America needed a magazine that reflected the life and desires of Black women, that they were going to call it *Sapphire.*[5] And one of the female advisors who heard that fell out laughing. She said, "No, you can't have a Black magazine for women called *Sapphire.*" They were doing a whole different approach to answering the question that Paul and I and others were trying to answer, which is what can we publish that represents and reflects who we are and

---

5 Sapphire Stevens was a caricature character from the *Amos & Andy* radio show; "The Sapphire Caricature portrays black women as rude, loud, malicious, stubborn, and overbearing. This is the Angry Black Woman (ABW) popularized in the cinema and on television." https://www.ferris.edu/HTMLS/news/jimcrow/antiblack/sapphire.htm last accessed 2 August 2022 11:08AM

what we want to be and what we want. We were looking at books. Ed and Earl said, "We're going to go for the magazine approach." And they were businesspeople. They were in love with making money, and they figured out that they could make some money by publishing magazines for Black businesspeople and Black women. And they did. And they still made 10 times more in a few years than Paul and I may ever make.

Paul Coates: Barry, Barry, speak for yourself, please, 'cause they probably made a thousand times more than Paul made. Maybe they made 10 times more than you, but a thousand times more than me, okay?

Barry Beckham: Yeah. Well, I used to have a statement when people would ask me about how we're doing. I'd say, "Ah, we did okay. We're only $4 billion less than Simon & Schuster last year."

Jodi Henderson: I have a couple more things that I want to ask about banning books. There's always been book banning, but it seems to have ramped up recently. And I just wondered if either of you have thoughts on that.

Barry Beckham: I don't have anything to say about it except that the sad part is that it's part of the culture that the division of the races in this country has been so exacerbated. Of course, it's something that doesn't make much sense in terms of a democratic society, but it doesn't surprise me. I look at that and so many things that's going on in this country and say, "that too will change." But the whole idea is absurd.

Paul Coates: Yeah. I think it's a misnomer—it's too easy, and it hides the villain to talk about book banning. When you say banning or book burning, the person that's doing it, even the reason they're doing it, is anonymous. It's hidden, and it's not understood. It looks like it's something that is just happening right now, so all we need is this temporary title on it. The truth of the matter is white people as a body, and I'm not speaking as an exclusive group of people, I'm speaking of representatively, white people who have oppressed Black people, or those who have had and shared that interest, have never wanted Black people to understand what was going on around them.

They were wedded to a particular narrative. Whether that narrative was that they were bringing civilization to the world, and consequently slavery was not bad, they wanted you to believe that. Anything that hid their real intentions of exploiting people, anything that hid the intention of lowering someone else and making someone else an Other who is lower than them, they put a name on it, and you were not allowed to change the name.

If you think about it, how is banning books any different than banning Black people from being educated? It's part and parcel of the same river. It's the same stream. And we're still wading in that stream. How is it different than saying we're not going to publish certain books because they don't reflect the things that we want to see?

It's not any different. So, I think when we talk about it as book banning, you have to talk about it as white racism. It is a fundamental feature of white superiority that its intentions be hidden from the people that it's being reflected on. But that's what oppressors do. Oppressors want to feed you shit and tell you you're eating donuts.

That's really what the deal is. They're not happy unless you say these donuts are good. But they're not going to eat them donuts. They're going to apply a whole different criterion to themselves. So, for me, leaving the name off, calling it what it is not, is dangerous for us.

We have to see it as a continuous act. What we're looking at is a group of angry parents who love Donald Trump; that's what we're looking at. But no, there's a history. This history goes back as long as Black people been enslaved in this country.

White folks have tried to hide their history. That's why that courageous group of whites, that courageous group of Blacks who fought against this and who are still fighting against it, that's why they're so important. But they're not fighting against book banning; they're really fighting against white superiority and white supremacy. So that's my take on that, yeah.

Barry Beckham: You know, Paul, one of the things that I loved about teaching one class at Brown, "American Literature from Mark Twain to the Present," is that in *Huckleberry Finn*, there's a moment when they have to think about what to do about Nigger Jim.

Paul Coates: Mm-hmm.

Barry Beckham: And they let him go. One of the statements I insisted on making in teaching that course and talking about thematic issues is that Mark Twain was, at the time, the only white writer who dealt with racism and did it with that scene.

Huckleberry Finn is banned because there's a Black man there, and he's got a little more freedom than he should, and it's not just Mark Twain talking about racism and the relationship to banning books, but it's also what about LGBT? What about the idea of sex itself? There's some banning approaches.

It's the idea that "there's something going on against what we as white men think is acceptable," and you could also say white men who are Republicans, "and that's what we're going to ban. And that guy named Mark Twain we're just going to dispense of him anyway. He's useless in our frame of mind." But Mark Twain is just an incredible example of how a man thought differently and wrote about it.

Paul Coates: Mm-hmm.

———————

Jodi Henderson: So, where would you like to see Black publishing now and going forward? Does it take on Random House?

Barry Beckham: I'm leaving it up to Paul now. I'm retired and not writing and not publishing.

Paul Coates: It's got to have a fierce independence. Because Italian publishing has a fierce independence. German publishing has a fierce independence, and whatever you want to look at. Publishing reflects the genius of a people. So, there's got to be a fierce independence and a center from which emanates works that are collaborative and workings that are collaborative. There has to be, I would think, a collaborative relationship at some point, but it can only be done once the center is secure. Here's what we're talking about at the center: a tradition of Black publishing. It doesn't matter whether Black Classic Press is here tomorrow. It doesn't matter whether Barry is here tomorrow. There has been a tradition of Black publishing that we're a part of, that people can look on, that people can draw from, and they can see the center there.

As long as people can see the center, there will be people that come to fill that center. If that tradition is in place, then there's always room for people to collaboratively lead that center outreach.

Some of the most successful books about Black people today are being published at Random House. And they're being published by a crew of Black people headed up by a young brother named Chris Jackson. Chris Jackson has produced book after book about the Black experience. And these are humongous sellers for Random House. That the whole conversation about being an anti-racist is Ibram Kendi. Chris Jackson produces both of his books. Chris Jackson produces the books for the brother that has the sanctuary in Alabama, I can't think of his name right now. He's the publisher of *1619*. He's the publisher of Ta-Nehisi Coates. He's produced all of Ta-Nehisi Coates's books, and Ta-Nehisi feels he can't live without that editor. That guy is working inside of a major white company, grooming talent and shaping talent and selling plenty of books. And he needs to keep on doing that.

At the same time, there has got to be a center. There's got to be a center for people like Walter Mosley to bring books to, for us to understand that we're responsible even if other people do publish it. Who's responsible for publishing Black books? We are. We're responsible for that stuff. So, when you ask "where does it go?", I see it as growing mature enough that it can lead, but not be dependent upon somebody having the last say over what gets published. Walter, for example, has published most of his books with white publishers, but we have a relationship, and that is to say "Anything they won't publish, Walter, you just bring it on home, and we'll get it published, okay. I don't care. And we don't care." It's important to have that center. And Barry, that's why Walter published with me in the first place, so that there could be the tradition that we represent in place.

Barry Beckham: Mm-hmm. Right.

Paul Coates: And that's it.

Jodi Henderson: Thank you both so very much.

Barry Beckham: Can I say one last thing? It's just a quick anecdote that has stayed in my mind. And Paul reminds me of it. Years ago, I was on the board of a magazine called *American Visions*; we had invited Walter Mosley to speak at a dinner, and he did. The director of the magazine asked me to drive Walter back to his hotel. We got to the hotel; Walter and I were talking, and he said, "So, you're publishing; you got some books coming along?" I said, "Yeah." He says, "I've got some things that haven't published. And I think you should call my agent. Here's her phone number." And I thought, "Is this really happening? Walter Mosley, who's with one of the large houses, just met me. He knows I'm a Black publisher, and he thinks I should look into things that he hasn't published yet." I thought that was, and I still think, what a tremendous spirit and a commitment to help someone who's in that area.

Paul Coates: He was very serious, Barry.

Barry Beckham: Oh I'm sure, yeah!

Paul Coates: He actually spent some time looking for what he used to call an independent press. You know, I didn't respond when he was looking initially, because I didn't see myself as an independent publisher. I saw myself as a Black publisher, and he never said Black publisher. He said independent publisher.

Barry Beckham: Right.

Paul Coates: We laugh about this today. You know what I mean? So, his thing to you was because he wanted to see Black publishing thrive. And that was the whole reason he published with me. It was precisely for that reason that he was looking to place that book somewhere. That there is a story that I often will recite.

We didn't have the money to publish it. This is the thing about large publishing, Jodi. You need a lot of money on every book, and one book is not going to make it. So, you can't just publish one book. We didn't have the money, when Walter gave me that book, to publish it properly. But we knew that we could find some money. So, we went looking for money, and we went to different places. And one of the places said they wanted to help with the book. This goes back to my earlier comments about being independent and at the same time collaboration. We were looking at white companies to collaborate with us. One of the companies that expressed interest was his publisher. We had a meeting with them, and it was at the end of the day. We had a room, and it was about, I don't know, Barry, maybe 10 or 12 white folks in that room.

There was me, there was Walter, and the young lady that worked with me as an assistant. We were the Black folks in the room. They were saying how they were going to help me do this book. I'm saying, "Damn, this is great, and they're going to do this, and they're going to do that." And in the middle of this stuff, Walter says, "No, y'all not doing that. Y'all not doing that because what you're doing by doing that is you're taking control from him. And the whole reason I selected him was so that he could have control. So that he could learn how to do this."

They wanted to control the negotiation of the international rights. They wanted all of the rights; they wanted to control that and keep it in-house. The distribution, they were going to keep that in-house. And Walter wanted me to have an experience of doing that stuff. He didn't care whether we made money. He wanted me to have an experience of doing it. So, he told them, "Nah, y'all not going to do that."

Now this is his publisher, who he's under contract with. And he basically is cussing them out and saying, "Look, y'all have the money. Y'all can keep that shit. You can keep it. If we have to stand on the corner with tin cans and beg for the money to publish this book, he's going to be able to do it. And he's going to have the whole experience doing it." And I'm sitting in the room saying, "Damn, bwah, why are you messin' up with the money?"

But he was so fierce. He was so fierce in this room of the people who theoretically controlled his money. He didn't care. He really didn't care. He was fighting for something larger. And that larger was that center that I was talking about, that independent Black publishing that I was talking about.

I will never compete with Random House on a book. But they could never get in the space that I'm in. You know, if they have all the money in the world, they will never get in this space. If the two of us are walking through the Black community, people will know the difference. And that's just that.

They can never own this. I can't own them; they can't own this space. And as long as I have life, as long as I breathe, as long as I can make it happen, the company that I'm affiliated with, the company that I've spent this time with, Black Classic Press, will be in that center and occupy the center.

LITERARY REVIEW OF THE WOKE 2019-2021

By Leah Creque, Ph.D., *Associate Provost of Pedagogy and Assessment, Morehouse College, Atlanta, GA*

There has been such tremendous growth in the production of African American literature and non-fiction during the two decades of the twenty-first century that cultural historians may soon designate the phenomenon with a name equivalent to preceding twentieth-century literary movements such as the Harlem Renaissance and the Black Cultural Movement—the book ends of the Civil Rights Movement. Amidst the backdrop of an entrenched popular culture of hip-hop and its bold rhythmic expressions, new writers penned the quest for social justice in a twenty-first-century context of modern-day slavery and the consequences of America's capital offense of 400 years of slavery.

It should be noted that this literary movement peaked precisely at the 400th anniversary of the 1619 arrival of the first African slaves in America and of the ensuing legacy of institutional racism. A very aware and literate citizenry of African Americans observed this somber anniversary and proclaimed themselves "woke," a term for being awake that comes from the hip-hop lexicon. The textual literacy that was denied to African Americans throughout history was broadened beyond text in this new iteration, extending to accessible electronic and digital media that brought global exposure to the plight of African Americans.

SLAVERY AND ITS CONSEQUENCES

Literature has played a prominent role in the freedom struggle of African Americans, from slave narratives such as those by Gustavus Vassa and Frederick Douglass to the works of Phillis Wheatley, who broke the chains of illiteracy to pen the humanity of the enslaved. The prohibition of teaching enslaved African Americans to read and write was sustained in substandard segregated schools during the Jim Crow era and beyond to the present day in which most black students are consigned to neglected school districts. Even Vernon Jordan, the late-twentieth-century activist, acknowledged in his memoir, *Vernon Can Read*, the fundamental power and status he derived from being able to read.

As slavery ended and the struggle for civil and human rights ensued, great leaders such as Booker T. Washington, W. E. B. Du Bois, and many others emerged with iconic texts and manifestos of social change. Into the twentieth century, great literary and cultural works explored the emotional depths of black life in America, from the writings of Langston Hughes and Zora Neale Hurston to works by Gwendolyn Brooks, the first African American Pulitzer Prize winner (1950), and Lorraine Hansberry, whose 1959 production *A Raisin in the Sun,* the first play written by a black woman to appear on Broadway, won the New York Drama Critics' Circle Award. Paule Marshall provided a glimpse into Caribbean culture with *Brown Girl, Brownstones* (1959). James Baldwin's works spanned the post-Harlem Renaissance era to the twenty-first century, and Maya Angelou's best-selling poetry and memoirs became emblematic of the seventies and beyond. Sonia Sanchez, Amiri Baraka, Nikki Giovanni, and Toni Cade Bambara were among the well-known authors of the Black Arts Movement of the '60s and '70s who ushered in an era of black nationalism and the reclamation of an African identity. Alex Haley broke ground with the publication of *The Autobiography of Malcolm X* in 1965 and his later groundbreaking work *Roots* in 1976. In theatre, *No Place to Be Somebody* (1969) by Charles Gordone won the first Pulitzer Prize for an African American play; this was followed by the Tony Award for the Broadway play *The River Niger* that was produced in 1972 by Joseph A. Walker. Ntozake Shange's choreopoem *For Colored Girls Who Have Considered Suicide / When the Rainbow is Enuf* (1976) was nominated for a Tony Award.

Charles Fuller's play *A Soldier's Story*, produced in 1981, won both a Pulitzer and the New York Drama Critics Circle Award for Best American Play, and the Outer Critics Circle Award for Best Off-Broadway Play. Literary artist Alice Walker won the Pulitzer Prize in 1983 for *The Color Purple*, and Toni Morrison won the Pulitzer Prize in 1988 and the Nobel Prize for Literature in 1993, signaling global awareness of the import of African American literature. August Wilson dominated theater with such extraordinary plays as *Fences* (1985) and *The Piano Lesson* (1987), both of which won Pulitzer Prizes. MacArthur Fellow John Edgar Wideman became a two-time PEN/Faulkner Award winner for fiction in 1984 with *Sent for You Yesterday* and *Philadelphia Fire* in 1990. MacArthur Fellow Ernest Gaines won the National Book Critics Circle Award for *A Lesson Before Dying* (1993). MacArthur Fellow Octavia Butler's award-winning collection of science fiction novels, among them *The Parable of the Sower* (1993) and *The Parable of the Talents* (1995), earned her the Lifetime PEN West Lifetime Achievement Award.

While this progress in literature was occurring, wide readership of black authors was moving beyond the confines of the educated middle class. The Oprah Winfrey Book Club, established in 1996 as a segment of her popular talk show, promoted reading as a worthwhile pastime and contributed greatly to the awareness of African American authors. It could be said that the Oprah Book Club spawned the exponential proliferation of community book clubs in which girlfriend groups gathered in the homes of their friends to explore the latest texts. Prior to that time, membership in book clubs was the purview of upper-class women who would scrutinize potential members by income and class before voting on their suitability.

The consumption of black texts grew as not only an intellectual exercise of the elite, but also a middlebrow activity of popular culture that emerged alongside the dominance of hip hop culture at home and abroad. The era of the black author and new young black voices was clearly at hand, as evidenced by the growing number of African American authors on *The New York Times* Best Seller list and as winners of prestigious literary prizes. *Brother, I'm Dying* (2007) by prolific author and MacArthur Fellow Edwidge Danticat won the National Book Critics Circle Award; *The Warmth of Other Suns: The Epic Story of America's Great Migration* (2010) by journalism Pulitzer Prize winner Isabel Wilkerson was acclaimed on *The New York Times* Best Seller list, as was *The New Jim Crow: Mass Incarceration in the Age of Colorblindness* by Michelle Alexander (2010). *Salvage the Bones* (2011) and *Sing, Unburied Sing* (2017) by two-time National Book Award winner and MacArthur Fellow Jesmyn Ward were lauded in the literary world. *New York Times* Best Seller, National Book Award winner, and MacArthur Fellow Ta-Nehisi Coates, author of *Between the World and Me* (2015), has been proclaimed the new James Baldwin, and MacArthur Fellow Colson Whitehead's *The Underground Railroad* (2017) captured the imagination of the American film industry. Bryan Stevenson's searing portrait of the carceral system in America, *Just Mercy* (2014), was listed as one of the 100 most notable books on *The New York Times* Best Seller list and became an award-winning film. In 2018, Tayari Jones's *An American Marriage* was an Oprah Book Selection and made *The New York Times* Best Seller List.

These literary achievements notwithstanding, in 2008, America elected its first mixed-race president, Barack Obama, who was the author of two significant works, *Dreams from My Father: A Story of Race and Inheritance* (1995 and 2004) and *The Audacity of Hope: Thoughts on Reclaiming the American Dream* (2006). Obama also won the Nobel Peace Prize in 2009, which further extended his audience worldwide. His renown as an author and that of First Lady Michelle Obama for her memoir *Becoming* (2018) have continued beyond his two-term presidency with *A Promised Land* (2020), the voluminous memoir of his presidency.

The presence of a black president who was a published author did not assure the dream of a post-racial society, as police brutality and vigilantism against blacks continued to dominate the media. The Black Lives Matter Movement came about to spotlight the 2012 murder of Trayvon Martin and the successive 2014 murders of Michael Brown, Tamir Rice, and Eric Garner. In 2015, there was the murder of Freddie Gray and the dastardly deed of the Charleston church massacre, in which nine blacks were murdered during a prayer meeting by an avowed racist. These are only a few of the multiple atrocities committed without impunity during this period. In this regard, the Black Lives Matter movement sparked a new generation's interest in tactics of mass demonstrations of protest reminiscent of the Civil Rights Movement, but with its own brand of fearlessness. The comparatively small number of coalitions with whites in the Civil Rights Movement was augmented by numerous white protesters in America and a growing international population, with protests staged all over the world in solidarity with African Diasporan communities and other marginalized groups.

The term "woke" became a part of African American slang to connote the positive attribute of someone who, in this information age, is fully aware of the political and socio-economic climate affecting African Americans, and, moreover, is well-educated, remaining current on the literature about this subject matter. Hence, the proliferation of consumed literature that whites and others who embrace the term allies in empathy with African Americans find essential to become anti-racists. Carol Anderson's *White Rage: The Unspoken Truth of Our Racial Divide* (2016), a National Book Critics Circle Award winner, excavated the root of the tensions in this country.

This sampling of iconic black authors, which is not exhaustive, provides historical context for the foundation that was laid for public awareness at home and abroad of the plight of African Americans denied the simple American constitutional rights of life, liberty, and the pursuit of happiness, a plight that has persisted since the commonly acknowledged historic marker of 1619, when the first African slaves arrived in Virginia. However, there is evidence that the presence of Africans in the Americas as explorers and as cargo on slave ships preceded that date by two centuries.

Historian Ibram X. Kendi laid the groundwork in his examination of the 300-year history of African Americans in his book *Stamped from the Beginning: The Definitive History of Racist*

Ideas in America (2016), which won the National Book Award. In 2019, his book *How to Be an Anti-Racist* (2019) topped *The New York Times* Best Seller List with clear definitions, categories, and evidence of prejudicial practices. Kendi explored this terrain again with co-editor Keisha N. Blain in the 2021 publication *Four Hundred Souls: A Community History of African America 1619-2019.*

Nikole Hannah-Jones, a MacArthur Fellow (2017) and an award-winning journalist for *The New York Times Magazine*, published *The 1619 Project*, a special issue to commemorate the 400-year anniversary of the 1619 arrival of the first slaves in America. The issue, which is an anthology of literary and cultural meditations on the grim anniversary in a variety of genres, was widely disseminated beyond subscribership to *The New York Times* to schools, colleges, and organizations. The digital version was made readily accessible as well.

The centerpiece of this special issue was Jones's essay that asserts that African Americans not only built this country with manual labor, but were also the architects and defenders of American democracy. Although Ms. Jones won the Pulitzer Prize for this work in 2020, and it was published as a book in 2021, the exploration of American racism that was first put forth in her essay caused a firestorm in American public debate that still rages in public policy and arguments about critical race theory and its appropriateness in school curricula. The Republican who was president at the time reacted by issuing an Executive Order banning federal support of programs, conferences, research, and so forth that provided training on America's systemic racism. Nikole Hannah-Jones's searing essay also affected her career as a professor of journalism at the University of North Carolina Chapel Hill, as the

Board of Trustees exposed themselves as racists by denying her tenure. Undaunted, Nikole Hannah-Jones left UNC to assume a tenured appointment at Howard University with an endowed chair.

The stunning historical marker of the second decade of the twentieth century is the death of George Floyd due to police brutality on May 25, 2020. Mr. Floyd's death brought forth a spontaneous international response of solidarity with African Americans' racial victimization by law enforcement and vigilantes that had become increasingly more prevalent with the preceding deaths of Ahmaud Arbery (February 23, 2020) and Breonna Taylor (March 13, 2020). Floyd's death was a watershed moment that sparked an unprecedented outpouring of global support from people from all walks of life who were united in misery by the global COVID-19 pandemic as well.

Despite the recommendations of quarantining and social distancing, people from all over the world, mostly young, took to the streets in massive protests. Law enforcement could not contain them. Though peaceful in intent, these protests sometimes erupted into violent confrontations with police and were infiltrated by troublemakers who committed the crimes of looting and destruction of property. All over the world, there were defiant acts to dismantle the statues of historic persons who promoted slavery and colonialism and upheld racist beliefs.

As if on cue, Isabel Wilkerson published *Caste: The Origins of Our Discontents* in August of 2020, though this book had long been in the works. This thoroughly researched work provided a vocabulary unfamiliar to most to uncover the roots of American racism and its long-term effects and manifestations. Again, Ms. Wilkerson's work topped *The New York Times* Best Seller list, and this book was the Oprah Book Selection for the Fall of 2020.

The wide reception of African American authors continued with the announcement of the 2020 Pulitzer Prize winner for fiction—Colson Whitehead's *The Nickel Boys,* which renders a story about the tragic lives of black boys in reform school—and the winner for poetry—Jericho Brown's *The Tradition*, which explores love, relationships, race, and sexuality in a new poetic voice. Reginald Dwayne Betts's *Felon: Poems,* which laid bare his emotions about incarceration, won the 2020 American Book Award. *The Dead Are Arising: The Life of Malcolm X* by Les Payne won the 2020 National Book Award for its in-depth treatment of Malcolm X's growth and development. Ta-Nehisi Coates's book *The Water Dancer* (2019) broke ground as a unique blend of Afrofuturism and magical realism.

The election year of 2020 was hotly contested. State of Georgia gubernatorial candidate Stacey Abrams, though unsuccessful for her bid, surprised many as she became a formidable foe to get out the democratic vote. Her success as an author did not wane as she published her tenth book, *Our Time Is Now: Power, Purpose, and the Fight for a Fair America* (2020). After the election, Abrams published a masterful work of political and legal intrigue, *While Justice Sleeps* (2021), which was number one on *The New York Times* Best Seller list. Many attribute the election of Democrat Joseph Biden to her tenacity.

Yet the insurrection at the U.S. Capitol dampened the spirits of this victory. Could we have foreseen such had we read *My Vanishing Country* (2020) by Bakari Sellers or *Long Time Coming: Reckoning with Race in America* (2020) by Michael Eric Dyson?

The Biden inauguration highlighted the poetry of Amanda Gorman, whose refreshing visage and vocal imagery provided hope and truth. Taking its title from that of the inaugural poem, Gorman's *The Hill We Climb* (2021) became a best seller prior to publication, as did her book of poetry *Call Us What We Carry*, published the same year.

The phrasing of Gorman's *Call Us What We Carry* aptly summons us to reflect and recollect the emotional and material artifacts that comprise our ethnic and national identity. In *All That She Carried: The Journey of Ashley's Sack, a Black Family Keepsake* (2021), historian Tiya Miles transports that theme literally through her narrative rendering of a sack and its contents that were an enslaved woman's parting gift to her daughter as she was sold away, never to reunite. For this she won the National Book Award. In a similar vein, *The Love Songs of W.E.B. Du Bois* (2021) by Honorée Jeffers recreates a historic and lyric epic narrative of the African American sojourn in America from its nascent origins to the present, from the scraps of ancestral legacy and lore to the inscriptions of black authors and intellectuals of the twentieth century whose texts were the soul and spirit of the people. From these fragments emerge a whole people who carry painful memories that cannot be erased by the enemies of critical race theory; nor can they be so crippled that they cannot walk into a hopeful future.

It appears that America is "waking up." George Floyd's killer is in jail; Ahmaud Arbery's killers are in jail. We have vaccinations and safety protocols against COVID. Yet, we are still living in tumultuous times, amongst a deeply divided populous beset with a disease that will not abate. However, there is a growing movement to learn more about each other. There are attempts at community dialogues and small dinners to promote understanding. There are movies and music that gain attention and shift our gaze to the lives of people different from ourselves. But nothing is like a book to transport our hearts and minds into the lived experience of the author's cultural expression of truth.

BLUEPRINTS TOWARDS IMPROVED COMMUNITIES

An interview with Dr. Lawrence Edward Carter Sr.

Dr. Tina Davis, Assistant Editor, Journal of Modern Slavery

One of the people who has worked tirelessly to keep the legacy of Dr. Martin Luther King, Jr. alive for several decades is Dr. Lawrence Edward Carter, Dean at the Martin Luther King Jr. International Chapel[1] and Professor of Religion at Morehouse College in Atlanta, Georgia. In the process of sharing Dr. King's philosophy, Dr. Carter has dedicated himself to fostering a deeper understanding of peace, non-violence, and equity in the United States and around the world. As part of his work, he founded the Gandhi-King-Ikeda Institute for Ethics and Reconciliation at Morehouse College and created the exhibition *Gandhi, King, Ikeda: A Legacy of Building Peace* to celebrate the community that comes from humanity's efforts to foster peace and equality through nonviolent means. The exhibition, which conveys the lives and work of these three architects of peace, has been shown at more than eighty locations on six continents and has inspired the more than 400,000 people who have seen it. I spoke with Dr. Carter about how the ideas and actions of Gandhi, King, and Ikeda have influenced his work and how they can be utilized today as potential roadmaps to create better communities.

---

1 https://morehouse.edu/life/campus/martin-luther-king-jr-international-chapel/

From years of following the path of an extraordinary mentor, Martin Luther King, Jr., your own work for peace and justice has reached all the corners of the world. Today I'd like to talk to you about the *Legacy of Peace* project that you initiated and the lives of the three men the project portrays: Mahatma Gandhi, Martin Luther King, Jr., and Daisaku Ikeda.

I'm curious to understand how their values and practices can offer a renewed source of empowerment and inspiration at a time when the US and indeed the world is faced with much uncertainty and unrest.

So, when you look at American society today, where would you say it is with questions related to racism and inequity, and what changes have you witnessed and experienced from the days since you were young?

Having reached the stage of being an octogenarian, which means that I came into this world when Franklin Delano Roosevelt was president and just five years from his own death, I was born in the southern United States when segregation was well established by law. That was a world where Negroes, as we were called then, understood very clearly the hierarchical relationship in America that was established based on race, skin color, and the superficially visible.

I was born in Terrell County, in the town of Dawson in the southwestern corner of the state of Georgia. And the first five years of my life, I was in the care of my maternal grandmother, because my mother, who had me at the age of eighteen, had to participate in the Great Migration north because there were few jobs for Negroes in the South. My mother followed her sister to Columbus, Ohio while my father, John Henry Carter III, was drafted into the military because of the World War II.

And so, the first role model I had for how to engage with the world in my first five years was my grandmother, who transitioned at the age of 55. That was the reason I was taken from Georgia to be with my mother and aunt in Columbus, Ohio in 1946. I got introduced to segregation in several ways in Dawson.

Every Saturday, my grandmother and I went to town. Town consisted of one street, very short, and it was paved. In my community, all the other streets were not paved; they were dirt roads. On Saturdays, our first stop was the undertaker, because by dropping into the mortuary, my grandmother could find out who had passed in town. It was another way of getting the news because we did not get newspapers. And on that street were stores where my grandmother shopped, and most of them were owned by Whites. So that was one of the early contacts I had with White people.

When my grandmother and I were leaving the downtown area, we would go right back past the funeral home, which is on the edge of the downtown area, and there was a filling station next door. On one particular day, I spotted the water fountain outside the filling station on the sidewalk, and I asked permission for my grandmother to go and get a drink. She granted me that permission, and she waited for me on the sidewalk. And as I approached the water fountain, I noticed there were a collection of bottles sitting on the ground, and it puzzled me. I instinctively knew that it was for colored people, but I wanted to drink from the water fountain, which was cleaner. I decided that I was going to do that, that I wasn't going to put my lips on those dirty bottles. And so I did.

And when I returned to my grandmother's side, she put her hand very firmly on my shoulder and spun me around in the direction of the water fountain, and she said, "young 'un, don't ever drink from the White man's water fountain again. Always drink from the pot bottles on the ground." At that very young age, something in me rebelled. Resisted. And I said to myself, "I will never drink from those water bottles." I knew at the age of five that I was "born to rebel," born to resist the cultural status quo of the American South.

Now the word racism I did not hear until I got to seminary, that was in my early twenties. We talked in terms of segregation. Hatred for Negroes and the whole idea of being unequal was everywhere. There were no Blacks in department stores working as clerks or Black transit or bus drivers. I don't remember any Black cab drivers. And through all of this lack of opportunity, lack of a chance to advance, it was amazing to me how positively predisposed Negroes were at making sure Whites always felt good. In all my growing up years, I never heard any of my relatives ever say anything negative or mean about White people. Successful White Americans were viewed as the standard for excellence, whereas evil Whites were not mentioned in public or in family conversations.

There is a world of difference between the world that I was born into and the world that I encountered in Boston in 1964 when I went to seminary. We lived and were governed by our understanding of what we believe Jesus would do. Sunday school and church, and the Baptist Training Union were very powerful institutions in my life. And I very naively thought that all Christian churches, Black and White, were like my church, and that everybody who was a Christian loved everybody who was a Christian, irrespective of their color.

My second major shift in my life, after moving to Columbus, Ohio was our family moving to an integrated community in

1951, when I was a fifth grader. We moved across town from the east side to the west side to a community called the Hilltop. And so, I got introduced to a whole different culture.

I remember in the seventh grade, I was in a music class at West Junior High School on Powell Avenue in Columbus. The teacher asked a question and I raised my hand, but I was in the back of the class, and there were many students in front of me who also raised their hand. When the teacher pointed, I put my hand down because I thought she had pointed to someone in front of me, but they didn't answer. Finally, the teacher made it clear that she was speaking to me, but this wasn't clear to me because what she did was call me a name that I did not recognize. She said, "Larry, I'm talking to you, I'm pointing you out. You may answer the question." Well, my name was Lawrence. My mother named me Lawrence, and I did not know that Larry was a nickname for Lawrence. Nicknames is a habit, maybe of White culture. When I didn't respond, the teacher became angry, and I explained to her that my name was Lawrence. That's why I didn't say anything. When I got home and told my mother about what had happened, my mother's response was "I named you Lawrence. You did the right thing. I did not name you Larry." Cultural differences.

Another one is when Black people meet each other on the street, sometimes we recognize people on the opposite side of the street. It's very common for Black people to throw up their hand and wave and to give that recognition and to do it several times in the course of a day. What I noticed about White people is that they don't give that recognition in a dramatic way. They wait till they get right up on you and may wave their hand without putting it in the air, if they do that at all. If you don't understand the cultural differences, you'll think

"My God, these people really don't like me. They're really racist." But it's cultural.

I learned how in the presence of Whites to be humble, not to be too dramatic or to move too quickly because Whites seem to be full of fear around Black people, especially Black men. And if you're too dramatic, they might think you're trying to hurt them, and out of fear, shoot you.

My mother was always afraid to send me back to Dawson, Georgia, to vacation in the summer because she said I talked too much. And I remember she said that to me at the time Emmett Till was lynched. She held up *Jet Magazine* where his coffin was open, and you could see how badly his body was mutilated. She said, "I do not want this to happen to you, and that's why I'm not letting you go to Georgia this summer, because I would have to come down there with a shotgun and kill somebody."

These are some very real ways that things have changed.

Many Blacks got elevated to positions of prominence after the assassination of Martin Luther King, Jr., but they were elevated out of White fear. There's always been a feeling demonstrated in White America that if Blacks ever got power, many Whites believe we would treat them the same way they've treated us. And most Blacks do not believe that. It's a dangerous thing when one person tries to speak for a whole race of people, but from what I have observed about my people, they don't seem to spend any time thinking about revenge. They think about upward mobility, taking advantage of opportunities, and not wanting their opportunities limited.

We want to have the same opportunities, rights and personal freedoms, social freedoms, and religious freedoms that all non-Blacks have who call themselves Americans. That is why we fought so violently after we were emancipated by Lincoln, and then recruited to serve in the Union Army. We fought with undying determination under the courageous leadership of Harriet Tubman because my slave ancestors, newly-freed slave ancestors, were fighting for their own freedom.

This is where the whole idea started that it will be the Negro, African Americans, who will save democracy, because if the newly emancipated slaves had not fought on the side of the Union, historians believe that the North would have lost to General Robert E. Lee. By emancipating the American Slaves, Lincoln saved the Union.

So, the changes that I have witnessed are numerous. You cannot live in the United States, regardless of your experiences and how cruel they may be, and deny that American democracy has become more real over the decades, but it has been hard-fought and hard-won. It has not been achieved without our nonviolent struggle.

Democracy and freedom are not free, and they're not won once and for all. George Washington warned us against tyrants masquerading as public servants and MLK Jr. said we are still fighting for what should have been guaranteed us at birth. We have voting rights that the Supreme Court is trying to limit. We can live almost everywhere we want to live if we can afford it. We can go to school almost everywhere, if we can afford it, and if we meet the requirements, grade-wise.

Just a few years ago, no African American owned a tall building on the skyline of any major city. Most of the skylines were created by White millionaires. For a long time, there were no Black businesses on Wall Street. One or two may be there now, but considering our numerical size in the population, there should be many more.

Through my whole life, I have just witnessed a series of firsts. The first African American to do this or to get that. And most recently, the first African American woman to be elevated to the U.S. Supreme Court. These things are long overdue. Many White people were horrified that Barack Obama was elected President. Well, he's the forty-fourth President. And it's accurate to say that his being president two terms, which the Right tried to stop, is the reason Donald Trump was elected. It was a huge backlash which literally shocked the nation.

So, it convinced most of us that the changes that we thought had occurred in the White cultural conscious- ness weren't as numerous as we had thought. But we were astounded when Obama in 2008 carried Iowa and beat Hillary Clinton. That was something we did not expect, because we never saw White people doing that much homework on them- selves in public. The nation had no truth and reconciliation commission as South Africa did, which was led by Archbishop Desmond Tutu. No open discussion on race. So, we figured that White people experienced an inner transformation in large enough numbers to elect a Black president. And we knew we couldn't. So, we decided to vote for Hillary until the state of Iowa, which probably was among the least integrated states in the nation, in terms of having Blacks in leadership positions, certainly in political leadership. That state went to Obama! We had to reassess the situation. Maybe we did not know White people as well as we thought. It's so easy to proj- ect stereotypes onto people because of what I earlier called, superficially visible skin color.

We decided between Iowa and New Hampshire to back Obama. He won Iowa, but he lost New Hampshire. Hillary won New Hampshire, but then he had hope, and he won South

Carolina, and she lost. Then we knew that his being president was indeed possible, because hope was born in Iowa.

From the days of my youth, I can say, I would have had personally a hard time hating White people, because all along the way from the fifth grade to getting my PhD, there were significant White Americans in my life who expressed a sincere, genuine interest in me achieving all that I possibly could.

It started in the fifth grade when a White teacher by the name of Josephine Clark discovered that I could not read well and kept me after class and asked me would I like for her to teach me how to read. If you could have seen the grin on my face when I heard that. The secrets were about to be revealed to me, because we had a little red bookcase at our house, full of books, and all I could do was look at the pictures. I was just as miserable as I could be because the secrets were not coming to me. So, she stayed after class every day for a long time, and I remember saying to her, "You're going to stay after school for me and not go home to your family?" And she said, "I sure am." Oh my God, you have no idea of how happy she made me. She was about to open up the world to me. But I had teachers in high school who said they didn't know how to teach me how to write, and they were English teachers with master's degrees from the great universities. I couldn't understand that, and I later thought, this is an example of racism, because they were teaching the White kids.

I brought that whole attitude to Morehouse College that I would never tell a student that I could not teach them. And so, I try to make things as plain and as clear as I can.

I have witnessed so much happen, nationally and internationally. But the biggest thing was the election of Barack Obama and Dr. King's magnificent nonviolent leadership.

How has your mentor, Martin Luther King, Jr., helped shape your life and your work?

By his example, his actions, his self-initiative, his preparation, his writings. Academically, he graduated from Morehouse College with a C average, but he graduated from seminary at the top of his class. His appreciation for language, words. And he used them in a powerful way to get through our defenses and our weak arguments. He had a transformative effect.

I met him four times. He was very humble. Very unassuming. Very regular. He was not pretentious or arrogant. In stature, he was not very tall, but he never gave the impression that he was coming from a place of inferiority, unless you wanted to attribute sometimes when he was speaking, he would stand on his toes. But when it came to the mic, he was a giant. And he was a giant not just because of his ability to communicate, to describe complex issues and causes and point to solutions that were a win-win for Negroes and for our oppressors.

He clearly had a very high self-esteem, and he transmitted, conferred, and bestowed something positive on everybody he met.

He was not condemnatory in the sense of demonizing difference. King could see pathology and schizophrenia in the American psyche and how we were founded. Beautiful words on paper in the nation-state papers of the founding fathers, and he could see the contradiction of how they were not living up to their own self-acknowledged ideals. These contradictions had plagued us, the whole nation, right through all of his days, even up until today.

Dr. King referred to racism as that hound of hell that was not just local and national, but unfortunately global, and that had to be rooted out. He demonstrated not a violent, but a non-violent approach. The thing that you were seeking, the thing you wanted, had to be reflected in the means that you used.

He did not believe like Frederick Douglass, "by any means necessary." He believed that the means you used and the ends you sought had to be a unity, not be separate.

So, he was a philosopher who I came to admire profoundly and I wanted so much to be like him, because I believed he was the closest I had ever seen of what the life of Jesus must have been like. I believe that Jesus was a prophet, and I believe that Martin Luther King, Jr. was a prophet.

We have many preachers, but we do not have many leaders in the pulpit who are as conscious as Martin King was of what the destination should be. He made this much more clear, understandable, and how we would get there. His blueprint was for everybody.

So, I tried to teach like him. I became very aware of my grooming. Sometimes this gave me great respect, and sometimes it didn't, but I never lost hope. There was never any doubt who my mentor was, because on the night that he died, when I was informed, it literally changed my life, and I made a commitment to do something significant for him before I closed my eyes. And I was granted two opportunities, one at Boston University, and now at Morehouse. For forty-six years, I have been working to help his cause. My achievement is much more tiny than his, but it is what it is.

When I got to Morehouse, I told President Gloster[2] that summer in 1979 that the Chapel has the wrong name. He was

---

2 Dr. Hugh Gloster was the seventh president of Morehouse College, from 1967–1987. He was chosen with the agreement of Dr. Martin Luther King, Jr., who was on the board of trustees at the time. Dr. Gloster was the first alumnus president of Morehouse.

startled and asked, "What name should it be?" I said, "the Martin Luther King Jr. International Chapel, not Memorial Chapel." So, he brought me before the trustees, and I persuaded them to change it. I told President Gloster, "If we are serious about Dr. King's dream, we have to think internationally. That means I don't just want a cosmetic change of the name, I want the name change to influence how we program."

That has taken me to thirty-eight countries speaking about peace and nonviolence, civil and human rights, freedoms and responsibilities. I am so happy, because I agree with Dr. King's vision in his last book and the last chapter of that book dealing with the World House.

As you mentioned, in his last book *Where Do We Go From Here? Chaos or Community*, which was published in 1967, Martin Luther King, Jr. wrote about the great World House that we have inherited where we all have to live together as a family, despite our differences in beliefs, ideas, cultures, and interests, and learn to somehow live together with each other in peace.

His vision of a free world free of violence and injustice was very strong. But at the same time, he was also pragmatic, which is reflected in his words, "We must learn to live together as brothers, or we will all perish together as fools." What did Dr. King mean when he spoke about the World House?

I think, for me, the primary thing that he was saying is our address is too small.

He was thinking about Jesus's question, who is your neighbor? And his response, I think, is correct. Now, this is interesting. If we are to answer this question in 2022, it means we are not just global citizens. When he talked about the World House, people primarily thought he was saying we're global citizens. That's what world commonly means. But today if he were here, he would be interpreting World House to be universe, cosmos. We are cosmic citizens. Why would he be interpreting World House cosmically? Because he was very oriented to responsibility and accountability, and he believed that responsibility checks freedom.

One of the reasons is that Americans and people internationally — no matter how many hurricanes sweep across the world, how many floods occur that the scientists blame on global warming — haven't believed it yet enough to want to do something about it. Dr. King would be emphasizing that by "world" he means "universe" and the cosmic community. Until people begin to see their address cosmically, they will never make the connection between themselves and the ozone layer, the stratosphere, and all the other spheres[3]. They will never feel that their human activity can influence climate change.

We are still struggling with a national identity: America, first. We were thinking more globally under previous administrations, but with the administration before President Biden, it drew us back to a political narcissism. Putting the United States at the center, we now know that we will "perish together as fools." We know this more today, because of COVID-19. The pandemic did not recognize any borders. No boundaries. And we needed the World Health Organization, the United Nations, any globally thinking institutions more than ever, because we were more dependent and interdependent on our global

---

3 Refers to troposphere, stratosphere, mesosphere, thermosphere, and exosphere. https://climate.nasa.gov/news/2919/earths-atmosphere-a-multi-layered-cake/

neighbors to solve the problem than we had been with any other problem that had hit us in a hundred years.

Dr. King was preparing us to get beyond nation-statism, beyond our neighborhoods being local. He wanted us to think of the broadest identification, with where we are in the cosmos. Look at what we just discovered recently. The American scientists shot a telescope a million miles into space; then they announced to us when the pictures started coming in that we were looking at 13 billion years ago; 13 billion years ago of history! It's hard to even wrap your mind around that. And yet, we are still speaking the language of "up" and "down" and "east" and "west" in reference to the sky. Oh my God, where are we? We are so infinitesimally small in the Universe. This announcement strengthens my belief in God because something is going on that the human mind has not yet comprehended. We are too local, and unable to solve our earthly problems without a bigger address.

How did Coretta Scott King play a part in your work and the actions that you've taken to transmit your mentor's vision?

Okay, I first saw her in person at the age of fifteen. She did a concert as a soloist in Columbus, Ohio at the Mt. Olivet Baptist Church. I didn't get to speak to her that day, but the next time I saw her in person was when I was the Acting Director of the Martin Luther King African American Cultural Center at Boston University. That was from 1971 to 1973. I traveled to Atlanta and went to her home to speak with her, but on that day, I discovered that she was not home. But by visiting her home and leaving the message as to who I was caused her early one morning, just past midnight, to call my apartment in

Brookland, Massachusetts. It frightened me, because usually when preachers get phone calls after midnight, it is bad news.

It was the operator who asked, "Is this the Reverend Lawrence Carter?" I replied, "Yes!" She said, "I have a collect call for you from Coretta Scott King."

If my teeth had not been rooted, I would've swallowed them. I was stunned. The operator asked, "Will you accept this call?" I said, "I will." She continues, "Mrs. King is not able to make telephone calls until after midnight when people are in place, and you'll have to wait thirty minutes, because Ramsey Clark, the Attorney General of the United States, is in front of you, and she's talking to him now."

Well, I had never heard that before or since. So, I waited, and she came on the line. After some preliminary remarks, she said that she wanted me to help her host the Board of Trustees of the Martin Luther King Center in Boston. And I agreed. And with all the activities, which included hosting Daddy King and Mama King and showing them the King Center at BU[4], and driving Mama King and Daddy King around town, the King family got to know me. Hence, when my name came up in the Board of Trustees meeting at Morehouse College to be the first Dean of the Chapel, Daddy King said, "Oh, I know Carter." And he told Coretta that the board had affirmed President Gloster's choice.

When I arrived that summer before school started, July 1, 1979, Mrs. King invited me to her house on Sunset Drive. That was where I had first tried to have an appointment with her that was unscheduled, and it didn't work [laughs]. So, the two of us sat in her dining room and talked, and in that conversation she

---

4 Boston University

challenged me to help keep her husband's legacy alive, and to make his philosophy a vigorously discussed issue.

I figured out how to do that for forty-three years. So that is how Mrs. King has played a significant role, and she supported me until her transition.

Why did you create the *Gandhi, King, Ikeda: A Legacy of Building Peace* exhibition, and was there a particular incident that motivated you to create the project?

Yes, the incident occurred on April the 20th, 1999. I was sitting at this desk where I am now. My phone rang, and the voice on the other end was a Morehouse alumnus clergyman by the name of Dr. Amos C. Brown, pastor of the Third Baptist Church of San Francisco.[5] He said, "Are you watching television?" I said, "yes." He continued, "So you've seen what just happened." I said, "I have." It was the Columbine High School shooting.

Then he startled me with the question "What are you gonna do about it?"

I had not thought so specific about what I was going to do. I held the phone back from my head and sort of looked at it, thinking that this was a question for Martin Luther King Jr., and he is not here to get that question. I am in his place. When I hung up, the question haunted me for the rest of the day. It really shook me. And as I walked around the King Chapel thinking about the question, I came up with the idea, probably not fully informed, that no one had really owned the nonviolent philosophy of Gandhi. And so, I decided to found the Gandhi

---

5 Dr. Amos C. Brown is also a civil rights activist and the president of the San Francisco branch of the NAACP.

Institute for Ethics and Reconciliation, and by so doing to begin programing more specifically about nonviolence and teaching it as a way of responding to the ever-increasing number of shootings that were occurring in schools and communities.

I thought that the King Chapel was the perfect place for this, and while I was planning for the inauguration at the end of the century, it got in the newspapers. One idea came from Martin Luther King Jr.'s sister—that I should make it the Gandhi-King Institute. So, I decided to do that. And then when we got in the newspaper, I got another phone call and it was from a woman I didn't know who was across the street from Morehouse at Clark Atlanta University's School of Social Work, Professor Ann Fields-Ford.

She said, "Is it true that you're about to do peace work?" Well, I had not thought about it as peace work. I was thinking about nonviolence, but the more I thought about it, I said, "Yes, it is peace work." She said, "Have you heard of Daisaku Ikeda?" I said, "no." "Have you heard of the SGI?" I said, "Yes, they've been here once." She said, "May I come to see you?" I said, "yes." And in a very short amount of time sitting at this desk, I heard, "Oh, wow, this is the biggest surprise in the AU Center."[6] I got up and looked out my office door into the Chapel library and there was Dr. Anne Fields-Ford. I said, "You got here very fast." We sat down, and she talked to me about the Soka Gakkai International and Daisaku Ikeda. And she said, "Would you like to know more?" I said, "I certainly would."

She arranged for a group of people locally to come to see me. And they brought a bag of Dr. Ikeda's books. We talked,

---

6 The AU Center is the Atlanta University Center Consortium, Inc., which is the world's largest consortium of private African American institutions of higher education. The Consortium is an NGO and operates on behalf of its member institutions: Clark Atlanta University, Morehouse College, Morehouse School of Medicine, and Spelman College.

and I interrupted at one point and said, "What do you really want?" And they said, "We want to establish a Soka Gakkai International Society at Morehouse or in the AU Center Consortium." I said, "Okay, we have other spiritual communities that have done that." This is very common across the nation in the academy. They said, "Would you like to meet some more of our leadership?" and I agreed.

I started reading some of Dr. Ikeda's books, and I was amazed. His writing seemed to be what I thought Gandhi and King would have been saying if they had lived to see the year 1999. So, when the second group came, they blew me away because they were from all over the United States: New York, Chicago, Miami, Houston, Los Angeles, and Tokyo. Someone flew all the way from Tokyo to see me. My idea of the Chapel being international was on steroids!

I thought that it was the universe telling me I had the right idea! Keep going!

I made the decision to broaden the Institute to the Gandhi-King-Ikeda Institute because I saw another opportunity for interfaith engagement since you had a Japanese Nichiren Buddhist, you had an African American Christian, and you had an Indian Hindu. Popularizing the global ideas of all three men, especially their exemplification of nonviolence and their embodiment of this power way of showing up in the world, has helped me to give a strong foundation to everything that I've done at the Chapel. It supports our interfaith assembly, our interfaith dialogue, my Christian Cosmopolitan theology, and that has been the most fun, finding the common ground between Hinduism, Christianity, and Buddhism around the world.

What do you see as the common thread in the lives of the three men: Gandhi, King, and Ikeda?

I see Ikeda as the long shadow of Gandhi and King. I believe if Gandhi and King were alive today, they would affirm everything that Ikeda has done and is still doing. He is in his mid-nineties. Dr. Ikeda became the third president of the Soka Gakkai International (SGI) in 1960. He started internationalizing what had been Soka Gakkai originally in 1960. It was five million people in Japan who were members of Soka Gakkai. Today there are 12.5 million people in 192 countries who are members of the SGI.[7] How did he do that?

Dr. Ikeda speaks one language, but with his ability to write, with the power of his pen, his publications have been translated into over twenty languages. Through his international travels, he has met and dialoged with scholars, experts, and authorities from a wide range of fields and disciplines on issues affecting our common humanity. Those dialogues have been published in hardback and paperback books. His genius is that he has been able to use his Buddhist philosophy to address global issues as Martin King used his philosophical theology to do the same and Gandhi used his Hinduism. He has published more than a hundred volumes on issues related to peace, the environment, human rights, women's rights, and more.

One of the most powerful things in my opinion that Ikeda has done for forty years, has been to send an annual peace proposal to the United Nations General Assembly, challenging

---

7 Soka Gakkai International (SGI) is a lay Buddhist organization. It was first established as the Soka Gakkai in 1930 and was established as SGI in 1975. Soka Gakkai stands for value creating society, and the organization's charter states that "SGI shall contribute to peace, culture and education. For the happiness and welfare of all humanity based on the Buddhist respect for the sanctity of life." Its members practice Nichiren Buddhism.

them to evolve, to mature what he calls the Parliament of the People towards bringing about global peace. These documents are very available on the internet, and they are brilliantly presented.

So impressed has the General Assembly been that they gave him their time-honored Peace Award from the United Nations. He's been nominated many times for the Nobel Peace Prize. He should have gotten it. Another thing that he has done is that he is the founder of two major state-of-the-art, world class universities. In 1960 he founded Soka University of Japan and a school system from the kindergarten through graduate school with schools throughout Asia. Soka University of America was founded in 2001 in Orange County, California.[8] It is magnificent. It is the first university in the United States to be founded on a pedagogy of peace. They are training their graduates to go into the world as ambassadors of peace.

So, to your question, all three of these men valued publishing, education, human rights, civil rights, and nonviolent practice. They did not make demands on anybody else that they did not make on themselves.

I think Ikeda has institutionalized the philosophies of Gandhi and King better than Gandhi and King did. He's carrying on their work at a higher level.

What was their motivation to work wholeheartedly for the sake of the people, even in the face of adversity and resistance, which all three of them have met?

---

8 Soka University is open to students from all backgrounds who meet the academic criteria.

The motivation was peace. What is peace? The wholeness of right relationships. At the heart of that is integrity, right relationships with yourself, with your neighbors, with your community, with the environment, with the cosmos, with all of nature. Today they all would decenter the person and they would center nature, because people are also nature. They would be highly influenced by the relatedness and the interconnectedness revealed in ecology. They all believe that life was meant to be beautiful. They all came from a personal place of do no harm, and they all believe that you can't have what you're not willing to be. So, they all wanted to show up a certain affirmative way in the world, and that meant that they had to work on themselves.

What would you say is the blueprint for living a life of nonviolence?

Gandhi, King, and Ikeda would all agree that the best life to live is an ethical life. They all are moral cosmopolitans, practicing cosmopolitan virtue-ethical options.[9] The ethical life is living a life that values all existence. The foundation of thinking is not reason. The foundation of thinking is value. If you can figure out what people value, then you'll better understand how they use logic and reason. What did Donald Trump value? Money, power, himself. So, you know what we've gotten, an insurrection. He didn't care anything about the law, nothing about the constitution, and nothing about the people around him.

The blueprints are values, virtues, ethics, and disciplined moral living. Nonviolence as a means. Respect for all life and overcoming personal anger.

---

9 Moral cosmopolitan involves seeing oneself as a citizen of the world, owing moral duty (commitment to help others) to everyone equally, and not just those close to you.

Dr. Ikeda focuses a lot on the need for inner transformation in order to influence positive, external change toward a peaceful coexistence. What does he mean by this, and how does it connect?

Now, this is very important, the need for inner transformation, which he often refers to as human revolution, in order to influence positive, external change and create a peaceful coexistence. Ikeda wants us to remember that spiritual work is an inside job, and everybody, he suggests, should move from making decisions from despair to making decisions from hope. Now here's the connection between that concept, which for him is Nichiren Buddhism, to what has operated among African American Christians, who said the same thing with different words. African American Christians would say we should work toward coming not from hopelessness, but from high expectations.[10]

White supremacists would have you believe that the Black situation is full of despair, hopelessness and low expectations. They would say they'd never want to be born Black because it's like saying they're eternally condemned. At Morehouse College, every commencement program has printed on it these words:

> There is an air of expectancy at Morehouse College. It is expected that the student who enters here will do well. It is also expected that once a man bears the insignia of a Morehouse Graduate, he will do exceptionally well. We expect nothing less... May you perform so

---

10 Despite their different backgrounds, Gandhi, King, and Ikeda all shared the belief that through the process of inner transformation, individuals have the power to change society, the environment, and the planet.

well that when a man is needed for an important job in your field, your work will be so impressive that the committee of selection will be compelled to examine your credentials. May you forever stand for something noble and high. Let no man dismiss you with a wave of the hand or a shrug of the shoulder.

Those are the words of Benjamin Mays, who was one of Martin Luther King Jr.'s most important mentors.[11]

For Mays, the chief ingredient in racism is low expectations. To overcome racism, racist mentalities that don't expect much from Blacks, all historically Black colleges emphasize for our students that regardless of how poorly they did in high school, if they got admitted to college, we believe the students can do what Martin Luther King Jr. did, go from a "C" average at Morehouse to the top of the class in graduate school.

The need for inner transformation means moving from acting from despair and hopelessness to hope. From low expectations to high expectations. If you're going to experience this inner transformation, you have to dismantle a deficit perspective. Put another way, if you're going to move from despair, you can't come from a place of feeling inferior.

Mr. Trump's presidency gave a lot of negative evaluations of Black people. The one most vividly that we recall was what he said about Haitians. He didn't want Haitian immigrants; he wanted them to come from Norway.[12] You heard me say earlier

---

11 Benjamin E. Mays was the sixth president of Morehouse College, and he is credited for laying the intellectual foundations of the American civil rights movement. Mays was also a Baptist minister, and Dr. Martin Luther King, Jr.'s admiration for Mays was instrumental in Dr. King's decision to become a minister.

12 In 2018, President Trump stated that he didn't want immigrants from places like Haiti, Africa, and El Salvador but instead wanted more immigrants from Norway.

SLAVERY AND ITS CONSEQUENCES

that in the fifth grade, I couldn't read. And a White teacher by the name of Josephine Clark offered to teach me to read. Not being able to read might be called a disability. The White teacher reframed it. That's what Black colleges do for students who are filled with low expectations. Reframe their thinking and self-perception. That's what for Dr. Ikeda is inner revolution through intentional acts of hope, which creates more hope. That's why historically, Black colleges are so necessary. It is not helpful that predominantly White schools are taking books about our history out of the library.

What was your vision for creating the *Gandhi, King, Ikeda: A Legacy of Building Peace* exhibition, which has traveled around the world?

I'll give you one sentence: to help people understand that these three exemplars—Gandhi, King, and Ikeda—led with their humanity, not with their race, their nationality, their gender, or with bombs. They led with their virtue, their character. You cannot practice ethics unless you exemplify virtue. You cannot practice virtue unless you're coming from a place of love. Love is not a virtue. Love is a norm that makes the practice of all virtue possible. Other norms would be integrity, justice, and courage, because you have to have the courage to practice virtue; you have to have the courage to forgive, and to love unconditionally.

Gandhi, King, and Ikeda are all firm believers and practitioners of nonviolence. And you founded the Gandhi Institute for Reconciliation at the King Chapel, which became the Gandhi-King-Ikeda Institute for Ethics and

Reconciliation . What do you believe is needed for a non-violent consciousness to take hold in the US and around the world?

Applied virtue-ethics, exemplars, and mentors. Healing comes from revealing. Being the thing itself. Taking it from the abstract to the concrete. People would rather see a sermon than hear one every day. Having a larger address.

We have too much structural violence, a Defense Department but not a Peace Department. We are in love with nuclear weapons and national security, but not human security. We don't trust the United Nations, but it is our last hope if we are to include the larger address.

And how do you believe reconciliation can happen in the US and in the world today to move society forward?

More diverse human affirmations on the internet and TV. Fewer hate posts on the internet. Less demonizing of people. Less use of the terms Black and White. Governments living up to the ideals in their nation state papers. Severe punishment of those who tried to institutionalize the limiting of rights. The Constitution is for expanding rights, not limiting rights. Many of the people under Donald Trump are being punished for January 6th. Our system will be in real trouble if Donald Trump is not held accountable. Being held accountable will bring about more reconciliation.

Here are some other specifics. Our government should do far more for the Native Americans from whom we stole their land. We should do far more than what we are doing for veterans of wars. I mean, they risk their lives. They and their families should be guaranteed education as high as they want to go, housing and pensions, all healthcare payments, because there's nothing good about war, but there's everything good about life. That kind of reconciliation would bring more people together to believe in their country, to get the government to identify with the people, and not just having the people identify with the government as a definition of patriotism. If we are the nation of the brave, then that bravery needs to be shown in how we treat each other, especially those who risk their lives. And as Gandhi said, if you wanna teach nonviolence to a nation, you begin with the children. Instead of having only armies, we need to have a Peace Secretary in the President's cabinet.

What would you like the legacy of your life work to be?

I want to be known as a moral cosmopolitan, full of hope and high expectations for all of humanity to achieve their greatest spiritual magnificence. I'd like my life to be a blessing to the world and to the cosmos, to all of nature.

How do you see your legacy as a continuation of your mentor's life work?

Well, I think that what I'm trying to do is institutionalize his work at Morehouse College. I want to institutionalize a pedagogy of peace. The King Chapel is the world's most prominent religious memorial to Dr. King. We ought to have a full program here that includes academic, vocational, pastoral training and more.

I've spent most of my time as an activist, helping people stay in school, raising money, staff salaries, scholarship money. I would like to put stronger foundations under the Gandhi-King-Ikeda

Institute for Ethics and Reconciliation. I would like to teach cosmopolitan virtue-ethical technologies, helping people understand that all theology needs to display an ethical edge.

Putting stronger legs under the Black social gospel justice tradition, which came out of Morehouse: Morehouse personalities helped to infuse this into the civil and human rights movement. This movement led by Dr. King influenced many other movements: the women's movement, the environmental movement, and strengthened the human rights movement.

If we were to take inspiration from the lives of these three men—Gandhi, King, and Ikeda—to help us navigate through the current challenging times, what would you suggest that to be?

Turning all our religious, educational and governmental institutions into affirmatoriums as exemplars of a needed love for people. You can't help people if you don't love people. I'm frustrated by what the Russians are doing in Ukraine, and what has happened all over the continent of Africa. How it has been exploited at the expense of the people. I'm very distressed over the scholastic racism and how European scholars have tried to take Egypt out of Africa and tried to suggest that Black Africans contributed nothing to world civilization. Nothing could be further from the truth.

I do believe the truth is going to win, but we cannot act like goodness is going to good itself into existence. We have to put actions behind all of our beliefs. I fear that I have not done enough in 83 years, and I have worked night and day. But I'm not hopeless. I do believe that Gandhi, King, and Ikeda's visions will prevail, because a lie cannot live forever.

TO HOPE, FOURTEEN YEARS LATER

Naje Lataillade

Fourteen years ago, I shed no tears. I was busy working. Keeping the subjects in focus. Checking the exposure. Framing the action. I'd been living outside of America for 7 years, and now I was back, filming the 2008 Democratic National Convention.

Fourteen years ago, I thought it was awesome that the Democrats nominated him. But the chances of him winning? That man, with that name? Barack Hussein Obama? Against military veteran John McCain? Still, Obama preached hope...

Fourteen years ago, that notion was beyond me. Just before I'd left America, the police murdered Amadou Diallo. And 7 years later, just before I came back, they murdered Sean Bell. Nothing had changed. Nothing would change. Hope was nice, but hope was powerless.

Fourteen years ago, I thought it was cute that my friends were throwing an election party. We knew Obama couldn't win, but it was fun to pretend. Then suddenly the world stopped. We looked around in disbelief... had it really happened? My sister called asking if this had really happened... We flooded the streets overwhelmed with the reality that it had really happened! Millions across the world rejoiced... it had REALLY HAPPENED!!!

Fourteen years later, far from Denver and that 2008 convention, I feel closer to these images and that moment than ever. The distance and time—and specifically the last four years—have given me a new proximity I hadn't thought possible.

Fourteen years later, as I sit here looking back at the images I took on that day, the tears run freely. Tears of appreciation for what was achieved. Tears of sadness for what has been lost. Tears of awe for what Obama symbolized. Tears of pride for who Obama actually was. Tears of reverence for the faces in the crowd that I photographed that day, many of whom had worked for years, or even decades, to make an Obama, a reality. Tears of shame, for doubting those efforts.

Fourteen years later, as I sit in a world seemingly growing ever more cynical, I understand that hope is not simply, nice. Today I shed a tear, understanding that hope is power.

THE SOUNDS OF FREEDOM

A dialogue on the poison of racism, the medicine of jazz, and a Buddhist view of life

Taro Gold

"Jazz is the ability to take the hardest realities of life and put them into music, only to come out with some new sense of hope or sense of triumph."

— MARTIN LUTHER KING JR.

Taro: Welcome Wayne Shorter, Herbie Hancock, and Esperanza Spalding. The underlying theme for our discussion today is the consequences of slavery in the United States, and the ripple effect of that horrible negativity from the past to the present. I'd like to begin, however, by focusing on the opposite, positive energy of freedom. What is freedom to you, as an individual and as a musical artist?

Wayne: One of my mottos in life is "zero gravity," which, to me, means freedom, means I won't let anything hold me back, and I'll keep striving to create something fresh and inspiring regardless of the past. The present moment is freedom to me, because it's the only place you can change your past and create your future. That's also a foundational concept of the Soka Gakkai[1] tradition of Buddhism that we practice.

---

1 Soka Gakkai International (SGI): A community-based Buddhist network for practitioners of Nichiren Buddhism with members in 192 countries and territories. The SGI promotes cultural exchange, education, and peace through personal transformation and social contribution. In Japanese, Soka Gakkai means "value-creating society."

I'm eighty-eight years old now, and every day I do my best to live with a youthful spirit, stay curious, and be present in the moment.

When I hear the word "freedom," I also think about the life force of babies. My grandson was born last year on my eighty-eighth birthday, and I see how he has ultimate freedom in his natural state, the freedom to go to sleep, cry, laugh, and let off what nature exudes from him. So, in the ideal state, all babies have that freedom, too.

But then adults start to move these kinds of freedoms away from the babies, hindering their speech and ideas and indoctrinating them in social ways and fairy tales, and something adults call "the truth." Whatever that is, of course, depends on the person who's telling it to the baby. And as the baby becomes a child and grows, a lot of the innate freedom that the baby has, or should have, has been stunted and cut off by adult human behavior.

Herbie: That's right. Babies teach themselves. They teach themselves to walk. To crawl. They teach themselves balance. You know, I totally agree with you that adults often push babies and children into a format that the adults are familiar with from their own history. And because we adults haven't learned to be free ourselves, it can stifle kids. I hope we're in the process of learning how to be better adults for the next generations to follow.

Wayne: You know, we adults could use some cognitive training on that. [*laughs*]

Herbie: [*laughs*] That's for sure!

Wayne: Anyway, when I think of freedom, I also think about the first time I went to Europe, after I got out of the Army. I was in a band called the Jazz Messengers. When we went to Europe, Art Blakey was the leader of our group.

He told me, in effect, "When you get to Europe, and you're playing modern jazz, and maybe the audience thinks it's such modern music and all that... don't try to teach and preach to the audience how much you know about music, don't flaunt how free you are coming over from the USA and running around in Europe. You're in Europe because you're free. You've been freer in your life than many of them have been, but they're not going to be moved by that. They won't remember all the little nuances you might want to drop on the audience, they won't remember things you want to tell them about the United States. The only thing they're actually going to remember is your behavior. Your behavior as a human being. Your behavior toward each other on stage, and your behavior toward the audience. It's all about behavior."

Taro: That guidance you received from Art Blakey is an important teaching in Buddhism, too, which says "The purpose of the appearance in this world of Shakyamuni Buddha ... lies in his behavior as a human being."[2]

Wayne: Exactly. Our behavior has the largest impact, because it shows who we really are. Another bookend to this lesson about behavior for me came many years later, when I was on stage with Miles Davis. Actually, it was a lesson in behavior as well as freedom and even democracy in a funny way. In

---

2 Nichiren, *The Writings of Nichiren Daishonin*, vol. 1 (Tokyo: Soka Gakkai, 1999), p. 852.

the audience that night—I'm not dropping names here, I'm name-lifting—was Sidney Poitier, and with him were Peter O'Toole and Richard Pryor. And of course those guys knew who we were. But there were a lot of people in the audience who had a question to ask us, they all asked the same thing, which really surprised me. The question was, "Which one of you is the leader?" Hah! [*laughs*]

We had gone from 1959 to 1976 or something like that and here people are still asking who the leader of the group is. Of course it was Miles, but the thing about jazz is, when it comes to freedom, leadership, and democracy, jazz is really democratic, because everyone has a voice. And we had made it so far up the ladder, our music was around the world, yet people still didn't know which of us on stage was the group's leader. We felt good about that.

Herbie: Yeah, that shows real unity and teamwork and respect for one another. Miles always demonstrated naturally so much respect for the musicians working with him that the audience couldn't tell who was leading. They expected the leader to stand out and to be up on a pedestal or giving orders or whatever. But Miles didn't do that. He would always push everybody else to the front of the stage and highlight them in various ways.

In my case, I couldn't move! [*laughs*] I had to stay seated behind the piano, you know? But there were other ways Miles would still do that, and highlight me, too. And so, we all felt like we were an equal team member and each free to shine. But we also felt his mentorship, because that's what a great leader does. He works in tandem with the people on his team.

Esperanza: I think the word "freedom" itself needs healing because it's been used in so many ways that have nothing to do with the actual liberation of humans, or the liberation of human potential from any kind of limiting belief or circumstances. So, when I think of freedom, I think about our responsibility to embody a healed version of the concept. And I also think of freedom not being contingent on anyone else giving it to you, which again plugs into this Buddhism we practice, that no one else holds the gateway to our liberation. We hold the keys; they are in us.

Herbie: In each individual person, right?

Esperanza: Absolutely. In every human being, whether they are Buddhist practitioners or not; every human being.

Herbie: Exactly.

Wayne: Yes! That's what I'm talking about.

Esperanza: So, I think that's part of the healing that the word "freedom" is asking for, to be liberated from the sense of something you must go achieve, or get, or even win, because it implies there's some circumstance that if it's altered in the right way, then you can have freedom. I feel like the concept, the spirit of freedom itself, is asking for a big healing and renewing to get more at the heart of the force of being liberated, of being free, being a spring that we can tap into. Maybe part of that is giving ourselves permission to tap into what is already there, to tap your innate infiniteness.

Taro: I know Miles was a very important mentor for you, Herbie, and Wayne, too. I'd like to ask all three of you, who have been your most influential mentors—the people who've served as examples in your musical journey and your spiritual journey?

Wayne: My first and most influential mentor was my mother, who taught me many valuable lessons and provided intellectually stimulating toys and tools to spark my imagination. She nurtured my curiosity and gave me my first musical instrument too, a beautiful clarinet that she and my grandmother got secondhand. She also gave me the belief that I could accomplish anything I set my mind to.

Then there was Achilles D'Amico, my wonderful music teacher at Arts High in Newark, New Jersey, who expanded my view of music and its potential. Later in my music life came Art Blakey and Miles Davis, of course, who both had their own wisdom. And most important to my personal life is Buddhist philosopher Daisaku Ikeda,[3] who has shown me through his own actions and through his written words in books and guidances how to live a life of indestructible happiness.

Esperanza: The person who comes up most strongly for me is Elder Malidoma Somé. Walking in Cambridge, Massachusetts, one day, I found myself wondering why I hadn't encountered any shamanic practitioners from an African lineage in my many years of researching and studying various healing technologies. I entered a store called Seven Stars Bookstore with this question in mind. My attention landed on a book that had

---

3 Daisaku Ikeda is president of the Soka Gakkai International (SGI), the world's largest community of Buddhist practitioners.

an interview with Elder Malidoma in it. Standing in the book-store and reading the first few paragraphs of his interview, I knew I had encountered someone who would become very important to me.

Learning more about his life and the worldview of his peo-ple (the Dagara people of Burkina Faso) has deeply altered and expanded my sense of the world, the role of artists within it, and my relationship to spiritual and community practice. I had the privilege of attending two of his workshops while he was still alive, and am forever impacted by his presence, depth of knowledge, and the grace and courage of the com-munity assembled to facilitate and learn in these workshops together. His teachings also moved me and inspired me to continue learning, because he orients his teaching in a frame that explicitly asks us Western students to acknowledge and address the roots of colonialism, often calling out how North American "spiritual-seekers" for the most part overlook our historical and present relationship—and obligation—to the very land from which we enjoy the privilege of encountering so many practices for supporting our spiritual development.

In terms of music, Milton Nascimento, Toninho Horta, Dr. Wayne Shorter, and Dmitri Shostakovich are some prominent figures coming up right now. Working closely and for many years with Leo Genovese has also had a profound impact on my musical sense and expansiveness. We've actually both worked with Dr. Shorter a few times, and feel like co-students in his vast musicianship and philosophy. I've also been greatly inspired and expanded by Geri Allen's work and approach to music making, especially the experience of playing with her, and feeling her kind spirit radiate in loving authenticity, despite the circumstance we happened to find ourselves in.

From her, I first encountered another form of feminine power, embodied and expressed on its own terms. She was a person who had divested—or was never invested!—in trying to make her value and power legible according to men's terms, opinions, or preferences.

Herbie: The most influential mentors in my lifetime are, musically, Miles Davis, and spiritually, Daisaku Ikeda as well. The freedom of style and teamwork that Wayne was describing about Miles is the same thing that happens with President Ikeda in the Buddhist philosophy that we practice. He works in tandem with all of us. That's the true spirit of mentorship.

I've been practicing the Soka Gakkai tradition of Buddhism for half a century, and I've found this practice is like jazz in that way. Also, both Miles Davis and Daisaku Ikeda share the spirit to raise many capable people, encouraging those they mentor to find their own answers in life. They've also taught me to reach up while reaching down, to grow while helping others as well.

There's one more thing I want to mention about freedom. And that is, life is full of opportunities and also challenges. Most people are afraid of the challenges. Or more specifically, afraid of the suffering that they perceive comes along with challenges. Nobody wants to actually suffer, consciously. But freedom—and I've learned this from Wayne, he captures it beautifully—true freedom is to not be afraid of the obstacles and the challenges or the sufferings, but to join forces with them and to understand that we can learn a lot from our challenges. Learning the way to turn the obstacles into benefits, that's also a fundamental principle in our Buddhism.

It's called the principle of "changing poison into medicine." When you can learn to change the "poisons" in your life into "medicine," to transform the energy of the obstacles into a source of strength, growth, and benefit for you, that's real freedom. If you develop yourself to the point where you have a complete realization of that power within you, that alchemy, and believe in yourself, then that's real freedom. Then you're not bound by anything, not bound by positives or negatives, by benefits or obstacles. As Wayne says, you make both of them your allies. Make both the positives and negatives in life your allies.

Wayne: Yeah, that's a good point, Herbie. You know, when I talk about that, I used to always use the analogy of how an airplane needs resistance from the air to get off the ground. But some people have a hard time imagining themselves as the airplane. So, here's another analogy. Say you're in a row-boat. In that case, the resistance is actually the water. How do you use that resistance to make the rowboat move—paddle! [*laughs*]

And from that, you can extrapolate so many examples. But you get really tricky ones sometimes, like people will ask me, *Well, what do you do when the "resistance" is a difficult person to get along with, like a boss or supervisor, or in-laws, or something like that. Where's my paddle in that scenario?* And that's when I say, it's chanting Nam-myoho-renge-kyo.[4] I've been chanting nearly fifty years now, and I know for sure that you

---

4 Nam-myoho-renge-kyo: Buddhism teaches that we have within us the enlightened capacity to transform any suffering. Nichiren, the 13th-century Buddhist reformer upon whose teachings the Soka Gakkai is based, awakened to this capacity and taught that anyone can manifest it by chanting "Nam-myoho-renge-kyo," the title of the Lotus Sutra. **Nam** comes from the Sanskrit *namas*, meaning to dedicate oneself. **Myoho** means "Mystic Law," expressing the fundamental life force of the universe. **Renge**, meaning lotus flower, is a metaphor—the lotus blossom is pure and fragrant, unsullied by the muddy water in which it grows. Similarly, the beauty and dignity of our humanity can be brought forth by chanting Nam-myoho-renge-kyo amidst the challenges of daily reality. **Kyo** indicates sound vibration and the teachings of Buddhism.

can manifest your inner wisdom, to find that paddle you need, find the way to transform the negative to a positive, to harness the resistance to lift yourself up, go higher, and never give up.

Herbie: That's total freedom. Then you're not afraid of anything, you're living a life without fear. "Be fearless," like Wayne so often says, right?

Taro: Yes, Wayne has encouraged me through difficult times with those exact words. "Be fearless!" and "Never give up!"

Wayne: In the SGI Buddhist community, we say "What is the meaning of faith? Faith is to fear nothing." And yes, never, ever, give up.

Taro: Like Duke Ellington said, "There are two rules in life. Number one: Never give up. Number two: Never forget rule number one."

Wayne: Precisely! I love wearing my T-shirts that say "Never Give Up." It's a hopeful motto that's timeless, too.

Taro: Esperanza, you often wear clothing with the words "Life Force" on them. What does that mean?

Esperanza: If you were always showing up on behalf of a company, you want people to know you were representing that company, and maybe wear the company logo on your shirt when you go out. For me, wearing "Life Force" is a way of reminding myself what I'm showing up on behalf of. This is the energy, the field, the strategy, the association that I'm affiliated with. I'm intending to show up as an emissary of Life Force.

Taro: Jazz is known around the world as "the music of freedom." Why is it called that, and what do you think gives jazz its universal appeal?

Herbie: Those questions, and the underlying topic of slavery and its effects over time, this all makes me think: What did the enslaved people do? How did they create internal freedom without external freedom? How did they respond to the evil and the negativity?

They created songs. They invented what evolved into gospel music. And gospel led to the blues, and they expressed their feelings about what was happening in their lives. In other words, none of us jazz musicians would be here—Wayne wouldn't be here, Esperanza wouldn't be here—had that not been our path out of the evil of slavery. Black people took the path that they took, which is through the arts. It wasn't called that per se, but that's what it became. The art of gospel music comes from the soul, and the blues definitely comes from the soul. If it weren't for soul music, there'd be no rock and roll. If it weren't for blues players, there would be no jazz. The blues, that's older than jazz. We know Wayne Shorter developed this great legacy throughout his whole life. But if a different path had been taken by the enslaved people, would there be any of our arts in soul music, blues, jazz?

And look at what happened in the 1920s, with the jazz age. Who built the foundation for that? Enslaved people. The jazz age affected not just America but the world. Jazz went to Europe and later throughout the entire world. I mean, the whole thing was a game changer for the musical arts. That's a profound legacy of enslaved people who tapped into their inner freedom, deep within themselves, and gave the artistic expression of that freedom to all of humanity.

That shows the value of being able to take the worst of circumstances and find a way forward, despite those circumstances. Now, *that's* changing poison into medicine!

Wayne: When you see jazz musicians playing on a stage, you never see one person doing everything. You don't really have an obvious leader, as we talked about. You may have a bandleader, especially in the old days, because of the music union laws and labor laws, and the way money was transacted, there had to be a bandleader. But when you are playing, you can see different people stepping out front speaking their piece, as we say, putting in their expression of what they want to get across. There's freedom in that, too, as well as in the way jazz is composed and performed to begin with.

In classical orchestra, you don't have individual musicians popping up to express themselves freestyle. You know, it's more like a solid mass of musicians, and you watch the conductor doing their thing and waving around. That's beginning to change a bit—certain orchestras don't have conductors now like the Orpheus Chamber Orchestra, and some others. But anyway, I'm getting a lot of feedback from Europe about orchestras and ballet companies, and they want to go at it like we do in jazz, they want to express themselves as individuals as well as with the group.

So, jazz has been having that "freedom" effect on other categories of music too now. In the early days, in the 1930s and '40s, a lot of people in America knew that jazz was about freedom of expression, so the uptight ones tried to resist it, tried to stop it from being played on the radio to limit record sales. They didn't want their children to hear what that kind of freedom was like on the radio, or see what it was like on television. Unless they could find something to make fun of, like having jazz players do minstrel songs and wear degrading makeup and all that, what do you call it?

Herbie: Blackface makeup and actually, sometimes, white-face makeup.

Esperanza: I'm thinking about what Wayne was just sharing about these European orchestras and companies reaching out and wanting to connect, and it makes me think of human beings around the world who are longing for a blueprint for transforming poison into medicine. And I feel what Herbie was speaking about, this alchemy, this profound alchemy for liberation within seemingly insurmountable circumstances. Right? I mean, that's an expression of freedom.

I heard you just describe people developing a pathway for their own artistic freedom, even if it was just with their voice in song, or a moment of sensing of who they were, creating freedom out of no freedom. It's hard to find examples of that in the world, like really embodied examples of transforming poison into medicine, and it makes me think that when people around the world heard jazz music, whether they were aware of the history or even aware of who was playing it, I imagine that their spirits felt that energy, they felt the blueprint of freedom inside of it, and felt like, oh, there's something in here that's an example of what I'm longing for. There's something in here that's the alchemy, and I can learn from this, even if I can't play the piano or an instrument, I can learn from what these individuals and these groups are doing.

Wayne: In Native American traditions, too, a lot of our people, a lot of Black people, I mean, and actually all people in the Americas, have interacted with the Native Americans, with so many tribes of indigenous peoples. Our ancestors also witnessed and were involved with some of the traditional Native American ceremonies and songs and music. I bet you some of the melodies from the Cherokee and the Apache and all the tribes that interacted with Black folks got into the young kids. Black, white, everything, and they'd be humming some of that stuff around the house. And their creative mind would put that together unbeknownst of where it came from. But it came from the mixture. And I think that mixing began to unify those sounds across the country. Then people start copying each other.

We know lots of people copied the blues. Just walking down the road, hearing folk music, walking down the road, hearing someone strumming a guitar, one chord [*hums*]. And from there, it reverberates into people's awareness, and twenty years later, or thirty years later, you got B. B. King and all them doing it. The mix.

When B. B. King came along, and a few others, that's when the rest of America opened up their eyes, finally praising the blues. Well, actually praising the money that the blues made. [*laughs*]

So, we gotta stay on our toes about this whole creative process. We can say what it is, what jazz is, what freedom is, the music of freedom, but actually acting it out, doing it moment by moment, that's the most important thing. Taking action to keep the music of freedom flowing around the world.

Herbie: I was thinking, Wayne, about how jazz actually evolves, too. It hasn't just stayed at one point. It's continued to evolve because, as certain conventions began to set in, those conventions kind of have cement on the bottom of them. They become so fixed that some individuals come up to challenge those conventions in jazz, and they start to create sort of a backlash against those conventions, because the music was not designed to stay in one place.

But as human beings, we can easily fall into the trap of conventions. Until some new people come along, and pretty soon, there's a team of new people, and then people from all different parts of the United States come around, because this is where jazz started. Each region has developed jazz from their corner of the country and, as they mix with other styles, a new direction begins to take place, and that spreads like wildfire for those musicians who are interested in expanding. That's the thing about jazz, it encourages you to expand. Some people want to hold on to the way they've been doing it, because it becomes comfortable. But the freedom of jazz pulls you to keep moving, keep growing.

Wayne: Yeah, until it eventually becomes rock and roll! [*laughs*]

Herbie: But that freedom of jazz is what allows for so much growth. I would just say that's how—for example, in my lifetime and Wayne's lifetime, but before Esperanza—the avant-garde jazz scene came up in the '60s and '70s. I wasn't interested in it at first. I didn't know what they were doing. But then I got a gig with an avant-garde musician.

Esperanza: Is it that record with Eric Dolphy?

Herbie: Eric Dolphy, right. I had no idea what he was doing. You know, I'd heard some avant-garde musicians, but I was more into bebop. I liked Charlie Parker and people like that from the '40s.

I even asked Eric in my first conversation with him. I said, "Do you play tunes?"

He said, "Yes."

I said, "Do you use chords?"

He said, "Yes."

And I was like, "Written chords? Chord symbols?"

He said, "Yes."

And I went, "OK." Meanwhile I was thinking, *It didn't sound like that to me!* [*laughs*]

Anyway, I got a chance to work with Eric Dolphy for a month, and in that one month of training with him I discovered something within myself that had never been activated, never stimulated before. And that is courage. Because in those days we played a lot in bars, and we were playing music that nobody in the bars understood. But I didn't care because I got completely wrapped up in the freedom of finding new things musically, searching and digging down deep within myself to find new ways to do things.

Even if we got criticized, I stood up proudly for what we were doing, because I knew that everybody in the band was trying to create something, something new, to climb a mountain, a new mountain that we had not climbed before. That's where I had to find courage within my own life because I got inspired by this new way of approaching jazz. And that brought out my courage.

Wayne: Talking about courage reminds me, I just saw the film

The United States vs. Billie Holiday. And I heard the director, Lee Daniels, say the US government wasn't going after Billie Holiday and other Black musicians because of illegal narcotics, like the feds claimed. What the government was really trying to do was silence a strong Black woman, to stop her and her collaborators from doing what they were doing.

And what were they doing? They were exhibiting "creative excellence." And that scared the racists in the government who didn't want people, and children, everyone across the country and the world to see the excellence of these Black jazz artists. And that sort of thing continues on, even to recent examples of excellence in rap and hip hop. Certain elements of the establishment don't want the public to know the excellence of it, the magnetism of it, and the messages in it. Not that I'm saying all the music itself is excellent, but the excellence of expression and creativity. It shows an excellent grasp of truth and reality, and urges listeners to reach further than your own grasp of whatever reality you're living in.

Anyway, Billie got a lot of attention across the country for taking a stand about racist violence. She sang the song "Strange Fruit" that describes the terror of lynching in the South that was going on in her day, in the 1930s and 1940s. People came to New York City all the way from Europe to hear her at Carnegie Hall, and that's when the powers that be really got upset. The feds told the public that she was a dope addict and tried to ruin her image. But the government didn't really care about her drug use. They just wanted to stop Black excellence.

Taro: I didn't know about the persecution Billie Holiday suffered before I saw that film. Federal agents hounded her until the day she died in 1959 at age forty-four.

SLAVERY AND ITS CONSEQUENCES

Herbie: Billie Holiday was truly brave, and I'm glad the true story of all that she went through is being told now. I also want to share that there's a whole thing, a history of gender discrimination against female jazz musicians, too, beyond the racism they faced. Even within the jazz world, which was mostly African American, women have had to fight a big battle, just to be there. Again, it's the same story of men subjugating women to a lesser class. Of course, regardless of skin color, that's been happening for millennia in all areas of life. But after thousands of years, it's time to pay the piper in every area of the fight for equality.

The same thing is true of jazz. When I came up, there were great female musicians, but they weren't treated the same way as the male musicians, and certainly not at all in the early days of jazz. Have you seen the documentary film called *The Girls in the Band*?

Taro: Yes, the story of female jazz and big band instrumentalists from the 1930s to now. The film's trailer quotes jazz critic George Simon who said in the late 1960s, "Only God can make a tree, and only men can play jazz."

Herbie: That's crazy, right? But that's what many men felt in those days. And those days weren't too long ago.

As men, we are kind of indoctrinated into this old concept of manhood, what it should be and what it shouldn't, right from when we are very young, and it's so damaging. Because it creates all kinds of prejudice against others, and it's like racism in and of itself, you know, making a class system based on superficial differences. Thankfully jazz has opened its doors to female musicians. But it was slow, too slow.

Wayne: Yeah, I know what you mean. There was a brilliant lady named Margie Hyams who was in the George Shearing Quintet in the early 1950s. Rumor had it she was the actual leader of the group, but the booking agents finagled a way to make George Shearing the leader and use his blindness, like a novelty, to make more money. They did that regularly with any female who was like the real bandleader or even with a whole female band, because they had to pretend a man was in charge. So, Margie had to pretend that the men were leading. The guys in charge and promoters in the 1940s and '50s, when Margie was coming up, would say they couldn't create a phenomenon around a female band leader or a female soloist. Sometimes you'd see them in the movies or on television, but they would subjugate the women and belittle the parts that she played.

Where I grew up, in Newark, New Jersey, there was also a brilliant Black lady pianist named Jacqueline Rollins, and she played all that great Bud Powell stuff, the bebop, which evolved from swing. Although I only encountered a few other female jazz musicians over the years, they were really open to new artistic stuff, and they were great, cutting edge. But most women were discouraged from performing, and even if they did, they were discouraged from going to musical places of experimentation. That's why I'm so glad Esperanza came along! She's carrying on a tradition of the few who made it through all the obstacles.

Esperanza: Yes, Mary Lou Williams, and Geri Allen, and...

Wayne: Yes! You know what I mean. Geri Allen and Mary Lou Williams and Margie Hyams, and there was also a British lady named Ivy Benson who was a bandleader, she formed an all-female swing band in the 1940s. And the first integrated female band came up in America then, too, called the International Sweethearts of Rhythm. Just imagine what it took to accomplish that in those days! Mary Lou Williams, she had her own band, too, when she was a teenager in Black vaudeville.

Herbie: Yes, yes. Mary Lou Williams was a brilliant jazz pianist and composer.

Wayne: And Betty "Bebop" Carter, too. All those legendary ladies, they had a lot of guts.

Herbie: And these days I'm happy we get to work with Terri Lyne Carrington and Esperanza, of course, and we got some others coming up.

Wayne: And we've got to invite more people out of whatever musical world they're in, classical or not, and pull them into jazz, too. Mix it up. Right now, I'm being commissioned to write something for a young pianist from Holland who's twenty-eight and doesn't improvise at all, but wants to do something to open up the classical world with jazz. So, I'm working on something with piano and seven other instruments, and the word came to me that they're interested in something called "optimistic chaos." I can deal with that, too! [*laughs*] It's going to be eleven pieces all together when we're done. I'm working now on other new ideas with Esperanza, too. Every time we work on something, we run into every question or subject that we're bringing up here, and it stretches our creativity.

Esperanza: Facts, yeah, I know.

Herbie: See, Esperanza is so brilliant, the only thing people have to do is open up their ears to listen either to what she has to say or what she has to play, and all the barriers and "-isms" just drop.

Esperanza: Thank you, Herbie, for what you said about my work.

Taro: Esperanza and Wayne, you've recently created a new opera, *Iphigenia*, together. What do you learn from working with each other from an inter-generational perspective?

Esperanza: When you look at some of these elders, like Wayne and Herbie who are in their eighties, still vigorously practicing, studying their philosophy—the Buddhism we practice—and the other philosophy—this music that we practice—it gives you a sense that there's no end destination to these devotions and their ever-expanding ways of living. Maybe in some other careers, there's a marker of achievement of, "okay, I graduated and I have a practice or I'm a doctor, I'm a lawyer," you can always keep expanding those skills.... But with Wayne and Herbie, they're modeling something that seems like it stretches even across their lifetime, ... and you witness how they continue to emerge and blossom as musicians and people. Seeing that as a person who's fifty-years-plus younger than they are, it tells me that it's not a destination, it's a way of living and of committing to these paths, these loves, these disciplines, these gifts of this music we love and this Buddhist practice, this teaching, that we're blessed by.

Also, as we all know, there's a heightened awareness that's brought out when you're doing your craft in the company of elders of that craft. In fact, they don't have to say anything, but you notice places where maybe you didn't practice as much or places where you're feeling really clear, really strong, or even sometimes hearing what you're playing through their ears, imagining how they might be hearing it, that brings a ... refinement to the way that you play. I've definitely experienced that with both of them—their presence brings out a heightened awareness of the potential for refinement of what we're doing, brings out a heightened presence in the music as we're playing, even studying and preparation for playing with either of them. They also model an equanimity, where they aren't imposing their authority as elders. It doesn't feel hierarchical when I am in their company. They're setting a tone of, "You're just my friend, you're my colleague." They're not hierarchical with their position as highly revered elders. That's also a very profound model, they are truly enjoying whoever is in their company. They're enjoying that person for who that person is right here in the here and now as equals, as equally valuable people, beings, and that's a profound teaching, too.

Wayne: I first met Esperanza when she was in her twenties, and I didn't think someone would ever come along that young who reminded me of working with Miles Davis. I thought she was another kind of "Lady Davis," but all her own style, creative inside and out. After our first encounter at my home, she left this little piece of paper behind upon which she'd drawn little five-ledger lines, with a vertical treble clef, and a tiny melody. That was her way of saying thanks.

I think she could be born in any era, and she'd be the same person she is in this lifetime, always forward looking. That inspires me, as does working with someone like her of a much younger generation who shows me how exemplary talent can be at any age.

Taro: Esperanza, you certainly broke down barriers and "-isms," as Herbie said, when you became the first jazz musician to win the Grammy for Best New Artist in 2011. What was the driving force that kept you going before you achieved that, and what keeps you going now when you face obstacles?

Esperanza: I feel that when we have the privilege of finding a thing that we love, like jazz, it can give us courage to keep going. It becomes like a vehicle or a way of seeing that can help you see through what may seem like the whole reality. Even if everybody else is talking about something that's happening, it can give you another vision. It's like... like...

Herbie: Like an encouragement, it becomes an inner encouragement.

Esperanza: Yeah, and whatever your experiences have been, maybe you had friends growing up that looked different than you and you still felt love for them and they still saw you as a full human being. Then we have another way of seeing our circumstances, whether it's facing sexism or ageism or racism or casteism. For some of us, even moving through it, being identified from the outside as a person who should be the subject of the oppression or repression. It's like we see the higher potential inside of it, choosing to create circumstances that actually embody what we know better, what we know is possible despite what's happening.

That's not to belittle the real trauma and suffering that we can experience, you know, going through oppressive systems. But it's a sense some of us have to go through this system. I'm noticing what's in all three of us, that we share this way of seeing. Like I'm thinking, OK, this is here, but here's what I'm going to build inside of that, because what's happening out there doesn't mean I don't get to have the experience I want to have, you know.

And I always appreciate men taking the initiative to speak out about sexism and patriarchy, so I appreciate how you guys dove in to speak about that. It's important because I do feel there's a lack of male voices speaking up about this much-needed shift among us, particularly speaking directly to other men about it. So, I appreciate y'all.

Taro: Herbie and Wayne, I'm wondering if you have any personal memories, perhaps a story you've never shared publicly, of an experience facing racism in day-to-day life.

Herbie: Growing up, although my parents didn't shelter me from racism, they constantly encouraged me that I could be my best self and succeed and achieve my dreams despite that. So, it's funny that, even though they taught me to follow whatever aspirations I had, my mother wasn't at all happy that I decided to be a jazz musician. Maybe she thought, "You can become whatever you want, and you chose *that*?" [*laughs*]

But seriously, even when I was beginning music, before I started playing jazz, my parents told my brother and sister and me that whatever we decided we wanted to be when we grew up, they would back us up, they'd encourage us and give us the freedom to decide what we wanted. They always said they would support us in whatever directions we chose.

Taro: And did they do that?

Herbie: To their credit, they did. Because of the unconditional support that I got from my parents, I truly believed in myself, and I believed I could become whatever I set my mind to. And because of them and their example of how they lived their own lives, I never looked for discrimination and I never held on to that, I've never held that in my heart. So, my tendency from childhood is, if something negative happens to me—a bad remark or someone behaves badly toward me or whatever it may be—I let it go, try to forget about it, and don't let it hold me back. If it affects me mentally, I try to stop any negative thought in its tracks and not dignify it by identifying it as this or that. Just let it go, it's someone else's negativity. And I never hold grudges.

Taro: That's a wonderful way you've developed to control your mind, rather than letting your mind control you.

Herbie: Fortunately, that's been my lifelong tendency. And my practice of Buddhism, which is really a practice for mastering one's mind, has helped me strengthen those positive tendencies even more.

As far as memories from my younger days encountering racism, there are some things I do remember. Once in the mid-1960s, I was in Washington, DC, with the woman who later became my wife, Gigi. She's from Germany and, as you know, she's white. We were dating then, and she came with me to Washington, DC, where I was doing a show as part of the Miles Davis Quintet.

Gigi and I stayed at a friend's house, and in those days we were both in the unhealthy habit of smoking cigarettes. One morning we ran across the street in the middle of the block to get more, and a police car came right up, stopped us, and told us to get in the back. So, in my head, I'm thinking, OK, here comes the racist stuff, right? Two white cops.

They asked for our IDs, but we didn't have IDs on us. So, they said they were taking us to jail. By the way, the policemen were sitting in the front seats of the car, and they never once turned around to look at us. I told them we were just going across the street to get cigarettes, but they said they didn't care. We hadn't crossed at the corner, so they said we had to go to jail. Unbelievable, right? Then at the police station, they said they were just going to lock *me* up in a jail cell, not her. And mind you, this wasn't Mississippi, this was our nation's capital.

Anyway, I knew what was going on, I could see it and read it in their faces—they just wanted to harass a Black guy for being with a white girl. The civil rights movement was in high gear then, and I thought, *Here's my little chance to be part of it, right?* Unreasonably locked up in DC. So, I said I wanted to make a phone call, but I didn't have any change. Could I borrow some? Actually, I did have change, but I wanted to see the policemen's reaction to me asking them for it. [*laughs*] Eventually, they did give me a dime to call a friend who came down and said something to get us out of there. Later I found out it wasn't even illegal to cross the street in the middle of a block in DC, so it was just racism.

Wayne: Yeah, I've had my share of experiences with racism, too, of course. But like Herbie, my mother taught me not to rely on color for anything—not for good, not for bad. She would say, "Skin color is a false premise for validating behavior." Both my parents taught me that there was segregation and discrimination across the board, but don't make excuses for your life due to color, just rely on your person, who you know you are inside, and do your best. Let go of the negativity you encounter from others.

But of course, that doesn't stop people from doing and saying racist things. One of the first experiences I remember of realizing that was when I was seventeen. I was playing saxophone at a dance in Elizabeth, New Jersey. The whole place was Polish. And here I am, this lone little Black kid with a few of my white friends from school playing songs for all these white folks. I'm the only Black guy there, and I'm just a teenager. This was 1950, and these Polish guys worked with my father at the Singer Sewing Machine factory, so that's how we got hired. I was told it was going to be "a nice party."

Pretty soon, we can see everyone is getting really drunk, and we just keep playing, and these people are getting drunker and drunker and now instead of just letting us play they start yelling out songs they want to hear. And one big guy came up right to me and said, loudly: "I want to hear 'The Saints Go Marching In!'" And I thought that was kind of racist, too, because in those days people always associated "The Saints Go Marching In" with Black people. But anyway, I didn't know what to do because we weren't gonna play that song.

Then this other guy came over to me and said, softly: "Don't you pay any attention to these drunk guys. Don't pay attention to what they say, because they're going to get rude and talk bad about your race." Then he said, "I don't care if you're black, white, or zebra striped, you just play what you want to play."

That was a turn-around for me, and showed me that there are ignorant people, racist people, but there are also wise people and openhearted people. He was older, too, which made it a surprising thing for someone of his age to say in 1950. So, I've always remembered that—"I don't care if you're black, white, or zebra striped, just play what you want to play." [*laughs*]

Fortunately for me, once I got to work with professional bands, everything was more or less set up for a younger person like me not to encounter racism in the raw. I was sheltered from the direct brunt of it. Also, we had Blacks and Caucasians playing jazz together. You know, Weather Report was a mixed band, and Dizzy Gillespie, too, later on. Miles Davis had all kinds of people in his band. Gil Evans and Miles Davis were a mixed team starting from the 1940s. They helped change things. So, in its own way, jazz helped support civil rights and public acceptance of integration.

Herbie: Yes, and Gil Evans, who was white, was one of Miles Davis's best friends, if not his best friend. A lot of jazz musicians got active in the civil rights movement. And many songs were created to express the soul of the movement, like Charlie Mingus's "Fables of Faubus."

Taro: Your album *The Prisoner* was about jailed civil rights activists, right?

Herbie: The title is a double-entendre about those who were jailed, and also about those who were imprisoned within themselves, trapped by their own inflexibility and distorted way of seeing. It also alludes to people's disbelief in their own power to change, to grow, and to transform their lives. I created that album as a social statement written in music, to express how Black people have been imprisoned in various ways for a long time.

Taro: And your song "I Have a Dream" was played at the public memorial service for Dr. King at Morehouse College.

Herbie: That's right, which was such an honor. I dedicated that song and the entire album of *The Prisoner* to the memory of Dr. Martin Luther King Jr.

Taro: Esperanza, you've dedicated some of your songs— including "Land of the Free," about injustice, and "Black Gold," about the rich heritage of African cultures—to social justice issues. What inspired you to focus on those themes in your music?

Esperanza: "Land of the Free" is about Cornelius Dupree Jr. When I first heard about him, he had served thirty years in prison for a crime he didn't commit, and then through new advances in DNA testing, the Innocence Project was able to prove his innocence. I was so overwhelmed by that story and learning about how many people are unjustly incarcerated, particularly people of color. And hearing about this impacted me very deeply.

My father is in prison for life, and something about hearing Cornelius Dupree Jr.'s story, then hearing about the tireless work that the Innocence Project was doing, I became overwhelmed. The way that I was able to process it and offer it forward was by writing "Land of the Free." I asked permission of the Innocence Project to send proceeds from the sale of the song to them, just trying to find a way to have the music engaged. Not that music on its own isn't enough, but that's the origin of that song.

Similarly, with "Black Gold," it was a metabolizing. I saw a difference in the encouragement that I was getting as a Black girl compared to how my brother was encouraged in school. That's what we experienced in Portland. I noticed that the boys seemed to get less, from what I could see in school, less programing support, less naming, less acknowledging "You are valuable and precious and capable and creative." So, I wanted to write something to speak to that.

In fact, Wayne says, you write what you wish for. So maybe that was a way of writing a song I wish would have been available for the little boys, and girls, that I went to school with.

Wayne: Your story about unjust incarceration reminds me of my first wife, Teruko. She was raised from a young age in the internment camps on the West Coast. Teruko and her family were Japanese American citizens, and like so many others they were ripped out of their home and bused to internment camps by the US government during World War II.

Taro: Around 120,000 people of Japanese descent in the United States were sent to those terrible camps during World War II. Did you know that jazz bands were one of the most popular forms of entertainment in the camps?

Wayne: It doesn't surprise me. The sound of freedom in jazz must have soothed the pain of being unjustly locked up because of other people's racist fears. I saw photos of Teruko and her sister when they were little behind barbed wire fences in those dusty camps. Incredible and sad that American kids, whole families and communities, were locked up solely because of their ethnicity.

Taro: This book project came about in response to some heartbreaking, tragic injustices of recent years, including the brutal murders of George Floyd, Breonna Taylor, and other innocent young Black people in the United States. Can you share how those events and the Black Lives Matter movement affected you, or your thoughts about the ongoing need for change?

Wayne: I'll tell you something—I knew since 1963, when the media started declaring "the civil rights movement is here," I thought, *Well, we've declared it before '63.* We thought civil rights was finally here when the '50s came. And my parents thought it was coming in the '20s and '30s and in 1933— that's when I was born. After the depression—the Great Depression—and the world was changing dramatically, Black folks thought, *Now things will change.*

Then after World War II, we thought everything was changing. The soldiers in the armed forces were integrated and all that. But I knew that we had a long, long way to go, from the late '40s to the '50s, and throughout the '60s. Not that I'm the only one that knew, of course, I knew lots of other people who were saying, "This is gonna be a long haul."

Taro: I met Coretta Scott King when she lectured at Soka University of America in 1995. She said then: "I guess we've thought that we had won these civil rights victories, but we must go back and fight for them over again. And once we do that, we must remember to teach the next generation, and teach every generation, that they have a responsibility to fight, to win the freedom again and again."

Wayne: Exactly. Today's movement is an extension of all that from throughout my lifetime. And if you listen to the music we were playing in the early days of the civil rights movement, it expressed what we were doing, how far we traveled, how we organized, how we united, even details like figuring out accommodations for the marchers and protesters. It was a huge effort behind the scenes.

For me, traveling the world as a jazz ambassador, the areas we traveled through—Japan, Australia, Europe, everywhere overseas—we were accepted. But even so, I saw there was a concerted effort to put new boundaries on artistic excellence. For example, we still celebrate "the Rock and Roll Hall of Fame" with major attention, which is fine. But the origins of those kinds of genre-specific things originate from people trying to set up barriers, to filter out the artistic excellence of "others," to limit what the public gets to see and celebrate. Why isn't there a "Music Hall of Fame" that's as globally honored? We should celebrate all types of music, all types of people, and make these kinds of social structures universal— open and egalitarian. The fight against racism is embodied in a universal attempt to just be universal.

Esperanza: [*snaps fingers*] Yes!

Taro: Esperanza and Herbie, how would you say the Black Lives Movement and the tragic events that I described have affected you?

Esperanza: It feels like the movement is more for individuals who weren't aware of what has been going on since and before the times Wayne was speaking about. And maybe also for individuals who were ready to get out and give their energy to a movement, a transformation, but maybe they didn't know which direction to go. So, I feel excited that the world at large is opening up, opening itself to reckon with these realities.

Wayne: You dig!

Herbie: Yes. After the murder of George Floyd, and during the pandemic, when I saw all the people supporting the protest movement led mainly by Black Lives Matter—I saw white kids, I saw Muslims, Asians, gay kids, transgender kids, I saw older people of every description, I saw people from every corner of humanity. And then around the world, especially young people were participating in marches and protests and it grew to dozens of countries. That's when I felt optimistic and said, "Ah, we're on to it." I've always realized that this is a much bigger fight than just relegating it specifically to Black people to handle. It's a big fight.

It's really a fight for the soul of humanity, and it's being led by the women who developed the Black Lives Matter movement. I mean, they were the catalyst. And it made me realize, when I see Australia and New Zealand jumping in, and they're thinking much more about people that they've marginalized— the Aboriginal people of Australia, and in New Zealand, the

Maoris. And here we have, of course, our Native Americans. In every country there are marginalized people.

So, to see this kind of movement on television and social media, expanding in a direction that really started with the Black Lives Matter movement, I feel that this is something the whole world can learn from. And this universal conversation that my generation has waited to have my entire life, as Wayne said, always feeling it might start now... nope... then now... no... then when? We wondered for decades, "When will *all people* start a *real* conversation about this?" And finally, finally now, the conversation has started in real and meaningful ways.

Some white friends of mine that I've known for many, many years, for the first time started talking about this topic with me and asked me questions about my life as a Black man in America. Just a few weeks ago, somebody I've known for several years now, a white guy, started asking me questions about not just the Black Lives Matter movement per se, but questions about racism. So, I feel hopeful that it's finally on the drawing board for many people who have been awakened to the reality.

But, of course, there is backlash fighting all of that, and that's one of the main reasons that the proposed voting rights bills (the Freedom to Vote Act and the John Lewis Voting Rights Advancement Act) are so necessary right now. If they don't get through, then we're not going to have an America that lives up to its promise and potential, the republic that we imagine we would like to live in, one that recognizes all people's rights. This is the key issue now, and I hope everybody gets involved. It is, as President Biden says, a fight for the soul of America. And I mean, the real soul. It's predicted that within a few decades, white people will not be in the American majority. Those scales are changing.

But one thing the pandemic has taught us is that we are all one family. In Buddhism, we talk about the fact that the external environment is also within your life as well as outside your life. So, if the world is hurting, if the external world is hurting, it's a reflection of pain within us, from the distorted views that emanate from humanity's collective lesser self. For example, climate change is in the external world, but it's going to lead to mass destruction of all life on the planet, and trigger a lot of suffering within us along the way. There's something profound to be learned from all of this—it's all related, every living being on this planet is part of one family. The virus is trying to hurt that family. It doesn't care who you love, doesn't care what the color of your skin is, doesn't care about your religion, doesn't care about any of that.

In our response to the virus, what we can learn from our greater self is that we need to take care of one another as a global family. We need to be part of a force that encourages the happiness of every other human being we encounter. This is what our practice of Buddhism is about, it's practicing for yourself and practicing for others.

In other words, helping to open our own eyes, and others' eyes, expand our vision, and nourish our Buddha nature, our enlightened inner potential, so that it grows and expands. It's so important to have a clear perception of the world and the importance of every being in it, because everyone is precious. No one on the planet is replaceable.

Wayne: Right on. And if everyone had that mindset, then we could create an anti-virus. Yes, and an uncle virus. [*laughs*]

Herbie: That's a great way to end that stream of thought. [*laughs*]

Taro: Many people are searching for practical ways to overcome trauma and strengthen within themselves a solid state of happiness. How has your practice of Buddhism helped you heal trauma and build resilience and joy?

Esperanza: That's such a massive subject you opened up, my answer can't be comprehensive. But, the healing process is a journey. Anybody who has suffered a topical wound knows that. To use the metaphor of a cut, there's a process to healing and supporting a process that has its own timeline that the body sets. It's also a process that's innate. So, when we recognize that we've been wounded and decide to attend to it, we're supporting a process that our body innately has access to. All human beings are naturally endowed with the capacity for healing, and we can become collaborators in the natural process of healing and the restoration of wholeness. I'm talking about the physical, psychological, and emotional.

This Buddhism has as a primary tenant the point that everything that imbues us with a sense of wholeness, connectedness, and wellness is already inside of us. Every human being carries the full, complex tapestry of personhood, which includes Buddhahood woven within it. And this practice encourages us to sink into and trust that. The practice of chanting Nam-myoho-renge-kyo and studying the Lotus Sutra helps us connect with that aspect of ourselves more and more. It's not like it adds it to us, it's not like it gives us Buddhahood. It supports us in encountering it within ourselves, witnessing the ways it brings transformation of whatever is happening in our lives, transforming whatever might be constricting or hindering or distracting, or even traumatizing us away from that innate aspect of ourselves.

And I use some of the tools of yoga, and some therapeutic somatic practices. I'm studying ways in which music and sounds support the processing and release of trauma, or trauma responses held in the body. Of course, I work with music as another tool and technology to release and process trauma responses that are percolating through this time-based phenomenon. All of these practices help us navigate through the ups and downs of life and not get attached to the suffering that they might bring. To hopefully reduce the impact of potentially traumatic encounters.

I also want to add that it's important to seek help from professionals too, like if you break your leg you need to go to a doctor. And one of the many ways that Buddhist practice can be utilized is to help tune our lives, so that we magnetize, like a navigational tool to help us encounter the right people with whom we can thrive. The practice also invites us to use any acute time-based issue, or challenge, or disappointment, into the raw material with which we apply this practice of Buddhism. Then even if our circumstances may seem hopeless or dreadful, actually they become opportunities for us to encounter an even deeper dimension of our own Buddhahood and our own sacredness.

Wayne: Yes, that's it. When I started studying and practicing Buddhism, I soon realized that resilience isn't something to be instilled in me, it was already in me to start. As Esperanza said, it's in all of us, just waiting to be realized and magnified, especially when something traumatic hits. Everyone has the potential for great resilience, whether they're consciously aware of it or not. It's just a question of how to manifest it.

In my case, practicing Buddhism has brought out more resilience than I knew I had, and I already felt I had a good supply. For example, long before I found Buddhism, I was working on the road a lot. I'd often stay after gigs to hang out in a nightclub drinking and having fun, sometimes the last one to call it a night. Even so, if someone from our group called me in the morning they'd hear my chipper voice answer, and everyone was perplexed how I wasn't tired and cranky. People started calling me "Mr. Activity," because I was so upbeat and active all the time, even mornings after a late night.

However, later in life, when I experienced truly tragic events, like prematurely losing loved ones—my wife Ana Maria died in a plane crash when she was only forty-seven, and we lost our daughter Iska from a grand mal seizure when she was only fourteen—that's when my usual resilience wasn't enough. I profoundly felt how my daily Buddhist practice helped me to open deeper levels of resilience. The trauma still hurt bad, of course, but even through times of suffering I was also able to feel joy in my heart again, as I'm sure my loved ones would have wanted. I was always able to keep moving forward and never lost my optimism or creativity. I gained an even deeper desire to help others who are suffering, to inspire goodness in the world, and keep changing poison into medicine. I'm very thankful for my Buddhist practice, which buoys me through every suffering in life, and for our SGI Buddhist community who've always offered me and my family emotional support along the way.

Taro: Esperanza, can you describe how the principle of "changing poison into medicine" could be adapted by social justice movements to create positive change?

Esperanza: That's a profound question. I think of the work of frontline cultural workers who are showing up regularly to advocate for social justice is such an intense and admirable way of moving this world, and responding to the injustices that perpetuate traumas amongst all our communities. So, I feel like I could only speak allegorically, because I wouldn't dare offer advice to people who are already in the pedagogies of social transformation.

Yes. What's coming up is, the principle of transforming poison into medicine I believe invites a spiritual intimacy with the poison. And I feel that for many of us who've been traumatized by certain social dynamics, or even people we associate with certain demographics, it can feel neurologically impossible to do that—because our bodies are revolted by the idea of becoming intimate with a person, situation, or event that's toxic, bristling with hate, ugliness, or vitriol.

We understandably have the instinct to try and affect it from a distance through the exertion of power. There's this instinct to collect power elsewhere, enough power that can be exerted as a counter force to affect things we see as harmful.

The concept of "changing poison into medicine" instead invites a radical intimacy with the poison. Because what it says is that by the willingness to show up in intimacy and engage what we recognize as a poison, then the poison will be transformed, and its capacity to poison us will be transformed. Now, I know that feels completely irrelevant and abstract if you're encountering people with assault rifles. I know we have really good defense mechanisms built into our bodily systems over the millennia of evolution for programming us to react in certain ways. I deeply understand the instinct and healthy neurological response to create distance between ourselves and sources of potential harm.

But this concept of "changing poison into medicine" is grounded in the idea of engaging whatever we recognize as poisonous so it can be transformed, and also recognizing that there's no phenomena that we can perceive outside our life that isn't also inside our own lives. This is also what we call "human revolution." It's the premise that by engaging with the poison with an intention of creating value—engaging for the sake of transformation—then it will transform that dimension within ourselves, too.

That's part of why I think this Buddhist practice is quite radical, more radical than it seems on the surface. Even in the Lotus Sutra, Shakyamuni Buddha basically says to his disciples, "This is going to be hard for people to believe." And when he tells them "Everything I've said up to this point has been preparatory. Now I'm going to expound the truth," many of his followers get up and walk out, because they don't actually want to hear it.

That shows how the practice of human revolution and transforming poison into medicine is really difficult to embrace. It requires depths of humility, compassion, and faith in the process of Nam-myoho-renge-kyo, faith in the process of transforming absolutely anything into value for your own life and for others. And to accept that Buddhahood unquestionably, irrevocably exists in all beings. If you truly believe that, then the only option is to engage with a person or a circumstance that you feel has the potential to bring a "poison" into your sphere and transform it into a "medicine."

Taro: One last question I wanted to ask you all today. What is a piece of wisdom or guidance that you personally return to, that lifts you up when you're feeling down or helps you get over obstacles you face in life?

Wayne: To fear nothing. That's a heavy-duty mission. But to fear nothing is to stimulate one's thoughts, to learn, to create, and not to fear, in real time. With that spirit, you can create ways of being and offer suggestions and have experimental interactions that demonstrate how fearing nothing is really not as hard as one may imagine. People's imaginations stop short of what they could really do. Open the door, come through imagination, and act on it.

Herbie: For me, this year is my fiftieth year of practicing Buddhism with our beloved SGI community of practitioners. So, it's a celebration for me, because this practice has helped me in countless ways to become a happier, healthier, more compassionate person.

Every day I get in front of my Buddhist altar and chant Nam-myoho-renge-kyo, which helps me to clarify my mind, to see myself and life clearly, to see the truth. It's what I do to lift my spirits, to encourage myself, to open myself up, to be able to see what has been unseen to me. So I share our SGI Buddhist practice with everyone my life touches and invite them to check it out for themselves.

We say in the Buddhist community, "use the strategy of the Lotus Sutra," which is referring to chanting, and to not letting your brain and ego try to convolute things, but to transcend the brain and ego, and to reach deeper into the core of your life force and soul through this practice. I have watched obstacles slowly transform themselves into something good in my life over and over for five decades. So, that's what I return to anytime I face an obstacle, and that's what uplifts me. It unfolds my wisdom, courage, and compassion each day.

Wayne: Right in there, that's it, right there!

Esperanza: Swoosh!

Wayne: That's the arrow hitting the bullseye.

Herbie: [*laughs*] It's really true, you know. With this practice, things come out of nowhere, or sometimes everywhere. Things that you never dreamed would be in your purview, that change the trajectory of your life toward your own North Star.

Wayne: Yes, even when you're in a rowboat with no paddles! Then, guess what, you use your hands. [*holds hands in prayer style*]

Herbie: That's how you row without paddles. [*laughs*]

Esperanza: Yes! [*laughs*] Well, I want to say both of these beings, Mr. Shorter and Mr. Hancock, have introduced me to this Buddhist practice, and I'm so grateful for that. And all that's coming up is just to listen, listen to what life is bringing through, to raise you up. All of us have experiences of how profound teachings have entered our lives. And we keep developing because we were present to listen. Wayne calls it "listening to life's dialogue," and that's all I can say. We're a part of the universe, and the universe also supports the bringing forth of our Buddha nature.

The universe is always trying to bring us the circumstances, whether that's a challenge or what seems like a blessing, to help raise the condition of Buddhahood from within our life. So, what always encourages me and what I would offer forward to others is just noticing the dialogue of life that you're already a part of.

Taro: Thank you all. Before we finish, is there anything more that you would like to share?

Wayne: One more thing I can say is, whatever it is that's an impediment in anybody's life, don't give up fighting to make it go in your favor. Turn it around, turn it around, because ain't nothing one dimensional. Or, let me say, it's two but not two—is your life half empty or half full? With that question at heart, you learn to be the director of your own life. You become a converter, a human revolutionist, a person who can change negatives to positives. Ain't that something? You can do it. Never give up!

INDEX

INDEX

INDEX

INDEX

INDEX

INDEX

INDEX

INDEX

INDEX

INDEX

INDEX

CONTRIBUTORS

Contributor Bios for Slavery and Its Consequences

Dr. Lewis V. Baldwin is Emeritus Professor of Religious Studies at Vanderbilt University. He received his Ph.D. in American Christianity from Northwestern University, with a minor concentration in cultural studies. He has written extensively on slave religion and culture and black church traditions, especially African Methodism, and he is widely known for his many works on the life, thought, and socio-political praxis of Dr. Martin Luther King, Jr. He has lectured on Dr. King and various aspects of African American religion and culture at academic institutions throughout the United States. His latest book is entitled, The Arc of Truth: The Thinking of Martin Luther King, Jr., which was recently released by Fortress Press in Minneapolis, Minnesota. Dr. Baldwin currently lives in Nashville, Tennessee with his wife Jacqueline.

Barry Beckham, distinguished novelist and founder of Beckham Publications, is considered one of our most innovative prose writers. As an English professor at Brown University, he directed the graduate writing program. While at Brown, Beckham edited the first of five editions of the *Black Student's Guide to Colleges* (Dutton, 1982)—also the first of its kind. His other guides include the *Black Student's Guide to Scholarships* and the *College Selection Workbook*.

He has written four novels including, *Runner Mack* and *Will You Be Mine?* and has published prose in *Esquire, Black*

Enterprise, Crisis, the *New York Times, Educational Record*, the *Washington Post, American Visions*, and elsewhere.

Beckham has been a board member of the Authors League Foundation for more than 10 years. A recipient of a National Endowment for the Arts Fellowship, Beckham has served also on the boards of the George Polk AwardsPEN American Center.

Orville Vernon Burton is the inaugural Judge Matthew J. Perry Distinguished Chair of History and Professor of Global Black Studies at Clemson University and Emeritus University Distinguished Teacher/Scholar and Professor of History and African American Studies at the University of Illinois. A prolific author and scholar (more than twenty books and nearly three hundred articles) and numerous digital humanities projects, Burton's books include Justice Deferred: Race and the Supreme Court (2021), The Age of Lincoln (2007), Penn Center (2014), and In My Father's House Are Many Mansions (1985). He has served as president of the Southern Historical Association and of the Agricultural History Society. A recognized authority on race relations, Burton is often called upon as an expert witness in discrimination and voting rights cases throughout the United States. In 2017 he received the Governor's Award for Lifetime Achievement in the Humanities from the South Carolina Humanities Council, and in 2021 he was awarded the Benjamin E. Mays Legacy Award.

Lawrence Edward Carter, Sr., Ph.D. was recruited in the tenth grade by Martin Luther King Jr. to come to Morehouse College. He has been the founding Dean of the Martin

Luther King Jr. International Chapel at the Morehouse in Atlanta, Georgia since 1979. He is also Professor of Religion, College Archivist and Curator. Carter is the author of *Walking Integrity: Benjamin Elijah Mays as Mentor to Generations* (Scholar Press, 1996, Centennial Festschrift Commissioned by Morehouse College; *Walking Integrity: Mentor to Martin Luther King Jr.*, Mercer University Press, 1998); *Global Ethical Options in the Tradition of Gandhi, King and Ikeda*, with George David Miller and Neelakanta Radhakrishnan (New York: Weatherhill, Inc., first edition 2001; New Delhi, Indian edition: Gandhi Media Center, 2004); *The Baptist Preacher's Buddhist Teacher: How My Interfaith Journey with Daisaku Ikeda Made Me A Better Christian* (Middleway Press, 2018), which has been translated into Japanese and Portuguese. Carter is also the founder of the Gandhi, King, Ikeda Institute for Global Ethics and Reconciliation, Director of the Martin Luther King Jr. College of Pastoral Leadership, Director of the World House Teenage Theological Summer Institute and Chairman of the Howard Thurman Educational Spiritual Trust at Morehouse College. Carter is the recipient of five interfaith honorary degrees internationally, and has traveled to 38 countries to address hundred of interfaith, intercollegiate, interracial and interdenominational audiences and congregations.

W. Paul Coates is the founder and director of Black Classic Press (BCP), which specializes in republishing obscure and significant works by and about people of African descent. He established the George Jackson Prison Movement to bring Afrocentric literature to inmates. By 1978, the program had transitioned into BCP. After receiving his M.L.S. degree from Clark Atlanta University, Coates joined the staff at Howard

University's Moorland-Spingarn Research Center as an African American Studies reference and acquisition librarian. A former member and Maryland State coordinator of The Black Panther Party, he was instrumental in the establishment of the Black Panther Party Archives at Howard University. In 1990, he was a contributing editor for the published work, *Black Bibliophiles and Collectors: Preservers of Black History.* In 1991, Coates retired from the Moorland-Spingarn Research Center; and, in 1995, he launched BCP Digital Printing to specialize in short-run printing.

Dr. Leah Creque is Professor of English at Morehouse College. She is an educator, cultural historian, and civic organizer. Though her personal and professional endeavors vary widely in scope, they reflect her commitment to promoting and preserving the culture of the African diaspora – particularly African American and Caribbean traditions – as well as the enrichment of the lives of women and African American youth.

In 2012, she was selected to serve as Director of the Morehouse College Howard Thurman Honors Program. She assumed the mantle of Chair of the Department of English at Morehouse in 2015 concurrently with her position as Honors Program Director. In January 2022 she was appointed as Associate Provost of Pedagogy and Assessment at Morehouse College.

Dr. Creque's writing has been anthologized in many scholarly journals and publications, including, *Recovering the African Feminine Divine in Literature, the Arts, and Practice: Yemonja Awakening* and *Crimes against Humanity in the Land of the Free.*

CONTRIBUTORS

Brandon Thomas Crowley is an African-American minister and scholar in religion and theology. Since 2009, he has served as the Senior Pastor of the Myrtle Baptist Church in Newton, Massachusetts, one of America's oldest Black congregations founded by freed slaves at the end of Reconstruction. Presently, Reverend Crowley is a Lecturer in Ministry Studies at Harvard University's Divinity School in Cambridge, Massachusetts. He earned a Ph.D. in Church and Society and a Master of Sacred Theology with a certificate in social justice from Boston University's School of Theology; a Master of Divinity from Harvard University's Divinity School, and a Bachelor of Arts in Religion and a certificate in moral cosmopolitan pastoral leadership from Morehouse College in Atlanta, Georgia. Reverend Crowley's manuscript is titled *Queering Black Churches: Dismantling Heteronormativity in African American Congregations* with Oxford University Press. He was ordained in the Progressive National Baptist Convention of America, Inc. and licensed by the National Baptist Convention of America.

Tina Davis, Dr. is a Special Advisor and Researcher at the Coretta and Martin Luther King Institute for Peace in Norway. An expert on modern slavery with 16 years' experience, Dr. Davis completed a global mapping on modern slavery for the Norwegian government in 2019 towards their Modern Slavery Development Program. Prior to this, she led the initiative for a Norwegian Modern Slavery Law in 2018, which came into effect as the Transparency Law in July, 2022. She was also part of a core group that advocated for the Australian Modern Slavery Act. Dr. Davis is currently doing empirical research on recruitment processes of migrant workers into the Norwegian food industry, which builds on previous policy reports on exploitation of migrant workers in Norway and in Australia.

She was part of the UN University, Delta 8.7 working group that developed a global policy on modern slavery and crisis. Dr. Davis directed the award-winning feature length documentary, Modern Slavery, which can be seen on Netflix Europe. She is the Assistant Editor for the *Journal of Modern Slavery*, and she holds a PhD in Sociology & Social Policy from University of Sydney. She is also a podcast host for the *Journal of Modern Slavery*, a writer, speaker and guest lecturer in migration, forced labour, modern slavery, business and human rights, and documentary-making. Dr. Davis is a member of Martin Luther King Jr. Board of Sponsors at Morehouse College.

Stephane Dunn, PhD, MA, MFA (University of Notre Dame) is the author of *Baad Bitches & Sassy Supermamas: Black Power Action Films* (2008), the screenplay *Chicago '66* (2020 Finish Line/Tirota Social Impact Screenplay winner) & the novel *Snitchers* (September 2022); Professor Dunn has written and co-produced short films and is a frequent moderator and commentator who has been featured on A & E Network, E! Entertainment, NPR and the documentary *Body Parts.* She is one of the co-founders of the Cinema, Television & Emerging Media Studies (CTEMS) major at Morehouse College. Her work has appeared in a number of publications including books, *The Atlantic, Vogue, Ms.* magazine, *Chronicle of Higher Education,* and *Best African American Essays 2009,* among others. She grew up in Elkhart, Indiana where she attended Pierre Moran and Elkhart Memorial High School.

Dr. Charles S. Finch III is an author, lecturer, and historian dedicated to the reclamation of ancient African history and culture.

Dr. Finch is the former Director of International Health at the Morehouse School of Medicine. A graduate of Yale University (1971) and 1976 graduate of Jefferson Medical College (1976),

Dr. Finch joined the Department of Family Medicine at the Morehouse School of Medicine in 1982 and then the Office of International health in 1989, leading four traditional healer research projects in Senegal between 1991-1995.

Dr. Finch has conducted independent studies in African antiquities, comparative religion, anthropology, and ancient science and has published more than a dozen articles, a collection of essays, and two books, *Echoes of the Old Dark Land* and *The Star of Deep Beginnings: Genesis of African Science & Technology.*

Taro Gold is the co-author of Tina Turner's inspirational memoir, *Happiness Becomes You,* and the author of seven other bestselling books including *Living Wabi Sabi: The True Beauty of Your Life, The Tao of Mom, The Tao of Dad, What Is Love?,* and *Open Your Mind, Open Your Life.* He has written extensively for Buddhist publications, including the *World Tribune* newspaper and *Living Buddhism* magazine. In his youth, Taro performed in the first U.S. national touring company of *Evita* and other Broadway musicals such as *Falsettos* and *Peter Pan.* Having enjoyed much of his life abroad, he developed an expansive worldview, traveling to more than forty nations and living in Australia, Spain, and Japan, where he became the first American man to graduate from Soka University of Tokyo.

In his sixth decade of musical innovations, **Herbie Hancock** remains at the forefront of world culture, technology, business, and music. As a member of the Miles Davis Quintet, he helped pioneer a groundbreaking sound in jazz, followed in the 1970s with albums, including "Headhunters," that combined electric jazz with funk and rock. He also explored acoustics with V.S.O.P. and electronic dance sounds with his best-selling album, "Future Shock." Hancock received an Academy Award for his "Round Midnight" film score and has garnered 14 Grammys, including the Grammy Lifetime Achievement Award and Album of the Year for "River: The Joni Letters." He is Institute Chairman of the Herbie Hancock Institute of Jazz, and the Creative Chair for Jazz for the Los Angeles Philharmonic Association. Hancock is also a UNESCO Goodwill Ambassador and Kennedy Center Honoree. His memoirs, "Herbie Hancock: Possibilities," were published in 2014.

Jodi L. Henderson is the editor in chief of the *Journal of Modern Slavery* and the Executive Director of SlaveFree Today. She has worked in the anti-slavery and human rights space for over a decade, as a consultant, speaker, writer, and editor. Henderson holds a Masters Degree in Psychology from the University of West Georgia as well as a license in professional counseling. Her work is informed by more than 25 years as a therapist, teacher and community activist.

She has been a part of SlaveFree Today since its inception and has been a driving force behind the *Journal of Modern Slavery* and the SlaveFree Today Podcast. Jodi lives with her loving husband, her brilliant daughter, and their three dogs. Jodi L. Henderson is a member of Martin Luther King Jr. Board of Sponsors at Morehouse College.

Dr. Joel B. Kemp is an Assistant Professor of Hebrew Bible at Emory University's Candler School of Theology. He holds a Ph.D. in Hebrew Bible from Boston College; an M.Div. from Andover Newton Theological School; a J.D. from Harvard Law School; and an A.B. from Harvard College. His first monograph, *Ezekiel, Law, and Judahite Identity: A Case for Identity in Ezekiel 1 - 33* (Mohr Siebeck, 2020), analyzes how the book of Ezekiel uses legal elements to advocate for the proper conceptualization of Judahite identity in light of the experiences of imperial domination. His current monograph, tentatively titled *Blackness in 3D: Biblical Race, American Law, and Contemporary Crises*, focuses on the racialized reception of biblical texts from the Primeval History and how those interpretations contributed to constructions of "Blackness" in America's legal system.

Naje Lataillade is a Haitian-American filmmaker and photographer based in Brooklyn, NY. His work attempts to push beyond entertainment or personal expression, engaging the viewer in reflection - exposing historical, social, cultural, political and/or economic conditions that have led to inequalities and injustices across class, race, religion, ethnicity, gender, sexuality and other areas. In 2020, Naje's series The Feels was nominated for three Emmys and won the Streamy for Best Indie Series. In 2007 he was selected by FADER magazine as one of the 50 filmmakers paving the way for the future of non-narrative film. He was also honored with a retrospective of his work at the Lens Politica Film Festival in Helsinki, Finland.Naje studied screenwriting at UCLA, documentary filmmaking at the EICTV in Cuba, and cinematography at the Filmakademie in Germany. He also studied Economics and Political Science while at UCLA.

Anthony B. Pinn is currently the Agnes Cullen Arnold Distinguished Professor of Humanities and professor of religion at Rice University. He is also Professor Extraordinarius at the University of South Africa. In addition, Pinn is a fellow of the American Academy of Arts and Sciences. Pinn is the founding director of the Center for Engaged Research and Collaborative Learning, and he served as the inaugural director of the Center for African and African American Studies both at Rice University. He is managing editor of Religious Studies Review. Pinn's research interests include African American religious thought, religion and culture; humanism; and hip hop culture. Pinn is co-editor of numerous book series, including (with Stacey Floyd-Thomas) "Religion and Social Transformation (NYU Press). He is the author/editor of over 35 books, including *The Interplay of Things: Religion, Art, and Presence Together* (2021) and the novel *The New Disciples* (2015).

Stephanie Shonekan is professor of ethnomusicology and dean of the College of Arts and Humanities at the University of Maryland. She earned a doctorate in ethnomusicology and folklore with a minor in African American studies in 2003 from Indiana University. Her dual heritage combining West Africa with the West Indies allows her to straddle the Black world comfortably. She has published articles and book chapters on afrobeat, Fela Kuti, Nigerian and African American hip-hop, soul music and country music. Her publications explore the nexus where identity, history, culture and music meet. Her books include *The Life of Camilla Williams, African American Classical Singer and Opera Diva* (2011), *Soul, Country, and the USA: Race and Identity in American Music Culture* (2015), *Black Lives Matter & Music* (2018) and *Black Resistance in the Americas* (2018).

Wayne Shorter has crafted a musical legacy for half a century, since the 1950s as a composer for Art Blakey's Jazz Messengers. Later, he joined the Miles Davis Quintet. In the 1970s, he cofounded Weather Report, marking the birth of fusion music. In the 1980s and 1990s, he released Grammy-winning works including "High Life," merging jazz with classical instruments. Since 2001, he's led the Wayne Shorter Quartet while developing symphonic works commissioned by orchestras including Los Angeles Philharmonic, Detroit Symphony Orchestra, and Philharmonie de Paris. In all, Mr. Shorter has more than 200 compositions that have been studied in music schools and performed globally. He's received twelve Grammys, including a Grammy Lifetime Achievement Award in 2015, and honorary doctorates from schools including New York University, Juilliard School, and Berklee College of Music. He's a recipient of the National Endowment for the Arts Jazz Master Award, and a Kennedy Center Honoree.

Esperanza Spalding is a being who has grown to recognize love in the abstract and aspirational, and is now fully dedicated to learning how she can serve and embody actualized love through honor for and receptivity to fellow humans, teachers, and practitioners of various regenerative arts. Bass, piano, composition, performance, voice, and lyrics are disciplines she is engaged in to cultivate her own channel for transmitting care and beauty through vibration, sound, and presence. She has cowritten an opera with Wayne Shorter, "Iphigenia," which premiered in 2021. Currently, she is researching liberation technologies in jazz and black dance, and continuing a lifelong collaboration with practitioners in various fields relating to music, healing, and cognition to develop music with enhanced therapeutic potential. She is presently paid by Harvard University to cocreate and learn with students enrolled there, working on developing creative practices that serve the restoration of people and land.

Ron Thomas has led Morehouse College's journalism program since 2007, and in July 2021 it expanded from a minor to a major named Journalism in Sports, Culture and Social Justice.

Professor Thomas teaches newswriting and sports reporting courses and helps advise The Maroon Tiger student news organization staffed by Morehouse and Spelman College students.

About 100 of the journalism program's former students and Maroon Tiger staff members work in the media or the sports industry, and 51 have earned master's degrees in journalism, sports management or related fields.

For 34 years, Thomas covered major college and professional sports at prominent newspapers such as the San Francisco Chronicle and USA Today. His book *They Cleared the Lane: the NBA's Black Pioneers* is the only one written about the integration of the NBA.

Thomas has a B.A. in Political Science from University of Rochester and a master's in Journalism from Northwestern.

ACKNOWLEDGEMENTS

First, we would like to thank you, dear reader. Our deepest gratitude for your time and attention. Your interest in the topics covered in this book is vital for making necessary changes to create more just communities.

We would like to express our heartfelt thanks to each and every person who has contributed to this book.

We are extremely grateful to:

Kimberly Brown, for her scheduling and organizational prowess and incredible patience.

Paul Coates & Barry Beckham, for their time and generosity in sharing their wisdom and years of experience in the publishing industry. That this book exists in tangible form, is because of these two.

Savannah Smoot, for proofreading & copy writing par excellence.

Benjamin Thomas Greer, for his insight and editing prowess.

Nicole Struth, for tenacious internet research and assistance with this project. Her patience and skill cannot be underestimated.

Alan Dino Hebel & the team at The Book Designers for their expertise and creativity in making our vision a reality.

BCP Digital Printing, for going above and beyond to bring you this beautiful book.

Dr. Marva Griffin Carter for her insight & recommendations in the area of musicology.

A big thank you to Matthew White for his thorough indexing, under extreme conditions and Kathryn S. Campbell for copyediting brilliance.

For your perspective and feedback, we would like to thank:
M. Nicole Horsley

Dr. Amanda M. Lawrence

Kathryn D. Blanchard, Charles A. Dana Professor of Religious Studies, Emerita, Alma College

We would like to thank Todd Tobias; Routledge, Taylor & Francis Group; Dr. Mikeal C. Parsons; Phoenix Mercury; John Horne & the National Baseball Hall of Fame & Museum who responded to requests and granted permissions that make this book richer.

We would also like to thank the Advisory & Editorial Boards of the *Journal of Modern Slavery* and everyone who invested their time & energy in this project.

LAWRENCE EDWARD CARTER'S PERSONAL ACKNOWLEDGEMENTS:

My service to Morehouse College is a labor of joy significantly because of the affirmative & supportive working environment of the college created by our 12th president, Dr. David Anthony Thomas.

Many thanks to Adrienne Harris, for her consultation & editorial brilliance without which this book would not have come to full maturity.

I'm immensely grateful for the typing skills and speed of my executive assistant, Kimberly Brown, who makes wonderful decisions regarding my rapidly improving computer skills.

Nothing would go well in my highly scheduled weekdays without the dedication, thoughtfulness & anticipatory genius of my loving wife, Dr. Marva Griffin Carter, whose proofreading of all my scripts move them to a higher quality.

TINA'S PERSONAL ACKNOWLEDGEMENTS:

This book came about as a direct response to the racial injustices in the United States and around the world that we have seen in recent years. The incident that for some may have been the tip of the iceberg and for others a new awakening, was the brutal murder of George Floyd. This horrific incident, the way it became widely accessible digitally, and the aftermath illustrated something I find interesting: that as human beings we are able to share, at a deeper level, common feelings regardless of where we are from.

Millions of people took to the streets to participate in the Black Lives Matter protests in countries around the world regardless of their nationality, ethnic and social backgrounds. What had started as the Black Lives Matter movement in the United States in 2013 against racism and discrimination quickly became a global mainstream protest in 2020, and regardless of whether people shared the lived experience or not, millions of people united against systemic racism. In much greater numbers than ever before, this became a shared struggle. And this fact gives me hope!

I also hope this book will forge a deeper understanding of the lived experience, the struggle, and how the Black community have played an integral and invaluable part in building and shaping the United States from 1619 up to modern America as we know it today. And if the book also encourages old and new discussions around what freedom and equity means, and feed into the larger, ongoing work of finding pathways to more just, inclusive and safe societies, then nothing will make me happier.

First and foremost, I wish to extend a heartfelt thank you to each of the contributors who so brilliantly and powerfully have shared their perspectives, experiences, knowledge and expertise in the form of a poem, an article, a dialogue, photo essay or interview in this book.

My deepest gratitude goes to my co-editors, Jodi Henderson and Lawrence Edward Carter Sr. for the incredible efforts, commitment, insights, creativity and generosity you have poured into this process. It has been such a pleasure to experience the passion, warmth and dedication you have shown throughout working with this book. I am very grateful.

A big thank you to Naje Lataillade for continuously supporting and contributing to my previous documentary work and now this book. It's a joy to work with you!

To each person and every person who in some way have been part of making this book. Thank you.

I wish to thank the Coretta and Martin Luther King Institute for Peace and Thomas Dorg for supporting my work.

To Ima, Wendy, Vivienne and my other friends who have shared painful personal experiences of racism and discrimination with me. You have helped me see that of course I can't understand, I never will. But I will always be an active ally and keep making causes for change.

I also want to thank my colleagues around the world who fervently and tirelessly work to improve human rights and labour rights every day to create fairer, safer and more equal communities with the current challenges without giving up.

Thank you to my nieces and nephews for all of what you have taught me by who you are and how you navigate your lives. I am proud of you: Victoria O'Neal, Alexandra O'Neal, Connie L. Davis Brekkli, Hugo Karol, Pratik Kachroo and Haakon H. Davis.

I wish to thank my mother, Turid Davis for her continuous support and for providing my life with much appreciated continuity.

To my friends and family for being there for me and caring for me. You all influence me in ways that make me better. I appreciate you!

To Maxwell Fraser (Maxi Jazz) 1957 - 2022. Thank you for the music, for your big heart, and your incredible belief. A great ambassador for unity and peace who practiced what you preached. I dedicate this book to you. Nam-myoho-renge-kyo.

Thank you to my life mentor, Daisaku Ikeda for encouraging me to constantly keep improving, moving, step out of my comfort zone, and grow.

And to Anurag, my life-partner, my love, my best friend: thank you for being there, for listening to me, for putting up with me at times when I am working too much, for offering me different perspectives, and for walking this windy road together with me. You are my gift from the universe, and I am eternally grateful!

JODI'S PERSONAL ACKNOWLEDGEMENTS:

"[I]n the end that's what legislation is. It is a letter written to our children. That's what public policy is. At the end of the day, the public policy you would make, or fail to make, is a letter to our children. And we could get more of it right if we would ask ourselves each time, 'What do we want that letter to say?'"
—Reverend Senator Raphael Warnock[1]

I believe that books, also, are letters written to our children. All of our children. What I hope this letter, this book, says to all of our children is that we are willing to have, in fact we are having, difficult conversations that should have happened many generations ago. That this nation, this world, belongs to each one of us, and that it is high time that the USA face all of its past, with honesty and humility, that rather than strive to remove uncomfortable chapters, we insist all of its history be taught, to reckon with that past in a spirit of truth and reconciliation.

I would like to thank my co-editors, Lawrence Edward Carter, Sr. & Tina Davis, for your generosity of spirit, passion, wisdom and compassion. I have learned so much from you. I am deeply grateful for this opportunity to work with you. It has been an honor.

Huge thanks to the very best home team:

Paul, for your love and unwavering support of me, the journal and this project.

---

1 quoted in Politico, "'There's Never Been Anybody Like Him in the United States Senate,'" https://www.politico.com/news/magazine/2022/08/05/raphael-warnock-georgia-senate-2022-profile-00049352 last accessed 9/12/2022

To my children Anna, Mags, Marin, for your presence, for all your help & feedback and for being the best cheerleaders anyone could have; you make me better. I am incredibly grateful. And I am so very proud of each of you.

My parents, Joe & Brenda, for life, the universe, and a love of books. If it's books, it's not hoarding.

Many thanks to:

Cynthia Gill-Wall, for always giving me a clear assessment of the situation and your honest opinion, then having my back when I dive in anyway.

Ely Diaz-Gonzalez for constantly reminding me that two steps forward, two steps back is not failure, it's a cha-cha (or at least an '80s song), for your constant support and also for making me laugh so hard that I can't speak.

Pete Zimowski, for years of building the plane while flying it, metaphorically, of course. It has been quite an adventure.

Daniel Reese, for your faith in me, your support, guidance, the list goes on and on. You are the mentor I don't deserve but am so very grateful for.

L. Carol Scott, for modeling how to create books and life and wholeness and joy.

Kathryn Falk Campbell, for being a light and a steady hand. Your clarity & hope mean more than you know.

Roger Trueba, for always asking the hard questions, challenging me to think it through one more time, from a different angle, while always making clear we're ultimately on the same side.

Rebecca Knight, your curiosity and presence are such a gift.

Logynn Ferrall, for really getting it.

April, Tom & Christopher, who hold the center.

Inge Myllerup-Brookhuis, who reminds me to breathe.

ACKNOWLEDGEMENTS

Laura & James Eric who talked me through the publication process.

And to Mrs. Jean Love, Ms. Virginia McChesney, Dr. Anne Richards, and Dr. Kareen Malone, for all you taught & continue to teach me, for encouraging me & pushing me to just do the thing.

Special thanks to Maria Hanson, David Perry, Joey Sanders and all my friends & loved ones who have supported me and shared their time & talents with me.

None of this would have been possible without you all. And I am grateful beyond words.

The Journal of Modern Slavery is a multidisciplinary journal focused on solutions to human trafficking and modern slavery. This peer-reviewed academic journal is dedicated to research, theory, and practical application in eradicating slavery and is staffed with subject matter experts from diverse professions, disciplines, nationalities, and cultures, all of whom are worldwide leaders in the fight against modern slavery and human trafficking.

Founded in 2018, SlaveFree Today (SFT) is a 501(c)3 nonprofit whose mission is to inform and illustrate practical steps toward a slave-free world. SFT provides an online forum for connection and information sharing for front-line service providers, educators, students, survivors and policy makers seeking community and solutions to implement locally and globally. Over 150,000 people visit our information-rich website each year.

SlaveFree Today offers the following resources at no charge to a growing audience: the Journal of Modern Slavery, the SlaveFree Today Podcast, a curated international resource library with links to current and past reports, media and additional means of staying informed, including training resources for victims, first responders, law enforcement, businesses, legal professionals, NGOs, and a blog featuring perspectives on current and emerging actions and ideas from around the world to tackle and eliminate modern slavery and related exploitative practices.